# With an open eye

# With an open eye

## Parables with meaning for today

Tom Gordon

WILD GOOSE PUBLICATIONS

First published 2011

Wild Goose Publications
4th Floor, Savoy House, 140 Sauchiehall Street, Glasgow G2 3DH, UK
www.ionabooks.com
Wild Goose Publications is the publishing division of the Iona Community.
Scottish Charity No. SC003794. Limited Company Reg. No. SC096243.

ISBN 978-1-84952-203-8

Cover photograph © Mary Gordon

The publishers gratefully acknowledge the support of the Drummond Trust,
3 Pitt Terrace, Stirling FK8 2EY in producing this book.

A catalogue record for this book is available from the British Library.

*Overseas distribution:*
*Australia:* Willow Connection Pty Ltd, Unit 4A, 3-9 Kenneth Road,
Manly Vale, NSW 2093
*New Zealand:* Pleroma, Higginson Street, Otane 4170, Central Hawkes Bay
*Canada:* Novalis/Bayard Publishing & Distribution, 10 Lower Spadina Ave.,
Suite 400, Toronto, Ontario M5V 2Z2

Printed by Bell & Bain, Thornliebank, Glasgow

To

**Cameron Martin Day**

a gift to the world
while this book was being written;
a new story just beginning.

# Contents

# Preface

'Edna's house was full of clutter.' So begins one of the earliest stories in this book, and immediately we are in a world that is familiar yet often unremarked, the world of the everyday life of ordinary people. Here are people ageing, experiencing the losses, but also the small moments of grace that can shine through bereavement, the onset of dementia, family worries and limited mobility. But these elders are far from being victims; they are spirited, wise and witty and they illuminate life for their neighbours and friends. Children too, direct and honest in their questioning, passionate in their dreaming and hoping, vulnerable to the harshness of life yet brave and full of wonder at its unexpected turns, and some of the loveliest stories are about the cherished relationships between the very old and the very young.

Few of the people in these stories are rich, few are high achievers (though a Moderator of the General Assembly of the Church of Scotland might be considered so, especially since he is gay). They are call centre controllers, shopkeepers, 'rodent operatives', social workers and youth workers, clergy and doctors, miners' wives and farmers. Some of them are those who are dismissed or demeaned at every turn in our success-obsessed culture. The things that happen to them are not the stuff of movies, but the tiny, insignificant happenings of daily life - painting a gate, a wet bus journey home, a child's broken bike, charity fundraising. Yet not really insignificant at all; seen in a different light, they become lucid with meaning and significance both for those they happen to and for the reader. Glimpsed through the prism of the Christian drama, it is as if what happens backstage or offstage has been brought momentarily to the centre of the stage and warmly lit, so we really notice them, perhaps for the first time.

A parable is a short story, told in either prose or verse (and the book uses both) which illustrates a deeper meaning or truth. It sketches a setting, describes an action and shows the results. It should be succinct, and though not explicitly stated, the meaning is not obscure or abstract but quite straightforward and clear. *With An Open Eye* fulfils all of these criteria with an authenticity which many will surely relate to. There are threads running through the book which are suggestive of the writer's own background and experience – a Highland childhood, the intensely pastoral eye of a parish minister, the steadfast inclusivity of a faith which is both mature and undogmatic, and, above all, the willingness and ability of a hospice chaplain to accompany dying and bereavement honestly. Some of the stories are profoundly moving in their simplicity – one of them sent me to reread messages I received on the deaths of my parents.

Above all, though it addresses serious and life-changing events as they are experienced in the lives of individuals and communities, this book is neither gloomy nor in any way preachy. It just tells a story and leaves us to make of it what we will. There are two excellent Christian Aid parables in it and one wonderfully funny tale which had me laughing out loud. But you will need to read the book for yourself to find it.

*Kathy Galloway*
*Head of Christian Aid Scotland*

# Introduction

I have always loved the poetry of Rudyard Kipling. From the first time I heard 'If', I was hooked. Drawn to his panoply of poems from the latter part of the 19th century, through the ravages of the First World War, to his reflections in the 1920s and '30s, I am devoted fan. This is not the place to offer a critique of Kipling's work as part of the canon of English poetry or to explore at length the reasons for the pleasure I get from reading his verses. But there are two things that stir me in Kipling's poetry and draw me back to his verses time after time: the first is his use of imagery – he paints some marvellous word-pictures; and the second is his use of rhythm – sometimes his verses just plead to be read aloud.

There are some who decry Kipling's language as being simplistic and his rhyming schemes as unimaginative. But for me, the imagery and the rhythm do it all.

One offering in which imagery and rhythm come together is a story-poem called 'Tomlinson'. It was written by Kipling in 1881, and dramatises the concept of 'karma', the principle that humans reap what they sow.

*'Now Tomlinson gave up the ghost at his house in Berkeley Square.'*

When Tomlinson dies, a Spirit comes to his bedside and carries him away, gripping him by the hair. They arrive at the gate of heaven, guarded by St Peter, who asks Tomlinson to account for how he had behaved on Earth, specifically what good he'd accomplished. At this command, Tomlinson grows 'white as the rain-washed bone', and answers that he had a friend, his priest and guide, who could testify to his good deeds. St Peter rebukes him by reminding him he is no longer conducting his life in his own neighbourhood of Berkeley Square, but is standing at heaven's gate and he must account for his own activities:

*'For the race is run by one and one and never by two and two.'*

So Tomlinson begins by reporting what he once 'read in a book'. But
St Peter wants to know what Tomlinson has done for himself – not
what he has read that others have said. Tomlinson then reports,

> 'O this I have felt, and this I have guessed, and this I heard men say.'

Again, Peter bitterly mocks this lame response and adds,

> 'For none may reach by hired speech of neighbour, priest, and kin
> Through borrowed deed to God's good meed that lies so fair within.'

St Peter can find no reason to admit Tomlinson to heaven, so dispatches him to 'The Lord of Wrong'. But as the forlorn Tomlinson
tries to enter the gates of hell, he is stopped by the Devil, who com-
mands him,

> 'Sit down, sit down upon the slag, and answer loud and high
> The harm that ye did to the Sons of Men or ever you came to die.'

Again, Tomlinson claims that a former lover could testify to his cruelty
on earth, and the Devil's reply is in chorus with St Peter's mantra –
that each must answer for his own sin,

> 'For the sin that ye do by two and two ye must pay for one by one!'

Just as the individual will be held accountable for his good deeds, he
will also have to answer for his bad deeds. But the Devil's attempt at
retrieving a full account from Tomlinson ends as unsuccessfully as St
Peter's. So Tomlinson is sent back to earth:

> 'Go, get ye back to the flesh again for the sake of Man's repute.'

Tomlinson was fit for neither heaven nor hell, so he had to go back to
earth to establish for himself a collection of virtues or sins. Both St
Peter and the Devil wished him well.

Marvellous stuff! It's a great and vivid read. In a much more
modest way, that is what I am trying to achieve in this, the final part
of my trilogy of books of contemporary parables to parallel the

three-year cycle of the Church Lectionary. I want, as Kipling does, to draw you into my stories, to share the efforts of many 'Tomlinsons', to make you smile and laugh, to ask you to wonder and be challenged, to expect you to worry and cry. And I want to do that with imagery, not about *a* heaven or *a* hell, but about your everyday struggle with the heavens and hells of situations and places that you can understand and relate to. And I want to make the stories readable, to make them come alive, with rhythm and vibrancy.

When I was preparing this book I heard that one of my stories from *A Blessing to Follow* – the first in this trilogy – had been read aloud, in dramatic form with different voices, in Iona Abbey as part of a Sunday morning worship service. You have no idea how encouraging that has been. So, as with Kipling's poems, it is clear that some of these stories plead to be read aloud. Try it for yourself, not just for public consumption but for your own involvement with them. I suspect you'll find some of the stories become even more alive that way.

Through all of this, I hope that the Tomlinsons in my stories will help you see old things in new ways, and offer you fresh insights into life's eternal issues and events, sorrows and joys, dilemmas and concerns.

When the Devil tells Tomlinson that he is fit for neither heaven nor hell because he has done nothing for himself, thought about nothing, believed nothing, or achieved nothing, he dispatches him back to earth, back to Berkeley Square, to try again.

*'Go back to Earth with a lip unsealed – go back with an open eye,*
*And carry my word to the Sons of Men or ever ye come to die;*
*That the sin they do by two and two they must pay for one by one,*
*And ... the God that you took from a printed book be*
*with you, Tomlinson.'*

I hope you find something of that in this 'printed book'. As you go back to your own Berkeley Square and ponder 'with an open eye' what matters most to you, as another Tomlinson having another chance, you might see things in your life and faith in a new and different way.

Thanks to Ed Daub, an Iona Community Associate from Wisconsin, USA, whom I've never met, but whose unfailing encouragement and insight have been both affirmative and enlightening.

Thanks to Christopher Bell, Nicola Bruce, Brian Embleton, Richard Leckerman and Duncan Morgan for permission to use their ideas and reflections in my stories, with the hope that I have done justice to their thoughts; to many others who have unwittingly been the source of ideas and concepts around which some of these stories have been built; to my wife, Mary, for the cover picture – and much more besides; to my daughter, Kathryn, for her insights into child development which helps me make sense of the childhood characters in the stories; to Lesley Walker for her helpful clarification of aspects of the birth of a baby at home; to the staff at Wild Goose for their unfailing encouragement and support; and to the unnamed people whose comments on my other books and stories continue to be encouraging and enlivening.

# 1 A change of mind

Cuthbert Clark had decided that Christmas should be abolished. And as he stood on the church steps on the first Sunday of Advent, his decision was more than adequately confirmed. He looked out over the church car park to the scene beyond, and his heart sank. Snow had come early this year. The last two weeks in November had been a nightmare. 'Snow had fallen, snow on snow' – in the words of the familiar carol – had been right enough. 'A cold front from Siberia,' the weather-forecasters had intoned. The view from Cuthbert's church steps was like a Siberian wasteland, that was for sure.

Cuthbert reflected on the struggles of the past fortnight – the hearse that had got stuck in the cemetery and had to be dug out by the mourners before the funeral could proceed – with Cuthbert doing his bit to help; the gravedigger who had slipped into the grave with the coffin and had to be rescued by the mourners – with Cuthbert doing his bit to help; the bus that had crashed into the church railings and the passengers who had to be looked after in the church hall – with Cuthbert doing his bit; Mrs Bowman who had fallen on the church steps and broken her elbow only last Sunday – with Cuthbert, etc, etc, before the ambulance arrived; the burst pipe in the church kitchen, and the flood that had to be mopped up – with Cuthbert … well, you know the rest.

It was all too much, and with no let-up in the bad weather predicted, it was only likely to get worse. And when Cuthbert pondered the four-week run-up to Christmas that lay ahead – visiting housebound parishioners; school services to attend to; a surfeit of good will and mince pies to be responded to at endless festive celebrations; all the additional services and preparations … Oh yes, Cuthbert had definitely decided that, if he had his way, Christmas should be abolished.

'Other people can do Christmas if they want,' he'd said to himself that very morning. 'But, if it was up to me, I'd have none of it – ever again!'

As the town's vicar, he had no real choice. But as Cuthbert looked over the desolate vista that stretched before him from the church steps, he knew that, if he had a choice, there would be no cards, no Christmas tree, no company, no presents, no special meal, no nothing …

Cuthbert was awakened out of his depressing reverie by the awareness of someone coming in through the church gate – twisted and barely negotiable as a result of the runaway bus (the gate, that is, not the approaching figure) – and tentatively making their way up the path to the front door. It was none other than Mrs Bowman. She was wrapped against the cold like Nanook of the North, Cuthbert only recognising her by her distinctive tea-cosy woollen hat. She had a shopping bag decorously draped over her right arm, and the left sleeve of her red coat swung limply by her side. There was a large bulge clearly visible under the front of her tightly fastened coat, a result, Cuthbert surmised, of a bulky, plastered broken elbow concealed beneath. Mrs Bowman had her head down, bravely battling onwards on her trek to the church. She almost bumped into Cuthbert before she realised he was filling the doorway. Lifting her head, she chirped cheerily, 'Morning, Mr Clark. Didn't see you there. Fine day, isn't it?'

Cuthbert chose not to agree, but to announce his surprise at his bold parishioner's appearance at worship so soon after her unfortunate accident. 'Mrs Bowman. It's yourself,' he offered, stating the obvious. 'I didn't expect to see you here today. Goodness, you've done well since your fall.'

Mrs Bowman smiled. 'Well, vicar,' she responded, 'what can you do? How could I *not* come to church. It's Advent, after all. Christmas just round the corner. So no stupid fall's going to keep me away.' And with that, she laid her shopping bag at Cuthbert's feet. 'And anyway,' she continued, 'I come bearing gifts.'

As she spoke, Mrs Bowman was delving into the bowels of her cavernous shopping bag, and, with a flourish, she unearthed a flat, square object, carefully wrapped in garishly bright Christmas paper. Holding it in front of her she proclaimed, 'This is for you, Cuthbert Clark. A small gift – to help you get through Christmas.'

'For me?' Cuthbert questioned. 'But …'

'I made it myself,' his parishioner responded.

'But,' Cuthbert continued, 'your broken elbow …'

'Och, no. I did it all before I fell. It's been ready for a while. But I had to give it to you this week – Advent, you know.' And then, in response to Cuthbert's obvious hesitation, she insisted, 'Go on then. Open it up.'

It didn't take long for the somewhat sceptical Cuthbert to remove the layers of Christmas and tissue paper, and to reveal … the biggest Advent calendar he had ever seen. Clearly home-made, it looked as though it had been put together from old Christmas cards, with windows boldly numbered 1 to 25 in red, felt-tip pen. Cuthbert was astonished. 'Mrs Bowman!' was all he could say.

The Advent-calendar-maker grinned widely, clearly delighted with the response to her surprise gift. 'Open the first window,' she instructed.

'Now?' Cuthbert enquired.

'Aye, now. It's the first day of Advent, after all. Go on. You'll get a nice surprise.'

Cuthbert carefully peeled back the marked window and peered underneath. And there, written in a neat, rounded hand, he read. 'Day 1. Here we go! Find the gift of a smile.' Cuthbert looked up from the calendar to find Mrs Bowman beaming at him from ear to ear. 'There you are,' she chirped, 'Day 1. Gift number one. And there's a lot more to come …'

Advent was different for Cuthbert that year. He had more gifts, and more pleasure, in Advent than he'd known for years. 'Day 6.

Coping OK? Pop in for a mince pie'; 'Day 11. Getting there? A miniature of Single Malt awaits'; 'Day 17. Looking for a sign? *Vicar of Dibley* Christmas Special'; 'Day 23. Nearly there. Come for supper'.

So, Cuthbert Clark got through the run-up to Christmas. And as he sat with his feet up on Boxing Day, he was genuinely glad he'd not abolished Christmas after all. And he was even *more* delighted that a very clever woman called Constance Bowman hadn't abolished Christmas either. He looked across at the home-made Advent calendar that had filled his mantelpiece since the first day of Advent, and at the 'Day 25' window he'd opened the previous morning. It boldly pronounced , 'Made it! Well worth waiting for. Have a great Christmas.'

**Waiting**

'Why is a waiter called a "waiter"?' my grandson asked.
'Why do you ask that?' I enquired.
'Well, we're waiting for our lunch.'
He was right, of course.
Well, you do that in cafés – wait, I mean.
Even fast-food has to be waited for – just a little bit.
'*We're* waiting,' he continued,
'so shouldn't *we* be called the "waiters", eh?'
He was right, of course.
He usually is.
'Well,' I began,
'to wait, like that nice man is doing for us,
also means to care,
or to serve by bringing us the things we need.
So, because he's waiting on us,
that makes him a "waiter", right?'
It didn't seem good enough.
It usually isn't.

'So he's a waiter *and* a server who brings things, eh?'
'I suppose,' I replied.
He was silent for a nanosecond.
'I know,' he exclaimed, triumphantly,
'I'll call him "Mr Bringer".
It sounds better, eh?
Because he brings us things, eh?'
So we waited,
until Mr Bringer arrived
with two cheeseburgers and fries.
There were no more questions –
not for now, anyway.
Burgers and fries tend to get in the way of questions,
for a while, anyway.
And the lunch was well worth waiting for.
Mr Bringer had seen to that.

### First in Advent

*Old Testament:* Isaiah 64:1-9
*Epistle:* 1 Corinthians 1:3-9
*Gospel:* Mark 13:24-37

# 2 Preparations

Edna's house was full of clutter. There was no getting away from it, if you were looking for someone to enter the Olympics in the 'owner of a small apartment full of stuff' competition, Edna would have won the gold medal hands down.

Edna had never been good at throwing things out at any stage of her life. So she'd been accumulating stuff for as long as she could remember. But it was following Bob's death that the clutter seemed to take over her life. For a start, she couldn't bring herself to dispose of his things. 'It would be like throwing him out with his stuff,' she decided. So Bob's things were still all around her. She liked that, of course, because Bob's stuff reminded Edna of Bob, and that was no bad thing. But there was so much of it …

Moving house had just compounded the problem. Decanting from a three-bedroom semi to a one-bedroom retirement apartment had been a sensible move … if it hadn't been for the stuff! She hadn't *actually* squeezed all that had been in four rooms into two. That would have been silly. But *most* of Edna's stuff had come with her to her new home. So, even more than usual, Edna's house was full of clutter.

The priest came to visit not long after she'd moved in. She has a picture of him indelibly fixed in her mind, standing by the door of her lounge, looking over to where Edna was sitting by the fire, and casting his eye over the clutter that stood between him and his new parishioner – working out how to negotiate the piles of magazines; the three pairs of shoes; the coffee table heaped high with books; the two wicker stools in the middle of the floor, one holding an ironing basket, and the other an open folder out of which were spilling envelopes, stamps, pens and writing paper; the newspaper-rack stuffed full of papers with the telephone perched precariously on top.

Yes, Edna's house was full of clutter. She just didn't have the motivation to do anything about it. Until …

Christmas was coming round, and Edna decided she would get herself a new Christmas tree. Now, it's not that Edna didn't have a Christmas tree already. She had one wrapped in a black bin-bag somewhere in the hall cupboard, and the little one she normally had on top of her TV – though she had no idea where *that* was. But Edna had the urge to get *another* Christmas tree.

She'd read a thing in the local paper about a new charity in the town called 'A tree for you, a gift for someone else', and their blurb ran:

> We sell good quality, fresh, locally-grown Christmas Trees
> that don't shed their needles.
> ALL profits made from the tree sales
> go to support local charities
> working to provide gifts for children
> who're having a tough Christmas.
>
> **DON'T MISS OUT. PLACE AN ORDER TODAY**
>
> Pick a date between 1st and 18th December,
> and we'll make sure your tree has been cut the previous day.
>
> **DON'T DELAY.**
>
> Order your tree now,
> and make a tree for you into a gift for someone else.

'That's for me,' Edna thought, and once she'd unearthed her telephone from under the pile of ironing on her settee, she phoned the number in the advert, and the tenth of December was agreed as the date her new Christmas tree would be delivered.

Edna looked round the room. Where on *earth* was the Christmas tree to go? There was not one square centimetre of available space. There was nothing else for it – some of the clutter would just have to go. Edna looked at her calendar. It was the first of December. She had ten days to clear a space for her Christmas tree, ten days to get ready. It was the longest and most challenging ten days of Edna's life. But the funny thing was, once she got started clearing a space for the tree, she began to deal with other things too. She cleared 'stuff' she hadn't looked at for ages. Out went the vase of dried flowers she'd kept since Bob's funeral. She threw out a whole year's collection of back copies of the *Radio Times*. She even found a new 'gloves, scarf and hat set' she'd been given by her niece the previous Christmas – or was it the Christmas before that? – still in its original packaging *and* in its Christmas bag.

When she finished – late on the evening of the ninth of December – Edna's house was still full of clutter. Now, though, not only was there less clutter than there had been before, but there was a space by the window where a new Christmas tree could be put on display.

Edna's priest came to visit the week before Christmas. She was amused to see him standing apprehensively at the door of her lounge, clearly expecting his journey to the chair by the fire to be as taxing as an expedition through the foothills of the Himalayas. But, as he surveyed the transformed scene, set off beautifully by a well-formed and magnificently decorated Scots pine by the window, a smile of pleasure flickered across his face. His eyes settled on Edna who was sitting grinning at him in her chair by a blazing fire, proudly wearing a matching set of gloves, scarf and a woolly hat. She knew right away what he was thinking, so she answered his question before he asked it. 'Sorry, Father John. I know I may look a bit strange, but, you see, I've just finished getting ready for Christmas.'

## So much

So much to get ready; so much to prepare;
So much to set up and to plan;
So much to provide for; so much to work out;
So much to arrange when I can.

So much to fit in when there's too little time;
So much that's expected again;
So much to accomplish; so much to create;
So much to uphold and maintain.

So much to be done as it's been done before;
So much that's the same as last year;
So much of tradition; so much that's the 'norm';
So much – though it feels insincere.

So much – so I'll need to take time out to think;
So much – yes, I'll try to unwind;
So much – how important the message to know;
So much – when there's meaning to find.

So much – when there's purpose I've still to recall;
So much – with more wonder to see;
So much – of the mystery, insight and love;
So much – and all given to me!

### Second in Advent

*Old Testament:* Isaiah 40:1-11
*Epistle:* 2 Peter 3:8-15a
*Gospel:* Mark 1:1-8

# 3 A deeper meaning

It was Christmas Eve in the workhouse – and all the other workers had cleared off home early for the holiday. Only Ivor was left, and it would be a while yet before he could get away. He had a report to finish – 'to be e-mailed to Head Office before Christmas', he'd been told. 'Before Christmas' was up to midnight on Christmas Eve, and Ivor reckoned it was certainly going to take him close to the deadline before he was done. 'I hate Christmas!' he muttered.

This had not been one of Ivor's best Decembers. His office team was struggling, trying to carry the same workload as before but with fewer staff. 'Voluntary redundancies' and 'natural wastage' in the face of cutbacks and a financial squeeze had taken their toll. Meanwhile, the work mounted up, the working day had become longer and longer, the pressure more and more stressful, and the job – well, that just wasn't enjoyable any more. As team-leader, Ivor had to carry the brunt of it. He tried to be as encouraging as possible for his colleagues and to cushion them, as far as he was able, from the harsh realities of the company's position. They worked long hours too, of course, but Ivor always felt he had to lead by example and be first in and last out each day.

Christmas Eve had been no different. The pressure didn't ease because of the holiday. He'd done his best to make sure everyone got home early. 'I'll not be long behind you,' he assured his colleagues as they left. But he knew the lie of that. The report was going to take a long time. 'I hate Christmas,' he thought.

It was just after 8 o'clock when Ivor slipped downstairs to get a filled roll from the corner shop to keep him going for the final stretch of his report-writing. He made his way out of the back exit of the building and it was well below freezing when he stepped outside. He pulled up his collar against the chill, and cursed that he forgotten his gloves that morning. 'I hate Christmas,' he muttered.

That's when he almost fell over the bundle in the doorway. Stumbling across the unexpected obstacle, and just about staying on his feet on the icy concrete, he cursed again, adding a few choice oaths to 'I hate Christmas'. He was about to kick the bundle closer to the wall when, to his amazement, the bundle moved closer to the wall all by itself, and out of the mess of polythene, cardboard and sacking poked a young, dirty face. 'Sorry, mister,' the face said quietly. 'I thought everyone had gone. There's no' usually anyone comin' and goin' through here this late.'

The face was half hidden by a dirty woollen beanie hat. But as it spoke, it clearly belonged to someone who wasn't yet out of their teens. And it was a female face. 'Sorry, mister,' the face said. 'Ah know ah shouldnae be here. But ah've naewhere else. This is a guid spot. There's aye a warm draft comes oot frae under this door. So, ah'm here regular. Like the night. Ah wis just settlin' doon. Ah'm sorry fur the bother.'

Ivor didn't need this, and it was nothing to do with him anyway. So, turning on his heel, he headed into the street, leaving the doorway-bundle to her own devices. 'I hate Christmas,' he muttered once more.

The corner shop was busy and Ivor had to wait in a long queue. Why he picked up a copy of the evening paper (which he was never going to have time to read anyway) and why he flipped inside (and not to his usual sports' pages at the back) and why he started to read 'A Christmas Thought' from a local minister (when he and ministers had little or nothing to do with each other) he'll not be able to tell you. But he did, and this is what he read:

I hate Christmas shopping! It was in this frame of mind that I found myself in the town centre one frosty morning earlier this month. Quietly grumbling to myself, and jostled by crowds of other equally 'cheerful' shoppers, I looked up and suddenly saw him – an 'old worthy', a good old-fashioned tramp, sitting on a bench in the middle of the pedestrianised area. Next to him was what seemed to be all his worldly possessions, a battered old rucksack-like bundle, stuffed full with goodness knows what. But what struck me was the hunk of stale bread, obviously his breakfast, that he was eating and sharing with the birds. Round his feet were darting sparrows, a couple of blackbirds, a robin, and it wouldn't be the town centre without a few starlings and pigeons. It was like an oasis amidst a crowd of miserably 'cheerful' Christmas shoppers. And you know what? No one seemed to notice the old man. Christmas swirled around him, and nobody gave him a passing thought. To stop myself staring I looked into a shop window resplendent in its Christmas display, and used the reflection to watch him. For every piece of bread he ate, he broke off another piece and threw it with a smile to the birds, quite oblivious to the crowds around. And I smiled for the first time that morning. For somehow, just for a moment, a deeper meaning about the sharing of Christmas returned. Christmas greetings to you all. Have a good one. Reverend E.

By the time he'd finished reading, Ivor was at the counter. 'I hope you're going to buy that newspaper,' the shopkeeper said accusingly. 'This isn't a public library, you know.'

'Oh, yes,' Ivor replied, 'I'm going to buy it – and a filled roll as well … no, make that two … yes, two filled rolls … cheese and pickle will do … and two pork pies as well … and two cartons of orange … and two bags of your 'turkey and stuffing' crisps … and two bars of chocolate … and … yes, two of those Christmas hats on the shelf over there …'

Ivor left the corner shop with two bags full of goodies. He knew who he was going to have a Christmas Eve meal with. He knew what report wasn't going to be finished by Christmas. He knew who he was going to tell to 'stuff it' if there was trouble. And he knew that, for a time anyway, thanks to an anonymous tramp, a jobbing vicar, and a young woman whom he was just about to get to know a lot better, 'I hate Christmas' had gone, and something of the true meaning about the sharing of it had come back.

## To share

When children are small,
so we're told,
they can play next to each other
and look as if they're sharing.
But they're not.
It's called 'parallel play'.
But it's not sharing.
They don't know how to yet.
It'll come,
so we're told,
when 'parallel play'
turns into proper sharing,
and children learn
to share as they should.

When grown-ups are small,
so we're told,
they can live next to each other
and look as if they're sharing.
But they're not.
It's called 'selfishness'.
And it's not sharing.
They haven't learned how to yet.
It'll come,
so we're told,
when selfishness

gives way to proper sharing,
and we all learn
to share as we should.

When nations are small,
so we're told,
they can exist next to each other
and look as if they're sharing.
But they're not.
It's called 'international tension'.
And it's not sharing.
They don't know how to yet.
Peace will come,
so we're told,
when power and might
turns into proper sharing,
and nations learn
to share as they should.

When Christmas is small,
so we're told,
we can prepare next to each other
and look as if we're sharing.
But we're not.
It's called not caring about anyone else.
And it's not sharing.
We haven't got round to it yet.
It'll come,
so we're told,
when all the preparations
remind us about proper sharing,
and Advent teaches us
to share as we should.

## Third in Advent

*Old Testament:* Isaiah 61:1-4, 8-11
*Epistle:* 1 Thessalonians 5:16-24
*Gospel:* John 1:6-8, 19-28

# 4 An angel in disguise

Miguel Filipe Gilberto Dominguez had never thought of himself as an angel. He had no wings and would never have considered himself good enough anyway to be labelled angelic. For another thing, he was a quiet kind of guy, whereas angels usually have plenty to say, don't they? Nor did he play the harp. In fact, he was pretty close to being tone-deaf. So, wingless, quiet, unsure, tone-deaf Miguel Filipe Gilberto Dominguez couldn't be an angel.

Miss Cameron-Hart, resident of Room 47 in the Hillview Nursing Home, had never really thought much about angels. It's not that she didn't *know* about angels. After all, weren't little red-cheeked angels leaning over fluffy clouds the most prized of all the pictures in her scrapbook when she was a girl? And hadn't she been an angel in her school nativity play *hundreds* of years ago, beautifully dressed in her white net frock and tinsel tiara? And didn't the amazing Angel of the North dominate the skyline when you drove around Newcastle? Yes, Miss Cameron-Hart knew about angels. But you couldn't say that they figured much in her daily thoughts or regular conversations – until, that is, Miguel Filipe Gilberto Dominguez appeared.

Miss Cameron-Hart had been a resident in the Hillview Nursing Home for over a year. She'd moved in a month before the Christmas of 1981. But she'd spent her first so-called 'festive season' in Hillview as miserable as she could ever remember. Not much improved in the New Year. Miss Cameron-Hart was, in her own words, 'thoroughly fed up with life.' Only two things kept her going. The first was Miguel Filipe Gilberto Dominguez. Miguel was a care assistant in the home, and with his gentleness, quiet voice, impeccable manners and politeness, *and* swarthy good looks, he quickly became a favourite of Miss Cameron-Hart. 'You are my angel,' she would say – and often. And her angel would just shake his head and smile.

The other thing that kept her going was her TV. And the only things worth watching – for 'there's never anything good on the television these days' – were news and current affairs programmes. Which was just as well, for the TV programmes were filled with a political crisis …

It was the spring of 1982. On the other side of the world, General Leopoldo Galtieri had become President of Argentina. The Argentine regime, in the midst of an economic crisis, pressed its long-standing claim over the British Overseas Territory of the Falkland Islands – *Las Islas Malvinas*. The tension between the two governments increased in the March of that year. And the rest, as they say, is history. The Argentine military junta ordered the invasion of the Falkland Islands on 2nd April 1982. And the Falklands war had begun.

Miss Cameron-Hart had always been a great admirer of Margaret Thatcher, the British Prime Minister, and she followed Thatcher's leadership through the seventy-four days of the Falklands conflict with a mounting sense of national pride. As the war unfolded, Miss Cameron-Hart bristled with self-righteous indignation. She came to hate the Argentines. She wept for the deaths of the 250 British troops. She wasn't bothered about the hundreds of Argentine dead. She loved Thatcher's style. In a very real sense, the Falklands conflict gave Miss Cameron-Hart some of her life back. Nationalistic fervour, Tory values, strong leadership, political success had all contrived to motivate her again.

The rest of 1982 saw Miss Cameron-Hart more settled in Hillview. Of course, the staff had to cope with her occasional outlandish and prejudiced views, but you can tolerate that occasionally from an old Tory, can't you? And while the approach of her second Christmas in the Home didn't really fill the resident of Room 47 with any great pleasure, there was always her angel …

Miguel Filipe Gilberto Dominguez didn't give much away. Miss Cameron-Hart knew he was a 'foreigner' and that he spoke Spanish. So one day she enquired as to which part of Spain Miguel Filipe

Gilberto Dominguez had come from. 'You are from Barcelona? Or Madrid?' she enquired. Her carer smiled.

'*No la ciudad*, not the city,' he replied gently.

'Ah, a country boy, then? Extremadura? Andalucía?'

'No, not there.'

'So, you are a Catalonian,' Miss Cameron-Hart exclaimed.

'Not from Catalonia,' her carer responded quietly.

'So, where then? Where in Spain do you come from?'

Miguel Filipe Gilberto Dominguez fell silent. Unusually, he avoided Miss Cameron-Hart's searching gaze. He could feel his cheeks reddening. Miss Cameron-Hart knew something was amiss. But still she pressed. 'Ashamed of your origins, are you?' she blurted.

Miguel lifted his head. 'No, not ashamed,' he whispered, 'but frightened.'

'Frightened? What on earth is there to be frightened about? You're not scared of *me*, are you?'

Miguel nodded slowly. 'Yes, even of you. You do not know, because it does not matter to how I care for you. But I come from ...' He paused for what seemed an age.

'Come on, it can't be that bad,' Miss Cameron-Hart encouraged. 'Angels have to come from somewhere ...'

'I come from ... from ...' The hesitation only served to increase the tension. 'From ... I come from ... Maria Pinto,' he blurted, 'a little village just west of ... Santiago ... in ... Argentina.'

The word, the very name, sent shudders through the frail body of Miss Cameron-Hart. She was stunned and, unusually for her, quite speechless. But Miguel Filipe Gilberto Dominguez wasn't finished.

'I have lived in your country for many years. I love it here. But I have heard you and others speak of my people with hate. So I do not tell you I am Argentine. I let you think I am Spanish. For it is easier that way.' He paused, and tears began to flow down his cheeks. 'But, you see, I too hate *La Guerra de las Malvinas*. I lost my only brother, Gabriel, in the war, and two cousins. My country lost 650 young men. I too weep for them. I hate the war. I hate what wars do. I am a peaceful man.'

Miguel could say no more. So a silent carer left a silent Miss Cameron-Hart to ponder what had just happened. And all she could think of was, 'An Argentine? And I called him an angel? But angels are supposed to be good, aren't they?'

### A visit from an angel

I once had a visit from an angel.
She'd trudged all the way down the street
to my house,
through two feet of snow, in the depths of the winter,
to bring me my mail.
I was waiting for an important message.
She thought of herself only as
'The local Postie'.
But I knew better.

I once had a visit from an angel.
He'd come all the way across town
to my house,
to see me when I was sick; the only one who bothered.
He brought me a bottle of whisky.
'We'll finish that together when you feel better.'
He thought of himself only as
'Your mate, Billy'.
But I knew differently.

I once had a visit from an angel.
He'd come all the way from next door
to my house,
to ask if I was OK, with Christmas coming up soon,
    and me missing Annie so much.

I enjoyed his quiet company – I always do.
He thought of himself only as
'Freddie from number 23'.
But I knew much more.

I once had a visit from an angel.
She'd phoned, and then come round
to my house,
to give me a break, and walk the dog,
and take the kids to the playpark,
because she knew I was struggling to cope.
She thought of herself only as
'Your little sister, Vera'.
But I knew the truth.

I once had a visit from an angel –
all the way from wherever angels come from,
to my house,
to bring a message and leave a gift,
to offer reassurance and help me to cope.
But there was always more than that.
They thought of themself as
'Just being me'.
But I know an angel when I meet one.

### Fourth in Advent

*Old Testament:* 2 Samuel 7:1-11, 16
*Epistle:* Romans 16:25-27
*Gospel:* Luke 1:26-38

# 5 Reminders

Molly McCracken always bought her Christmas cards at the January sales. For one thing, she could get them at half price; for another, when Christmas eventually came round, she was well ahead of the game. Of course, she didn't leave the cards lying about the house for eleven months. People would have thought she was mad if they came across Christmas cards in the McCracken home in the middle of the summer. So, when the January-sales purchases were brought home, they were stored away safely until early December when card-writing was the order of the day.

Molly McCracken always bought her Christmas cards at the January sales and unearthed them from storage in time for Christmas. Until, that is, she went to look for them one year and they weren't there. *Now, that's strange,* she thought. *They're always in the bottom drawer of the dresser in the lounge.* But there were no cards anywhere in the dresser, or anywhere else in the lounge for that matter. Molly searched around the house, but she couldn't find them at all. Eventually she had to admit defeat and head into town to buy some more. *Unless there's an invisible Christmas card thief around the house, I'll probably find the blooming cards when I'm not looking for them,* Molly mused. Dutifully, she bought her replacement cards, wrote and posted them, had a good Christmas, and bought next year's cards at the January sales as usual … and, of course, stored them away safely.

Until, that is, she went to look for them in the December of *that* year, and they weren't where she thought they should be. She'd never found last year's lot, and now this year's had gone too. *There's definitely a Christmas card thief in this house,* Molly decided, and reluctantly went into town to buy another batch of cards.

When Christmas was over, she bought next year's cards at the January sales and hid them in the house. But could she find them when it came time to write them later in the year? Of course not. With *three* lots of Christmas cards now missing ... *Maybe the Christmas card thief is building up a store of cards so he can start his own retail outlet,* Molly thought. *Or maybe it's me ...*

When she thought about it, she'd been forgetting other things too. Why, only the other day, when she got on the local bus, she'd asked the driver for a half-pound of sausages and two pork chops, just because she'd been thinking of her shopping list rather than the fare into town. And hadn't she paid her gas bill twice a few months ago because she'd forgotten she'd paid it already? It was all a bit worrying.

And it was even more worrying when she realised she'd lost the lovely present her sister had given her for her birthday. She *knew* she'd put it somewhere, but she couldn't remember where. It was a special gift for her seventieth birthday, a leather-bound journal, a lovely book with a patterned cover and blank pages. Molly and her sister were always going on about writing down things from their child-hood, reminders of past days, before they were forgotten for ever. Molly was to start it off while she still remembered the details, and then they would sit down and work on it together. The leather-bound journal would be just the ticket − if only Molly could remember where she'd left it. It wasn't in the bottom drawer of the dresser in the lounge, or anywhere in the dresser, or anywhere in the lounge for that matter. Molly was distressed. *How could I lose such an important gift?* she thought. *I'll just have to turn the house upside down until I find it.*

And that's just what Molly McCracken did. And having looked in all the obvious places − to no avail − she began to look in the obscure places too. She looked behind her record collection on the top shelf of the cupboard in the hall, and there she found ... two packets of Christmas cards that she'd bought in the January sales. She pulled out the two big casserole dishes from the corner kitchen unit − the ones she *never* used. And when she took them out, what did she find inside? A bundle of Christmas cards she'd bought two years before. She burrowed under the sheets and blankets in the chest in the spare bedroom, and with a squeal of glee she held aloft a box of Christmas cards she remembered buying half-price in town only last year. She took down all the paperbacks in the bookcase in the hall, and there .... was a pristine, leather-bound journal.

Molly sat on the bottom step of the stairs with the journal in her hands and surrounded by bundles of Christmas cards and she wept with joy and relief. *I will never lose this precious gift again,* she decided.

The leather-bound journal now resides permanently on Molly's kitchen table. And occasionally she jots down on a blank page, 'I remember going to the seaside on the train with the children from the Sunday School,' or 'What was the name of the man who lived next door who had pigeons in a shed in his garden?', and knows that she and her sister will fill out the details later.

Molly McCracken always buys her Christmas cards at the January sales. She can get them half price and, when Christmas comes round, she's well ahead of the game. Of course, she doesn't leave the cards lying about in the house for eleven months. People would think she was mad if they came across Christmas cards in the McCracken home in the middle of the summer. So, when the January-sales purchases are brought home, they're stored away safely until early December when card-writing is the order of the day.

Molly knows she'll forget where she's hidden them. So, when she comes home from the sales with her cards and hides them away, she goes straight to a leather-bound journal which always sits on the kitchen table, and writes, 'Reminder – Christmas cards in the cleaning cupboard behind the dusters and the polish.' And she knows that the message will always be there. And she smiles to herself as she wonders where she's left her half-pound of sausages and two pork chops, and reckons she should have written down a reminder about that too.

### Reminders

I remember the story I heard long ago
In innocent childhood, believing it; so
Amazingly different; as clear as a bell –
Oh yes, I remember it well.

I remember the story shared often since then,
Through frequent reminders, again and again;
Those great Bible stories; their meaning so clear –
Oh yes, I remember each year.

I remember the story – traditional words;
Familiar old carols; I never was bored
With shepherds, and angels who came from above –
Oh yes, I remember with love.

I remember the story – the manger; the babe;
Three wise men who travelled; the gifts that they gave;
The wonder enshrined in the Bethlehem boy –
Oh yes, I remember with joy.

I remember the story – but what does it mean
To me now I'm hearing it over again?
Will it have an impact; a message, or not?
Oh yes, I remember – so what?

I remember the story – so now I must search
To know it's as fresh as I found it at first;
To feel the excitement, the mystery too.
Oh yes, I remember – it's new!

I remember the story ... So this is the deal –
Engage with its newness, and know that it's real;
Be changed by the wonder; be moved in the 'now'.
Oh yes, I remember – and how!

I remember the story – but not from the past;
It's modern; still topical; with us to last.
So come now – discover a meaning that's new.
Oh yes, I remember ... Will you?

## Christmas Day

*Old Testament:* Isaiah 52:7-10
*Epistle:* Hebrews 1:1-12
*Gospel:* John 1:1-5, 9-14, 16-18

# 6 Duke Street, Number 9

It was one of Logan's set-piece occasions as Moderator of the General Assembly of the Church of Scotland, the figurehead, for a year, of his precious Kirk. The theme was 'Jesus presented at the temple', welcomed by a couple of old folk waiting for his arrival. Logan looked out at the grey heads of the majority of his congregation. *'Plenty of oldies here,'* he thought.

Logan couldn't remember a time when he didn't go to church. With his mother a Sunday School teacher, his father a Kirk Elder, and two older brothers to accompany him, going to church had always been part of his life. Indeed, in his upbringing in a village in the Highlands of Scotland, it was an integral part of the life of many families and children his age. Going to church was just what you did.

Sunday – long before the family had a TV and social patterns had irrevocably altered the shape of a weekend – was a day of rest. As such, in the 1950s' housing estate of his later childhood, it had a set routine – a light breakfast, the church service at 10am, Sunday School to follow, a 'cooked breakfast' thereafter, a Sunday-afternoon walk, a Scottish 'high tea', evening worship at 6.30pm, then bath and bed. As regular as clockwork, the routine of Sunday would be the same every week. There was something greatly reassuring about that. It was safe and secure.

In his earlier years, however, while the *routine* was the same, the church building in which the family worshipped was quite different from the modern 'hall church' of Logan's later youth. The presentation at *his* temple was at an old, traditional Highland Kirk, up on the hill above the village on the shores of the loch. It was, to a small boy, a magical place. The dark-stained pews were so different from the modernity of his home and his school, but there was nothing old-fashioned or intimidating about that. The musty smell of the place was quite distinctive, creating an atmosphere all of its own. The high pulpit, the massive, gold-eagle lectern, and the carved stone font all added to a sense of wonder for a small boy. And, of course, the massive stained-glass window at the front – and at the sides and the back as well, though Logan was told often enough that it was rude and disruptive to keep turning round to look at them – was a joy and a delight. He had never seen the likes before, and with its huge, stylised figures and fancy patterns, its old-fashioned writing and its myriad of different-coloured glass pieces, he was regularly transfixed with wonder.

The worship, of course, was what he'd come to know as 'traditional Presbyterian' – long, wordy, brooding, fierce and adult-orientated; and the singing – mostly psalms – was dirgy, slow, heavy and lacking in anything that smacked of modernity. But what did he know then of alternatives? Nothing at all. And he loved it, the pace, the style, the difference, the depth …

There was an organ in church too. Logan learned later that this was quite a 'modern' innovation. For his father's generation, singing had been largely unaccompanied. But he loved the organ, with an elderly lady, fit-to-burst with exertion at times, pedalling like billy-o on the bellows, and producing a wheezing, melodious sound that he just adored. The singing was always slow, but it carried a dignity that he would never forget.

There were always things to see and do in church. The words were largely lost on him then, of course, the sermon and prayers being 'adult-orientated' and all. But there was more than enough fascination to keep him going. Counting the panes of stained glass in the windows; adding up the numbers of the psalms in the praise-board; looking up the tune by the number the minister always announced – 'Duke Street, Number 9', and the like; learning off-by-heart the words of the familiar psalms; making sure his penny for the offering didn't roll away under the pew; counting the number of people with hats on; watching some folk nodding off to sleep and trying not to himself.

But his all-pervading memory was of rightness. It was a good place to be. He felt at home. And as Logan mounted the steps of the church for another set-piece sermon in his Moderator's Year, he was eternally grateful for ministers, deaconesses, caring people and a loving family who helped with that.

The Kirk for Logan was very different now, and his 30 years of ministry had seen many changing patterns both in Church and society. But as he rose to address his congregation, he was convinced that at the root of it all, and what continued to matter most, was the value of what he had learned as a child – feeling at home; knowing he belonged; being in a holy place; a time apart from everything else.

He only hoped now that he would be able to create something of that for other people through his current responsibilities, in different settings and in different ways. If *he* felt included, then he hoped he could help others feel included too.

Logan was gay. The Kirk of his childhood had allowed him to feel at home. It valued who he was and what he could offer. His choice as Moderator of the General Assembly was the ultimate outcome of that. And as he looked out over the grey heads of his congregation that day, he began, 'When Jesus was presented at the temple, that was the beginning for him of feeling included, don't you think? My theme today, therefore, will be inclusiveness in the Church ...'

### The man in the choir

The man in the choir was asleep –
not while the choir was singing ...
now, that would be silly ...
but during the sermon,
while the minister was droning on;
sound asleep, he was,

his big, bald head lolling forward,
his bristly chin squeezing even more chins
out of his neck.
The man in the choir was asleep.

*I* never slept in church,
not while the minister was droning on
or even when the choir was singing.
*I* never slept like the man in the choir –
not ever.

How could you sleep
in a place like this?

Counting all the red pieces of glass
in the stained-glass window at the front,
for ages,
and losing count,
and having to start again,
even when the minister was droning on,
and the man in the choir was asleep ...

Trying to work out
what the minister wore
under all his black robes ...
a black vest and black pants
to match his black look
and his big, black beard
while he was droning on
and the man in the choir was asleep?

Wondering who James was –
King James, my dad told me it said
inside the front cover of my Bible –

and why he was important enough
to have his name there ...
Did *he* once go to church
while *his* minister was droning on
and the man in *his* choir was asleep?

Watching the people outside –
kids from my class in school
whose parents never took them to church ...
the man next door
coming back from the shops
with his Sunday papers ...
the girl from number twenty-two with her baby ...
what they could have learned
being here,
even with the minister droning on,
and the man in the choir being asleep!

How could they not be here
in a place like this?

The man in the choir is awake ...
'Duke Street, Number Nine'
is the tune we're all to sing,
from the book Mum gave me
with the split pages –
the tunes with the dots and squiggles at the top
and the words in the bottom half,
and me not being able to understand
either one.
But I knew the words anyway
*and* the tune ...

How could they not be here
when there's things like this to sing,
when the minister's stopped droning on
and the man in the choir is awake
and 'Duke Street, Number Nine' is your favourite?

It'll be the same next Sunday,
and the next,
and the one after …
with the minister droning on
and the man in the choir being asleep,
and me …
loving it
when 'Duke Street, Number Nine'
interrupts me at
One Hundred And Twenty Four,
and I'll have to start counting
the red pieces of glass
in the stained-glass window at the front
all over again.

### First after Christmas

*Old Testament:* Isaiah 61:10-62:3
*Epistle:* Galatians 4:4-7
*Gospel:* Luke 2:22-40

# 7 More than a marathon

To this day Jamie doesn't know why he let his mates persuade him to run in the marathon. It had all started with a bit of banter in the office. Ely was a runner, a proper runner, and even went out for a half-hour's run at lunchtime. 'Bloody mad,' Jamie had said – though, if he was honest, he had just a tinge of envy for the way Ely looked after herself. Terry was a runner too … not as passionate as Ely, but he played rugby at weekends and trained every Wednesday evening. So he was pretty fit.

Brenda? Well, she wasn't the running type, nor did she have the running build. 'D'you need a prop-forward for your rugby team, Terry?' she had once enquired. But no one had taken her up on her offer, and Brenda never minded.

So why Jamie was persuaded to run in the marathon is beyond him. Ely was planning to sign up, so she informed her three colleagues as they shared an end-of-the-week drink in *The Jolly Jack* after work one Friday. She'd run marathons before but fancied doing this one with some mates. 'Anyone up for it?' she asked. Terry was enthusiastic.

'Yeah. Sounds good. I've always fancied having a go. And if you run just in front of me, Ely, I can watch your little bum all the way round and that'll give me encouragement to keep going.' Ely hit him with a beer mat and turned in mock disgust to the other two.

'Well, you guys, what do you think?'

'How long's a marathon?' Brenda enquired.

'A tad over twenty-six miles,' Ely responded.

'Twenty-six miles? You've got to be joking,' complained Jamie. 'That's from here … as far as … there …'

'*And* back …' Brenda added.

'Oh, come on you two,' Ely chirped. 'It would be good for you,' only to be greeted by two very sceptical faces. But Ely was not to be deterred. 'I tell you what,' she continued, 'we can enter a team, four of us, one leg each …'

'I'm running nowhere on one leg,' Jamie quipped.

'No, you silly bugger, there are four sections for the marathon teams, and we'd all do one each. That way, you don't have to kill yourself running the whole thing. There were over a thousand teams last year. Surely we could do it. Yeah? We could call ourselves … "The Jolly Jack Joggers", or something like that.'

'More like the Jolly Jack *Crawlers*,' Brenda suggested.

'Or more like the "Stay-in-the-Jolly-Jack-for-another-pint-ers",' offered Jamie, only to be struck by another carefully directed beer mat. But as the evening wore on, it was agreed – four colleagues would run the Edinburgh Marathon in six months' time. Jamie doesn't remember agreeing. But the others – including Brenda – insisted he had. So, that was that, 'The Jolly Jack Joggers' were born.

The team part of the Edinburgh marathon was called the 'Hairy Haggis Team Relay'. The event was for teams of four (so far so good …) and each team had to have a team name (done …). There were four legs, two long, and two short (well, it's the haggis theme, obviously …). Ely and Terry would run the two longer legs – Ely'd start off and do 8.1 miles ('The Royal Leg', round Holyrood Palace and the like …) and Terry would handle the third leg of 8 miles ('Gosford', out along the East Lothian coast and back …). And that left the two shorter legs for Brenda and Jamie. Brenda on number two would do 5.4 miles (from the city to Cockenzie and Port Seton) and Jamie would finish off the last 4.7 miles (the 'Glory Leg', to the finish at Musselburgh racecourse).

*Glory*? That was *very* far from Jamie's mind as he struggled with the basic training. 'Keep it short and simple at the start,' Ely had advised. Short? Five minutes was all he could manage before he was out on his feet … Simple? Yes, he'd decided he was *extremely* simple in the head to have been conned into this. 'Remember to do your warm-up,' Terry had coached. Warm-up? It would have been better to keep warm by a cosy fire or in a nice bath than to be dragging yourself out into the street on a cold evening for another training run. 4.7 miles? That was a marathon of itself. Glory? No bloody chance ...

The only thing that mattered – the only, single, important, valuable, motivating, positive, helpful, creative, sensible thing that really mattered – was that The Jolly Jack Joggers were doing it for charity. Brenda's sister worked for an AIDS charity in Botswana – SOS Children's Villages. 'Sixty thousand children have been orphaned because of the AIDS epidemic,' Brenda had informed them. The decision had been an easy one. And it was the only thing that kept Jamie going.

On the day of the marathon, everyone was in fine spirits. They hadn't set themselves any target time or anything like that. 'I just hope I can finish,' was all Jamie could say.

'You done your full 4.7 miles in training?' Ely asked before she set off, jogging up and down on the spot to keep her motor running.

'Oh yes, no problem,' Jamie lied. And the marathon was under way.

Jamie was *very* nervous as he waited with Terry on the Port Seton esplanade for the second-leg runners to come through. The field was pretty well strung out before Brenda arrived. She was exhausted, and it was all Jamie could do to give her support as Terry raced off on his eight-mile loop out to Gosford House and back. In the hour it took Brenda to recover, Jamie felt a sense of mounting panic. What if he couldn't make it? What if he let people down? What if he failed to finish? What if he made a fool of himself?

He was on his fifty-third 'What if?' when Terry appeared. He'd done well. 'Over to you, pal,' he shouted. 'We'll see you at the finish.'

The 4.7 miles from Cockenzie to Musselburgh was the most agonising of Jamie's life. After two miles – the most he'd ever run before – Jamie hit his own personal wall. The 2.7 miles that remained were absolute agony. What kept him going? What kept him dragging one foot in front of the other? 'Sixty thousand kids in Botswana' who had their own marathon of survival. *What's 4.7 stupid, mad, too-long, too-hard, bloody miles in comparison to that?*

Well, Jamie actually managed to finish 'The Glory Leg'. And as he collapsed into the arms of his three welcoming friends on Mussel-burgh racecourse, they all shared in the glory of the day – and the SOS Children's Villages in Botswana had benefited to the tune of £4693.75p.

'Good effort, everyone. That was some marathon, eh guys?' Ely commented as the team sat in *The Jolly Jack* later that evening.

'Aye, more than a marathon, I reckon,' Terry responded.

'Never again,' Jamie insisted, as he downed his beer.

'Shoot me if I say yes to next year,' suggested Brenda.

'Me too! Even *I* was struggling,' Terry confessed. .

'C'm'on, you wimps,' Ely exclaimed. 'We could *all* do the *whole thing* next time. The Jolly Jack Joggers will live on.' But she shouldn't have been surprised that she was bombarded with a hail of beer mats.


### A gift

I gave a gift the other day,
fifty pence, it was,
dropped into the battered hat of a homeless man,
in a shop doorway in the High Street.
What's fifty pence?
I don't know what it meant to him.
He never even said 'thank you'.
But I'd given a gift of giving to myself ...
That's OK, isn't it?

I sent a gift the other day,
twenty quid, it was,

in an envelope that had come through the post,
and I don't usually open junk mail.
What's twenty quid?
I don't know what it'll be used for.
I don't expect I'll find out.
But giving it made me feel good.
That's all right, isn't it?

I offered a gift the other day,
a wee visit it was,
to an old friend I hadn't seen for a while.
What's forty minutes out of my day?
I don't know what she made of it.
She never said.
But giving my time felt right.
That's fine, isn't it?

I delivered a gift the other day.
I don't know what it was.
I just felt I had something that I could offer.
Was it any use?
I don't suppose I'll ever know.
But giving it gave something back to me,
more than I had ever given ...
Now, that's kind of strange –
and OK – isn't it?

### Epiphany

*Old Testament:* Isaiah 60:1-6
*Epistle:* Ephesians 3:1-12
*Gospel:* Matthew 2:1-12

# 8 Hours and hours

Stephanie had a vestry hour once a week – though that was a distinct
misnomer in so many ways! For a start, the said event was only programmed for *most* weeks because it didn't happen during the holidays; Stephanie was always known as Steph, or more often 'Rev
Steph'; there wasn't a proper vestry in her run-down church and so
the event took place in what was exaggeratedly dubbed 'the office';
and the thing could last anything from a few minutes (rare) to a
couple of hours (more common). But, none the less, Stephanie held
open house as regularly as possible – what was traditionally known as
her weekly 'vestry hour'.

The purpose of it was to allow a young minister to be 'available'.
It was like a doctor's surgery, but without appointments, when people
could come to arrange a baptism, plan a wedding, or simply pour out
their troubles. And you just never knew who was going to turn up.

'The office' had no waiting room, so people waited their turn in
the corridor. There were always the regulars, and one of these was
Reginald. On busy nights or quiet, at the last minute or first in the
queue, Reginald was a regular. And every time Stephanie saw him
waiting, she knew she would get the same story she'd had a dozen
times before. It would never change, and neither would he. For Reginald was what Stephanie's granny would have called 'a poor wee soul'.

Stephanie first met Reginald not long after she'd come to her
bedraggled inner-city parish. He was living with, and caring for, his
elderly mother. It had been that way for years. He'd never worked, as
far as Stephanie knew, and he put all his troubles down to the fact
that he was tied to caring for his mother. No chance of socialising –
Mother to get home to. No time with 'the burds' – Mother to give
time to. No time for Reginald – Mother came first. Everything
would be fine – if it wasn't for Mother.

Stephanie got all of this regularly at the vestry hour. At the beginning it took ages. In time she got it down to ten or fifteen minutes. But, even with a corridor full of impatient locals, Reginald would have his time, and pour out his troubles, and Stephanie would be bored witless once again.

When Reginald's mum died, Stephanie had taken the funeral. Sad though Reginald was at his loss, this was to be his new beginning. A new world would open up. The possibilities would be endless. But there wasn't a new beginning. The new world was pretty much like the old one. It wasn't Mother who'd been the problem, it was Reginald. He was just an inadequate man, and he struggled to come to terms with that. So Reginald kept coming to the vestry hour, and he kept pouring out his troubles, and Stephanie's heart kept sinking.

Stephanie was doing some paperwork one night when there was a loud knock on the office door. When she opened it, standing in the doorway was the most pathetic sight – an unkempt young woman carrying a small bundle in her arms, with the bold Reginald standing by her shoulder. Stephanie beckoned the young lass to take a seat – and Reginald came in too. 'Just give us a minute, will you Reginald. I'll be out in a moment. I'll see to the young woman first.

'But we're together,' Reginald announced, and stepped further into the office. There were only two chairs in the room. The woman took one, and Reginald took the other. And with all the dignity she could muster, Stephanie sat on the table. No one spoke. Stephanie looked at the young woman, and the bundle in her arms wriggled and squeaked. The squeaking bundle was unwrapped to reveal the most gorgeous little baby. Stephanie grinned. The lassie grinned too. The wee baby gurgled on cue.

'This is Sharon,' Reginald announced. 'She said she wanted to see you, Rev Steph, but she didnae know where to come to. So ah sez ah would bring her wi' me.'

'Thank you, Reginald. That was kind of you,' Stephanie replied.

And turning to Sharon, offered, 'I'm glad you've come, Sharon. And what can I do for you?'

'It's the baby, Rev Steph,' Reginald replied.

'Goodness,' said Stephanie. 'That's very clever, Sharon. You said that without moving your lips.'

'No, Rev Steph, that was me, no' her,' Reginald responded.

'I know that,' Stephanie assured him, trying hard to conceal her irritation. 'But it would be better if Sharon were to speak for herself, don't you think?'

'Aye, it would,' Reginald replied. 'But, see, she cannae.'

'What do you mean she cannae – I mean, can't?'

'She cannae. She cannae speak, like. And she cannae hear either. She can do that signin' stuff you see on the telly late at night, but she's not much cop at it yet. So when ah kent that she needed tae come to see you wi' the bairn, ah said ah would talk fur baith o' us, ken?'

And that's the way it was for the next hour or so … Reginald doing all the talking – as usual. But not about his troubles this time. Someone else needed his words. How Sharon knew what Reginald was on about, Stephanie never figured out. But she did, and the nods and smiles clearly indicated she was happy with the conversation.

And that's the way it was when they planned a baptism for Daniel O'Donnell McCann … And that's the way it was when Sharon McCann responded to the baptismal vows with her nods and smiles – and Reginald's voice … And that's the way it was when a baby was handed to a young minister beside a marble font on a sunny Sunday morning, in a run-down church, in a bedraggled inner-city parish, by a godparent called Reginald, and Daniel O'Donnell McCann was welcomed into the family of the Church.

The following Wednesday evening, Reginald was first to arrive for Stephanie's vestry hour. But, unlike his usual visits, he was only there for five minutes. He just wanted to say thank you to Stephanie for 'doing the necessary' the previous Sunday. 'I cannae stay, Rev Steph,' he insisted. 'Ah promised Sharon ah would read the bairn a story. I could be there for hours and hours. So I cannae hang about here a' night, can I?'

Stephanie smiled. She had a picture of Reginald reading to a squeaking and gurgling little Daniel O'Donnell McCann. And from somewhere – and she didn't know where – she heard a voice whispering, 'This is my beloved son in whom I am well pleased.'

## A screaming baby

In the middle of the baptism the baby decided to scream –
a full-blown, lung-bursting, ear-piercing scream.
The minister was struggling to be heard –
and hated it.
The young parents were embarrassed –
and looked it!
The congregation mumbled and tutted –
and meant it.
And one old lady turned to her neighbour
and smiled.
No disturbance or embarrassment,
no complaints from her.
No ...
She whispered to her friend the truth of it all –
'Looks like there's one child
who wants everyone to know he's arrived,
don't you think?'

And she thought of a God
who wasn't disturbed or embarrassed either;
no complaints from Him.

No …
Instead, she was *sure* she could hear,
even above the noise,
the truth of it all,
'This screaming baby is my child,
in whom I am well pleased.
Shouldn't you be too?'

## Baptism of our Lord

*Old Testament:* Genesis 1:1-5
*Epistle:* Acts 19:1-7
*Gospel:* Mark 1:4-11

# 9 A call worth responding to

There was snow on the hills when Ahmed got the call. There had been snow on the hills for a while, so there was nothing particularly noteworthy about that. But the snow had been falling heavily all day and the roads were now pretty bad. Ahmed's journey was going to be a tough one. 'As if being a locum doctor in such an out-of-the-way, friendless place isn't bad enough,' Ahmed muttered to himself as he pulled his woolly hat tightly over his ears. He checked he'd got all his medical supplies and headed out into the cold to his 4x4.

'The top of Glen Arthur,' the call had said, 'Inverarthur Estate – the croft house right at the far end – the Cunninghams' place – two miles off the main road – make an assessment – paramedics on their way – may take a while …'

Dr Ahmed Chowdry knew the Cunninghams' croft well. Old Jimmy Cunningham had a dodgy heart, but refused to come out of the croft. 'I'll die in my own bed,' was his mantra. 'A stubborn man' was the gentlest of titles Ahmed could have used for his uncooperative patient. The son-of-the-croft, Jamie, worked in all weathers and was the rudest man Ahmed had ever met. Thankfully, Jamie was on the hill more often than he was at home, which meant that Ahmed hadn't had much to do with him. Aileen, Jamie's wife, was a quiet kind of soul, well cowed, it would seem, by the dominance of her two male companions.

Ahmed liked Aileen but had never had much of a chance to develop anything close to a warm relationship. She was pregnant with her first. She'd been insistent she had the baby at home. All had been going well … But now? Ahmed had to get there quickly. And there was snow, lots of it. And the Cunninghams didn't care much for their locum doctor.

Ahmed felt that he wasn't cared for much by anybody. He'd been around for about three months – halfway through his locum contract – and had taken the job on after the local GP had died suddenly. Ahmed was well qualified and was delighted with the appointment. But he'd been far from delighted with the reaction of the locals. 'Not like Doctor McCrae … Funny accent, can't understand a word … Paki, isn't he … And Muslim to boot …' Ahmed had heard it all.

He'd tried, of course. Wouldn't his good doctoring skills win people over? Couldn't they respond to his pleasant nature? Shouldn't they appreciate someone with his experience coming to this remote corner in the first place? No, no, and no … and 'no' to almost any other question that arose. So Ahmed steeled himself to see out the rest of his contract. And now there was a crisis … and there was snow … and the Cunninghams didn't care much for Dr Ahmed Chowdry.

Thankfully, the 4x4 did its job through the snow and along the two-mile track from the road, and it didn't take Ahmed long to reach the Cunningham croft. It was getting dark when he arrived. 'No chance of Jamie being on the hill, then,' had been Ahmed's first thought. He was right, and Jamie Cunningham made sure he knew it. 'About bloody time,' was the welcoming greeting, 'Aileen's in a hell of a state.' While the greeting was less than friendly, the medical assessment was pretty well spot on. Aileen was distressed. Ahmed knew it could be an hour before the paramedics arrived. There wasn't going to be time.

'I need this place warmer. Bring a heater in here, and I'll need some pillows to support Aileen's back,' he instructed. Jamie stood in the bedroom doorway and didn't move. '*Now*, man,' Ahmed said, as forcefully as he was able. Old Jimmy had appeared at his son's side. 'And if you've got baby clothes, wrap them round a hot-water bottle to keep them warm. We'll need them sooner than you think. You two need to do your bit. I can't do it all by myself.'

At last the men were galvanised into action. The croft's bedroom was being transformed into a makeshift labour suite. Ahmed was talking quietly with Aileen while the men were away. She'd been in labour for a while, she said, and didn't want to be a bother … Ahmed reassured her things were fine, just moving on pretty quickly. 'Breathe slowly,' he suggested gently, 'you need to stay calm.' Aileen held his hand tightly as she did as she'd been bidden, and visibly relaxed.

'There's been an amniotic rupture and Aileen's tachycardic,' Ahmed announced when the men returned. 'Talk English, man, for God's sake,' Jamie snapped back. 'Waters have broken … Aileen's heart-rate is high … the baby may be distressed …' Ahmed translated. 'The labour is far on … not much time …' more to himself than to his apprentice labour-suite staff. From then on Ahmed swung between telling two gormless men what to do and keeping Aileen as calm as possible, while all the time making sure a home birth went more or less as it had been planned.

It all worked out OK. James Donald Cunningham saw the light of day – or, at least, the dim light of a croft bedroom – at eight fifty-five on the evening of October the twenty-second, and was wrapped in the swaddling bands of a cot-sheet and a knitted jacket that had been suitably warmed round a hot-water bottle. The paramedics arrived at nine fifteen. Aileen and her baby were on their way to the hospital at a quarter to ten. Ahmed took his leave of the Cunningham men at nine fifty-one. He was back home before eleven.

There was still snow on the hills six weeks later. There had been no news of the Cunninghams, not so much as a word of thanks. 'Such is the way of things,' Ahmed had mused, as he'd done often before, and was glad that his locum stint was close to its end. That's when the call came …

The phone's ring was incessant. 'Is that the doctor?' a gruff voice enquired.

'Yes,' Ahmed responded with diffidence.

'Doctor Chowdry?' the voice enquired.

'It is,' Ahmed responded with his usual politeness. 'How can I help you?'

'It's Jamie Cunningham.' Ahmed's heart sank. In an instant, he rehearsed in his mind the several scenarios which could be about to unfold – 'It's my father … I need you for Aileen … The baby …', or maybe some rudeness that wasn't worth contemplating. Ahmed took a deep breath.

'Yes, Mr Cunningham. And how can I help you today?'

'Aye, weel, doctor, it's like this …' There was a pause. Ahmed wondered if some reassuring words should be offered to break the silence. He didn't have to wonder for long.

'Weel …' Jamie Cunningham continued, finding his gruff voice again. 'Ye see, the wee laddie's tae be christened in the local Kirk the Sunday afore Christmas. An' me an' Aileen – an' ma faither tae, ye ken – we wid a' like ye tae come an' join us fur the christenin', an' the wettin' o' the bairn's head …'

Ahmed *almost* responded with a firm 'Talk English, man, for God's sake,' as he wasn't sure he understood much of what Jamie Cunningham was asking. But he didn't. For he knew *exactly* what was being said, and he was sure that this was a call worth responding to after all.

### The call

The call comes in a feeling …
a stirring;
an awareness;
a growing sense;
a persistent thought.
Oh, how I wish the call would be clearer than that.
So I'll wait for the call to come …

The call comes in a whisper ...
a prompting;
a gentleness;
a consistency;
a constant awareness.
Oh, how I wish the call would be louder than that.
So I'll wait for the call to come ...

The call comes in a sign ...
a coincidence;
a surprise;
a connectedness;
a confirmation.
Oh, how I wish the call would be more understandable than that.
So I'll wait for the call to come.

The call comes in a word ...
a suggestion from a friend;
a phrase in a book;
a verse from the Bible;
a line from a song.
Oh, how I wish the call would be more distinct than that.

The call comes in a shout ...
a definite bidding;
a dominant force;
an inescapable roar;
a clear statement of intent.
Oh, how I wish the call would be ....

And the call comes,
'Look!
I've been calling you for *ages*.
Aren't you listening?
What do you want?
Clarity?
Oh, come on!
I'm still waiting …'

## Second after Epiphany

*Old Testament:* 1 Samuel 3:1-20
*Epistle:* 1 Corinthians 6:12-20
*Gospel:* John 1:43-51

# 10 Strange but true

Freddy Buchan was a plant for the Special Branch – at least that was his story when he appeared in the front foyer of the Social Work Department one day and dived inside Jack Gormley's office.

He was an odd little man was Freddy, a kind of Walter Mitty character, and Jack was never very sure whether he was for real or not. Unemployed, Freddy had a penchant for 'a wee line on the geegees', at which pastime he was, it had to be admitted, moderately successful. He and his wife Tanya were well known around the estate, and well known to Social Services too.

Freddy wasn't particularly bright. One day Jack saw him coming towards him in the shopping centre car park, limping badly on his right leg and leaning heavily on a stick. He greeted Jack warmly and the two exchanged good wishes. When Freddie continued on his way, Jack was surprised to see him carrying his walking stick jauntily on his shoulder – *and* limping on the other leg!

But back to Freddy and the Special Branch … There he was, having just dived inside Jack's office. 'Shut the door, man, and quick,' he whispered. 'Did anyone see me, eh, anyone out there?' *More chance of being noticed by all and sundry if you keep acting like this than if you were walking through the shopping centre with a redundant walking stick,* Jack mused.

Before Jack had a chance to reply, Freddy was across the office behind Jack's desk and was furiously pulling the blinds closed – at 10 o'clock in the morning! 'I mustn't be seen. No one's to know I'm here.'

'Good grief, Freddy,' Jack protested, 'are you in trouble? Rent man? Bad debts? Wife? Bad accident with your leg? What on earth's the matter, for goodness' sake?'

Freddy sat down at the desk. *Make yourself at home, why don't you.*

*Cup of tea? Gin and tonic? Cushion for your back? Stool for your feet?* He took out a grubby tissue and mopped his brow. 'No, Mr Gormley, no trouble. But I need to get to Fettes HQ right away, and I need a lift.'

*OK. No problem. Taxi for Buchan?* Fettes was the Headquarters for Lothian and Borders Police and was a ten-minute drive away towards town.

'But why?' Jack asked. 'A summons? A witness to a crime? You can deal with all of that up the road at the local nick.'

'Naw, man, I need to get tae Fettes, tae see my contact. See, I'm a plant for the Special Branch, and I have tae report in.'

Now, Jack had heard some bizarre things in his time as a social worker. But wee Freddy and the Special Branch? No, that just didn't square. He looked somewhat incredulous, and Freddy, picking this up, looked equally offended. 'Naw ... It's right enough, Mr Gormley Gen! Straight up! I've been chosen, specially selected. I'm a plant at the local Communist Party. I go tae the meetin's, right, and if I pick up anythin' interestin' I've tae report it back, see? So, they had a meetin' last night, and they were plannin' a protest wi' leaflets an' a' that, about the rent increases, an' stuff. An' Red Willie *(William Walters, of this locality, well known local political activist, and scourge of anyone in authority ...)* telt me this mornin' that the leaflets are away gettin' printed an' they'll be banged roon the estate by the weekend. An' they're organisin' a public meetin' tae drum up interest. So ...'

Wee Freddy was breathless with excitement. 'So, I need tae get tae Fettes pronto. Gonnae gie us a lift? I cannae get the bus and hop off at Fettes. That'd be too obvious. An' if I was tae get a taxi, Red Willie wid find out soon enough. An' a cannae afford that anyway. So, I thought ... Mr Gormley's my man! Eh? So ... a lift? We could jook intae the car and we'd be offski. OK?'

'Are you sure?' Jack asked, lamely. 'Special Branch, Freddy? Fettes?' Freddy looked even more offended.

'Mr Gormley, would I lie?' Well, it would have been answers-on-a-postcard time, if it wasn't for the fact that Freddy was on his feet again and up at the window twitching at the blinds – obviously with a view to checking if any of Red Willie's entourage might be lurking in the bushes outside. So … yes … Jack Gormley drove Freddy to Fettes police HQ.

'Drop me at the front door and you can park over there,' Freddy suggested, indicating the empty parking place boldly labelled 'Deputy Chief Constable', then nipping quickly from the passenger seat and disappearing through the revolving door into the bowels of the police headquarters. Jack slipped the car past the place reserved for the second-top polis, and sat gingerly on a yellow line near the exit gate. He sat there for twenty minutes, keeping an eye on the rear-view mirror for Freddy's return, or for the arrival of some officious custodian-of-the-law who would seek to move him on. In time, Freddy did come back, slipped into the seat beside Jack and announced, 'Cheers, Mr Gormley That's that sorted. Home, ma man!' Meekly and without question, Jack drove Freddy back to the estate. 'Just drop me here,' Freddy indicated, as the car came to a stop three streets away from the Social Work Department. 'Now, not a word, OK? An' if anyone asks, you've never seen me, right?' And Freddy Buchan was off, ducking into the nearest stair, doubtless to embark on another piece of Special Branch surveillance.

The leaflets were duly delivered round the estate to fire up enthusiasm for complaints to the Council about the rent increases. There were ten people at the public meeting – Red Willie, two other members of the local Communist Party, the Community Centre janitor, two old ladies, a young couple who'd got there on the wrong night and thought they'd come to the prize bingo, Freddy – and Jack Gormley.

The next morning Freddy was at the door of Jack's office asking for a lift to police headquarters. Jack declined. He told Freddy he had a funeral to go to. He lied. Freddy looked very disappointed. And, as he left, Jack wondered if the Special Branch would get to know about the meeting the previous evening, and he wondered, just for a moment, if they'd be told that one of the local social workers had chosen to be there.

### Here

Here is the place; this is the call;
A gentle voice asks for my all.
Here, where I am; dare I say no?
This voice has come, but must I go?

Here I set forth; now I begin;
An urgent voice, my soul to win;
Here, I respond; this I must do;
To heed the voice, 'My way for you.'

Here I must trust; this is my will;
The strength of voice is sounding still.
Here is the truth; now, when it's good;
This voice for me; my life renewed.

Here life begins; now I obey;
A voice that's clear; this is the day!
Here is the lead; nothing's the same;
This voice is clear; it calls my name.

### Third after Epiphany

*Old Testament:* Jonah 3:1–5, 10
*Epistle:* 1 Corinthians 7:29–31
*Gospel:* Mark 1:14–20

# 11 Eradication

Donald had mice in his kitchen. He could hear them scuttling along the worktops when he switched on the kitchen light, and would occasionally catch a glimpse of a small, furry rear-end with accompanying tail disappearing into a gap between the kitchen units. A packet of washing powder in the cupboard under the kitchen sink had had one of its corners chewed through, and he knew *he* hadn't done that. And, just yesterday, he'd found mouse droppings on the window sill. So Donald knew for certain he had mice in his kitchen.

It wasn't just Donald who had mice in his kitchen. Eileen had mice in her kitchen too – given that Eileen was Donald's wife and, consequently, shared the kitchen of their vicarage. That being the case, Kirsty and Ewan had mice in their kitchen as well. But since they were Donald and Eileen's eighteen-month-old twins and didn't really claim ownership of *any* kitchen, they really knew nothing of a mice infestation. They were happy to leave that to people who had it in their job description to worry about these things – like Donald and Eileen.

If the kitchen had been Donald's sole concern or responsibility, he would have been inclined to barricade the kitchen door and never enter the room again, even if he was reduced to living off carry-outs from the local chip shop or Chinese takeaway, or cooking on a camping stove in his front room. For Donald hated mice. A peaceful co-existence with a three-foot-thick wall between invading mice and a vicar with a mouse phobia would have been fine. But this was a vicarage, and Donald had his wife and children to think about, and he had his reputation ... and so mice in the kitchen was a problem that had to be faced.

The problem came to a head one cold, autumn afternoon when

Donald returned to the vicarage after visiting in the parish. Coming in through the back of the house, he was surprised to see that the kitchen lights were out. 'Strange,' he thought. 'No loving wife preparing a family meal or feeding the adorable twins. No noise … No sign of life … Mmmm … Very odd, very odd indeed.'

The quiet, unlit kitchen was amply explained by the scene that greeted him in the lounge. For there was Eileen standing on the sofa, with Ewan under one arm, Kirsty on the sofa beside her clinging to a maternal leg, and a brave vicar's wife ready to fend off all-comers as she brandished a rolled-up copy of The Times in her free hand. And Donald could see at least three mice running up and down the lounge's patterned curtains.

There was no screaming from Eileen, the silent adversarial type. There were squeals of glee from Kirsty and Ewan, who clearly thought the whole thing was just some great game. But Donald, perceiving that the situation was way out of control, let out an ear-piercing scream, slammed the lounge door shut, and hot-footed it to the refuge of the upstairs bathroom. 'Come back here you wimp! Donald! DONALD! Get down here this minute, or you'll get more than mice,' were the cries he heard wafting their way to the top of the house as a threat to his temporary security.

So the problem had to be tackled. Eileen hadn't *actually* reduced it to 'it's the mice or me'. But when she said she was taking the twins to spend a few days with her mother 'in a mice-free environment, which I may come to enjoy permanently …' Donald got the message. And the following day *Rodents-R-Us* got his message too, for within hours Donald was introducing two white-paper-boiler-suited 'rodent operatives' to the intricacies of his kitchen.

'It's a bad one, vicar,' one of the men pronounced.

'Got them everywhere, it seems,' reported the other.

'Time of year,' informed the first. 'Soon as the frosts come, they're inside before anyone can say Korky the Cat.'

'Rapid reproduction rate,' assured the second. 'One pair can give you up to 12 in a litter, and after only 20 days. Females can get pregnant right after the litter appears. A female mouse can be fertile after 12 weeks, you know. So, there you are … today a happy couple, and in a few weeks you have your whole bloody army of mice. Sorry, vicar, but when I get going …'

'Not to worry,' Donald reassured him. 'But can you get it sorted?' He knew that eradication of his mouse problem was *much* more pressing than an occasional oath in the vicarage kitchen.

'No problem, vicar,' the first man said reassuringly.

'What you have here is your common house mouse,' his erudite colleague continued, 'your *Mus Domesticus*. Too large an infestation for your common traps. No, we'll have to use your tamper-proof bait-station, strategically placed along the little blighters' runs, with your multi-feed anti-coagulant poison … that's your *Warfarin* or your *Flocoumafen* in layman's terms if it's really bad – sorry to be technical, vicar.'

Donald had no idea why he was being assigned the slightest 'ownership' of these matters with the persistent use of the personal possessive pronoun. All he knew was that his stomach was beginning to heave at the very thought of it all.

'Better than your prayer in this case, vicar,' the first man added.

'And Robert's your auntie's husband,' the second continued, clearly unaware of his customer's discomfort, 'you have your decaying mouse. Sorted! We'll be back every couple of days for the next week or so to make sure all is well – with you, vicar, if not for our little furry invaders – and you should be clear in a few weeks.' And Donald offered a quiet but heartfelt 'thank you' as the two specialists went about their business.

He was just about to depart the battleground when operative number one called him back. 'A word to the wise, vicar,' he said. 'If you don't want a recurrence, you have to keep the buggers out – sorry vicar. It's like a boat leaking water. No matter how much you bail it out, if you don't plug the leak, you're in trouble. Mice can get in through ridiculously small holes, you know. They can flatten their whole body and squeeze through gaps as small as a pencil. So, anything bigger than your biro pen, seal it up. Keep them out in the first place, and then you won't have this bother again.' Donald nodded.

'It's like sin, vicar,' number two suggested. 'Once you start, you can't stop, so you're better not to start at all.' Donald smiled weakly.

'But then, you'll know all about that, ''cause sin's your business, eh vicar?' said the first. But Donald had already gone, and was pondering how sin getting in through a gap the size of a pencil could be introduced as a metaphor for his homily this coming Sunday.

### Sin

So, there are two ways of dealing with sin –
First …
don't let it sneak under our defences in the first place.
No …
sorry …
that's not on!
We can't stop being sinful.
Even when we try, we're bound to fail,
fallen sinners that we are.

So,
second option?
Deal with it when it happens;
acknowledge the mistakes;
face up to the failures;
recognise the infestation;
name your demons …
That way you keep on top of things
and stop evil taking over.

OK?
Oh, and before I forget,
it's helpful in option two
to say you're sorry ...
sorry to yourself;
sorry to those who've been hurt by your mistakes;
sorry to ...
well, you know what I mean.

## Fourth after Epiphany

*Old Testament:* Deuteronomy 18:15-20
*Epistle:* 1 Corinthians 8:1-13
*Gospel:* Mark 1:21-28

# 12 Against the law

'It's against the law,' Alex pronounced to the little lad who was sitting on the pavement outside his gate. 'It's against the law.'

'No it isn't,' the lad protested. 'I've never heard of a law about that. And anyway, I've been doing it for ages and ages – and you've even seen me – and nobody's ever said "It's against the law" before. I think you just made it up.'

'Made it up, is it? Made it up? Well, I'll tell you this, young man, if you go on breaking the law you'll be in trouble,' Alex insisted. A continued exploration between Alex and the little lad from next door was interrupted by a distant call. 'Frankie. Frankie. You out there? Come on. You'll be keeping Mr Morgan back. Come on in. It's tea time.'

'That's my mum,' Frankie announced, lifting himself up from the pavement where he'd been engaged in conversation with Alex Morgan for some time. Mr Morgan was usually in his garden when Frankie Beaton came home from school. They usually had a chat. Frankie liked that, until Mr Morgan started to wind him up about something or another – as he usually did. 'I have to go in for my tea now,' a relieved Frankie affirmed.

'Well, don't let it happen tomorrow. It'll still be against the law then, just as it is today. So beware, young man, beware.'

'Nah, I don't think so. And anyway, I'll ask my dad when he gets home and *he'll* tell me it's not against the law to wear your shirt outside your trousers on the way home from school.'

And with that, Frankie Beaton was off home, with the tail of his school shirt flapping behind him. Alex Morgan smiled. He loved his times with Frankie – especially when he could wind him up about something or another – as he usually did. 'Against the law …' he called after Frankie, broke into a wide grin, and got back to his gardening.

★ ★ ★

'It's against the law,' Frankie pronounced to his fellow councillors who were gathered in the grandeur of Committee Room 1 in the council offices. 'It's against the law.'

'No it isn't,' the ruling party's spokesman protested. 'There's never been a law about that. And anyway, councils have been doing it for ages and ages – and you've been party to it as well – and nobody could ever say, "It's against the law." You're just making it up.'

'Making it up, is it? Making it up? Well, I'll tell you this, Councillor Highfield, if you go on breaking the law and flouting the rules of this chamber, you're going to be in trouble,' Frankie insisted. A further exploration between Frankie and the ruling-party spokesman was interrupted by a bang of a gavel from the committee chairman. 'Councillor Beaton. Resume your seat. Councillor Highfield has the floor. Please sit down, or I shall rule you "out of order".'

'Well said, Mister Chair,' Iain Highfield announced, lifting himself up from the seat in which he'd been the target of Frankie Beaton's tirade. Frankie Beaton was usually on the attack from the 'opposition benches', especially when Iain Highfield had something controversial to propose. They usually clashed head on. Iain liked that, until Frankie Beaton started to wind him up about something or another – as he usually did. 'I will continue now, if I may,' a relieved Councillor Highfield affirmed.

'Well, there will always be tomorrow. It'll still be morally indefensible then, just as it is today. So beware, Mr Highfield, beware,' Frankie Beaton muttered as he resumed his seat.

'Nah, I don't think so. It's not against the law to cut the housing repairs budget. It's pragmatic. There's a recession on. The cloth has to be cut ...'

And with that, Iain Highfield flapped his copy of his party's budget proposals across the table. Frankie Beaton smiled. He loved his times with Councillor Highfield – especially when he could wind him up about something or another – as he usually did. 'Against the law …' he called out once more across the room, broke into a wider grin, and got back to his committee papers.

★ ★ ★

'It's against the law,' Iain pronounced to the large invited audience gathered in the conference centre. 'It's against the law.'

'There's nothing illegal about it,' the woman sitting two along from him at the table announced. 'There's never been a law about that. And anyway, countries have been doing it for ages and ages – and you've been party to it as well – and nobody could ever say, "It's against the law." You're just making it up.'

'Making it up, is it? Making it up? Well, I'll tell you this, Lady Glenborough, if we go on breaking the law and flouting the rules of International Conventions, we're going to be in trouble,' Iain insisted. A further exploration between Bishop Iain Highfield and Lady Mary Glenborough was interrupted by the voice of the TV presenter who sat between them. 'Restraint, Bishop, restraint. Let Lady Glenborough have her say. You'll have your turn soon enough.'

'Thank you, Christine,' Mary Glenborough said, leaning forward in her seat to engage better with the crowded conference centre and the TV audience beyond. The Bishop was usually on the attack when it came to the legality of the invasion, especially when people like Lady Mary Glenborough were spouting forth. They'd been clashing head on at many meetings in recent months. Mary actually liked that, until the Bishop started to wind her up about something or another – as he usually did. 'I will continue now, if I may,' a relieved Lady Glenborough affirmed.

'Well, there will always be tomorrow. It'll still be morally indefensible then, just as it is today. So beware, Lady Glenborough, beware,' Iain Highfield muttered as he leaned back in his chair.

'Oh, I don't think so,' Lady Glenborough was continuing. 'It's not against the law to do what is right – even when military action is required. It's our role. We have to combat evil, stand up for right and truth …'

And with that, she wagged her finger admonishingly straight into the TV camera lens. Iain Highfield smiled. He loved these kinds of debate – especially when he could wind up people like Lady Mary Glenborough about something or another – as he usually did. 'The invasion is still against the law …' he said out loud just off-camera, broke into an even wider grin, and scribbled notes on his pad in preparation for his next contribution.

### Laws

I've been given the Law and the Prophets,
From the Medes and the Persians, and all,
And the laws of the land to direct me,
All my wayward intents to forestall.
Yes, I follow the rules of society;
And the precepts my family's ordained
Will ensure that I act 'right and proper'
So their standards are always maintained.

I'm extremely well versed in behaviour
That's ethical, moral and true;
And codes for directing my conduct
Mean I'll do all the right things by you.
Yes I'm upright and just; law-abiding;
An exemplar; a benchmark for all;
A paradigm; one to look up to;
A mentor, whate'er may befall.

But what do my laws say of justice
And meaning for those who're oppressed
By an imbalanced world, where resources
Are kept by a few, while the rest
Cry out for their share, and get nothing,
And are begging for crumbs that fall down
From the tables where laws are created
To keep them down there on the ground?

I can walk with my head high above them,
And look down my nose with a sneer;
Being righteous and holy is easy –
As long as the poor are not near
To plead with their tears for compassion,
And call me to be more aware ...
What good are my laws and good-living
If I've never been bothered to share?

## Fifth after Epiphany

*Old Testament:* Isaiah 40:21-31
*Epistle:* 1 Corinthians 9:10-23
*Gospel:* Mark 1:29-39

# 13 Vic's disease

Dr Allan Galloway was a retired GP – though semi-retired would be more accurate. He was delighted to be asked back to do some sessional work in the surgery. Turn up, do the 'shift', swan off to the golf course for the afternoon, and leave the others to cope with the hassle ... Great! So Allan took a surgery twice a week. It was the times in the week when people could come without an appointment. You just never knew who was going to turn up. That's what still made being a GP enjoyable.

The 'heart sink' people were the regulars. And one of these was Victor Arkwright – or Vic, for short. Vic always seemed to be carrying the troubles of the world on his shoulders. Early in their acquaintance, Allan had become convinced that Vic's education was entirely based on back copies of the *Readers Digest*. Occasionally he would trot out three or four jokes in a row, and end with the quip, 'Aye, Doctor, Life's Like That ...' as if he were offering some new and wonderful insight into the human condition. From time to time he would regale his GP with the story of someone with one leg who had climbed Everest, or a teenager who had rescued an entire fishing party from a stricken yacht by swimming ashore and raising the alarm, or some new breakthrough in cancer treatment. And he was red hot on the benefits of Stannah Stair Lifts.

But the most worrying times were when Vic's *Readers Digest* stories served to fuel his hypochondria. One week he'd have read a story about 'John's Prostate' and was convinced he had prostate cancer. The next, he'd have absorbed some information about a new treatment for arthritis, and was sure he needed a replacement hip-joint. So when Vic Arkwright told his doctor that he was suffering from leprosy, Allan Galloway didn't know whether to laugh or cry.

'I think I've got leprosy, doctor,' had been Vic's opening gambit. Resisting the temptation to enquire what edition of the *Readers Digest* Vic had been perusing this week, the GP replied with a non-committal, 'Oh.'

'Aye, doctor,' Vic continued. 'Leprosy. That's what it is right enough.'

'And what makes you think that, Vic?' the doctor's gentle diagnostic probing began.

'Well, see,' Vic went on, warming to his tale of woe, 'it's like this ... First off ... I've got these red blotches round my waist. And, second of all, I've got this dryness on the palms of my hands. And ...' Vic paused for dramatic effect. 'And this is the worst one, doctor – I've got these white patches on my neck and behind my left ear. The wife spotted them in bed this morning. She jumped away that quick too. She said it could be catching, and she wouldn't go near it to tell me what it was like. So, here I am, doctor. And when you put it all together, well ... it's leprosy, right? I was just reading the other day ...'

Allan chose to interrupt the flow before Vic suggested his fingers might be falling off at any minute. 'OK, Vic. Take off your shirt and let me see these blotches.' While Vic was divesting himself of his top, Allan pulled on his rubber gloves in preparation for his examination of Vic's torso.

'Very worrying, eh Doc?' Vic suggested.

'Mmmm,' was the uninformative reply. 'OK. Let me see your hands.'

'Bad, eh?' Vic offered.

'Mmmm,' Allan repeated. 'Now turn around and let's see these white patches.'

'Are they horrible, Doc, just like the wife said?' Vic enquired.

'Mmmm,' Allan responded once again while he was removing his rubber gloves. 'OK, Vic. Put your shirt on. Now, here's the story.'

'Bad, Doctor?'

'No, not bad.'

'Leprosy?'

'No, not leprosy.'

'No? What then, what's the matter with me?'

'Vic, you've got fleas. The red blotches are flea bites. Get some flea powder and dust your bed and your clothes. Wash everything. And keep the house clean.'

Vic looked suitably sheepish. 'And my hands?'

'Dry skin,' Allan retorted. 'Too much washing-up. Let your wife take a turn. Or use moisturiser on your hands. That'll sort it.'

'But … the white patches on my neck …' Vic questioned.

'Vic. Have you been painting the house?'

'Aye. How did you know?'

'Because you've got white emulsion paint on your neck and behind your ear. Get your wife to give it a thorough wash and you'll be as good as new.'

Vic looked crestfallen. 'So, no leprosy then?'

'No leprosy, Vic. No leprosy. The last confirmed case of leprosy in the UK was in the Shetland Islands in 1901. So, no leprosy.'

Vic rose to leave. 'Oh, but while we're on the subject,' Allan continued, 'take this magazine home. It'll tell you all about leprosy and the *real* effect it still has on people in South America and North India and elsewhere. And you'll read about organisations who work to combat it. Go on. It might widen your knowledge.'

When Vic had gone, Dr Allan Galloway wondered whether his magazine would be able to compete with the wonders of the *Readers Digest*. He never found out. But he only hoped that the *Readers Digest* compilers never decided to do an in-depth piece on the symptoms of the bubonic plague.

**Thanks**

The doctor never complains –
at least, not to me –
that I never say 'thank you' for the way she's sorted me out.
Oh, I knew it hadn't been life-threatening …
But it was bad enough,
and I can't be doing with being not well.
She did a good job.
The advice and the tablets did the trick.
I was better in no time.
But I never bothered to say 'thank you'.
I was just relieved to be OK again.
I just got on with living …
Until I got 'not well' again,
and I had to go to see the doctor to complain about being sick.
But she never complained –
at least, not to me –
that I never said 'thank you'
for the way she'd sorted me out last time.
So, doc, if you're reading this,
'thank you' for sorting me out.
You did a good job.
And I'll try to remember to say 'thank you' the next time.

My God never complains –
at least, not to me –
that I never say 'thank you' for the way she's sorted me out.
Oh, I knew it hadn't been life-threatening …
But it was bad enough,
and I can't be doing with being not well.
She did a good job.
There was a healing from somewhere that did the trick.

I was better in no time.
But I never bothered to say 'thank you'.
I was just relieved to be OK again.
I just got on with living …
Until I got 'not well' again, and my God got it in the neck
when I complained about being sick.
But she never complained −
at least, not to me −
that I never said 'thank you'
for the way she'd valued me and my life the last time.
So, God, if you're hearing this,
'thank you' for making me what I am.
You did a good job.
And I'll try to remember to say 'thank you' the next time.

The people who work with lepers never complain −
at least, not to me −
that folk don't often say 'thank you'
for the way they're sorting things out.
Oh, I knew I didn't have leprosy …
Well, it's not around my society any more −
there are other kinds of 'being not well'.
Leprosy organisations do a good job.
There's a healing they can offer that makes a difference.
It's better in our time.
But I never bothered to say 'thank you'.
I was just relieved that leprosy happened to other people.
I just got on with living …
Until I got 'not well' again, and I felt it's all gone wrong
when being sick's such a nuisance.
But they never complained −
at least, not to me −

that I never said 'thank you'
for the healthcare throughout my life
while people still die of leprosy.
So well done for fighting against leprosy.
'Thank you' for doing what you do.
You do a great job.
And I'll try to remember to say 'thank you'
the next time –
and put my hand in my pocket
and offer you some practical support.

### Sixth after Epiphany

*Old Testament:* 2 Kings 5:1-14
*Epistle:* 1 Corinthians 9:24-27
*Gospel:* Mark 1:40-45

# 14 Heroes

When Josie heard that her favourite DJ from the local radio station was to come to her village, she was ecstatic. Jaguar Jerry was the best ever, and it wouldn't be too much to say that Josie worshipped the ground he walked on.

Jaguar Jerry was a flamboyant, over-the-top, loud, brash, zany character who was, quite clearly, Radio WK202's best asset. Since his arrival at the station, listening figures had soared, advertising revenue had exceeded expectations, and teenagers like Josie had a new hero.

She had Jaguar Jerry's posters all over her bedroom. The colour-scheme, much to her parents' displeasure, was clearly influenced by the DJ's typical yellow and black. She carried a signed photograph of him in her school bag. And the best moment *ever* in her fifteen years of life was being able to speak to *the man himself* on a radio phone-in quiz, even though the conversation lasted no more than thirty seconds. She wondered sometimes whether Jaguar Jerry would remember talking to Josie from Little Barnsworth. But, even if he didn't, she remembered talking to *him*, and that was more than enough.

So when word went round that Jaguar Jerry was to visit her village as part of Radio WK202's promotional tour round the area, Josie was ecstatic. 'Jaguar Jerry here ... in my village ... I just can't wait ...'

The visit was to happen on a Sunday. Sunday June the 18th. Sunday June the 18th at 10.30am. Sunday June the 18th, 10.30 to 12. Sunday June the 18th, 10.30 to 12, on Little Barnsworth's village green. Josie had it ringed in red on the calendar in the kitchen. She had it programmed into her mobile phone. She'd marked it with a star in her diary. She checked off the days, from three weeks before, on a chart on the wall of her bedroom. She'd fall asleep thinking about Jaguar Jerry. She'd wake up knowing she was another day closer to the momentous event. It just couldn't come quickly enough for Jaguar Jerry's greatest fan.

So when Josie ruptured her Achilles tendon in a school hockey match on the afternoon of Friday the 16th of June at 1.47pm, it was a disaster beyond disasters. She screamed in pain as she fell; she wept in the ambulance all the way to the hospital; she sobbed uncontrollably during the investigation of her injury; she was unable to take any consolation from anyone. The assumption was that the injury was bad, or that Josie wasn't good with pain, or that a fifteen-year-old was just being a wimp. But Josie knew better. It wasn't the pain of her injury that mattered. Her distress was the pain of all her dreams being shattered, the ruination of her carefully crafted picture of the best day of her life.

She had the operation to repair the Achilles tendon tear late on the Friday evening. She had to stay in hospital overnight and her leg was to be encased in plaster to hold her foot in place so that the tendon had time to heal. Two months – minimum – she was to be in plaster, with crutches for later, but a wheelchair for now. Josie was inconsolable. She didn't sleep on the Friday night, and when she went home on the Saturday afternoon she insisted on being taken upstairs to her bedroom and being left alone. Josie cried herself to sleep on the Saturday night. She woke early on the Sunday morning feeling awful. She refused to come out of her room once her mum had helped her to dress. Her conversation was monosyllabic. If she never spoke to anyone again she wouldn't have minded.

So when the doorbell rang around 10 o'clock, Josie hardly bothered. Until, that is, her father came upstairs. 'OK, young lady. Up-an'-at-'em. We're going out.'

'But ...' Josie protested, to no avail. For her burly father had already lifted her in his arms and was carrying her downstairs. Her mum was there, with Josie's yellow and black jacket, standing beside Josie's wheelchair.

'Your chariot awaits, my dear,' she announced.

'But ...' Josie tried again. But by now she'd got her jacket on and was secured in her chair.

The footrests appropriately adjusted, the wheelchair was spun round by her mum, who boldly proclaimed, 'Ready? Then we're off.' And when Josie was unceremoniously bumped down the two steps at the front of the house, she was surprised to see the school minibus parked at the garden gate.

'But ...' Josie attempted once more. But no one bothered. And there by the gate was Mr Cargill, her hockey coach; Daren, the captain of the school rugby team; Mr Rollinson from two doors down; and her dad, grinning from ear to ear. In an instant, Josie was being lifted, wheelchair and all, into the back of the bus. And, with no one being too concerned with health-and-safety, four strong men held the wheelchair firmly in place as Josie and her entourage were driven off in the bus. The destination? The village green, of course. But when they got there, there was no way Josie was going to see for the crowd. There were *masses* of people. It was bad enough being stuck at the back, but when you're in a wheelchair, how are you going to see anyway? But that had clearly been thought of too, because Josie was now being pushed in her chair, through the crowd, from the back, right to the front. Well, being pushed proved to be more difficult than expected – no solid path; wet grass; a heavy chair. Undeterred, Josie's four strong men simply lifted the chair aloft, and with two of them on each side, Josie was carried, shoulder-high, like some queen in a sedan-chair, right to the barriers at the front.

The rest was a blur for a bewildered Josie. She remembers her mum sticking a camera into her hand. She remembers the loudness of the cheers when Jaguar Jerry appeared. She remembers bouncing up and down in her chair as much as she was able when the music was playing and Jaguar Jerry was encouraging the singing-along and chanting of the crowd. She remembers shouting out the answers to the quiz questions as loud as she was able. She remembers it being over all too quickly. She remembers crying a lot. She remembers it being *pretty* much the best time of her life ... But now she has lots of pictures on her bedroom wall of the day Jaguar Jerry came to her village, on the 18$^{th}$ of June. There he is waving ... There he is looking right in Josie's direction ... There he is brandishing his yellow and black flag ... There he is in front of Radio WK202's banner ... There he is blowing kisses to the whole crowd ... *And* there's a photo her mum took on the way home – of Josie in her wheelchair, being carried high by Mr Cargill, Daren, Mr Rollinson and her dad, with a label beneath it boldly designating them as 'Josie's heroes'.

## Heroes

I have a little hero; her name is Sarah Jane.
She comes on Friday nights and stays for tea.
She knows I can't get out because I'm still in too much pain.
So she's promised now that she will come to me.

She's always bright and cheery; she gives me all her news,
She makes me feel I matter while she's there.
She listens to my stories; she never yawns or frowns;
She doesn't rush; she takes the time to care.

We need our little heroes; we need them every day;
Like Sarah Jane – or maybe you and me;
They're not in stained-glass windows, or found in history books;
They're the here and now; the current crop, you see.

The ones who're bright and cheery; the ones who lift us high,
Who help us reach from darkness to our sun.
We know them when we see them, and thank them
    when they come;
Yes, let's hear it for the heroes, everyone!

## Seventh after Epiphany

*Old Testament:* Isaiah 43:18-25
*Epistle:* 2 Corinthians 1:18-22
*Gospel:* Mark 2:1-12

# 15 The old place

There was no doubt about it. The old place had been transformed. Ramsay Fenwick never believed it would have been possible. Others had said that it would happen one day, but he was too sceptical for that. But now, here he was, seeing it for himself, and it was quite a transformation.

The 'old place' in question had been the 'old place' of his youth. Indeed, as a familiar landmark, it had been the 'old place' for generations of people in that part of the town. The foundation stone read '1843', so it had been the 'old place' for more than a century and a half. 'Old place' wasn't its proper name, of course. 'The Old Parish Church of St John' was its correct title, and that was boldly announced to passers-by on the large noticeboard at the corner of the street. But for the more 'knowing' locals, the 'old place' it was, and 'old place' it would stay.

The trouble with the 'old place' was that it was old, and, in recent years, had begun to fall into disrepair. It was in a part of the town that was just being redeveloped, but the congregation of St John's were as old as the nickname of their church, and there was neither the money nor the energy to restore the 'old place' to anything close to its original grandeur. Things got worse when dry rot was discovered in the roof. There was nothing else for it. The 'old place' would have to go.

There were howls of protest, of course. How could the area be the same if 'the old place' wasn't there? OK, people didn't go to the church any more. So? Shouldn't the Church authorities preserve an old building? Or maybe the Council ... Yes, the Council should keep it going ... a day centre ... nursery ... anything that would keep 'the old place' as it was.

Ramsay Fenwick had followed all of this from a distance – a 3000-mile distance, in fact, from his home in Canada. The Old Parish

Church of St John had been his childhood church and had remained his family's place of worship long after Ramsay had emigrated. He, too, wanted the 'old place' to stay. He'd not been actively involved for ages, of course. But it still mattered to him.

Things came to a head when it was decided the building should be pulled down – 'Not fit for purpose'; 'dangerous to keep in its present state'; 'an eyesore to be got rid of'. There were those who were pro and those against; those in favour of demolition and others who believed a renovation might be possible; those who wanted it out of the way and those who fought for preservation. There were campaign groups and public meetings; newspaper headlines and delaying tactics; claims and counter-claims; factions and rumours. From his 3000-mile observation point, Ramsay hoped the 'old place' could be saved, but, to be honest, he didn't believe it could.

When he heard from his mother that the 'old place' was to be transformed, Ramsay couldn't believe it. 'An entrepreneur,' his mother had breathlessly revealed during their weekly Skype call. 'Once lived locally ... made his pile ... keeping the shell ... transforming the frontage ... the new from the old ...' and much more besides.

Eighteen months later, having followed the progress of the transformation with fascination, Ramsay couldn't wait to see it for himself. There was to be a 'grand opening' of 'The St John's Centre'. The top two floors had been renovated and turned into low-cost housing; the basement and sub-basement had been divided into office space for community projects and sheltered workshops for adults with learning difficulties; the ground floor was a community hall with a small chapel area off it for local worship services; the caretaker's home had been sold as a desirable townhouse; and the minister's manse had been divided into luxury flats. Ramsay knew all of this because his mother had kept him informed at every stage. But he wasn't really prepared for the transformation.

The impact the frontage of the St John's Centre had on Ramsay was quite breathtaking. The glass and steel front of the building shone and sparkled in the sunlight; the bold signage demanded your attention; and the striking nature of the whole enterprise completely altered the character of the surrounding area.

Ramsay was stunned. 'What a transformation!' was all he could say – over and over again. 'Who would have thought that the old place could shine like this?' And as he looked at the original foundation stone reminding him that 1843 marked the beginning of the 'old place', it just didn't seem right any more. He wondered if someone would create a new foundation stone with today's date, and whether the locals might take to calling it 'the new place' from now on. After all, that's what a transformation deserves, isn't it?

### Old?

What's old, when there's still
A chance of change, and newness
Can always appear?

### New?

What's new, when the gift
Of newness is around us
Every single day?

### Transfiguration

*Old Testament:* 2 Kings 2:1-12
*Epistle:* 2 Corinthians 4:3-6
*Gospel:* Mark 9:2-9, 12-17

# 16 Ashes

Anthony collapsed on the sixth day of the trek up Mount Kiliman-jaro. He and his three colleagues were on the Machame route and were only two days from the summit when it happened. Thankfully they weren't on a steep part, and had only just set off from their overnight camp. But Anthony's collapse was dramatic enough. He just dropped like a stone.

It had all been going so well since they started out from Moshi, a town on the plains below the 4600-metre mountain in Tanzania. The trek was a charity event for the local hospice, in memory of the head-master of Anthony's and his friends' old school. The climb had been two years in the planning, and the logistical arrangements and fitness of the men were unquestioned. Anthony was, arguably, the fittest of them all. At thirty-eight he still played rugby, jogged and played squash regularly, and was, of course, a keen walker and climber. He was the last one anyone would have expected to collapse.

Oxygen deficiency was the obvious cause. The climbers had been well warned that they should rest up for a bit if anyone was affected, to give their bodies some more time to acclimatise. But as the day wore on, Anthony didn't improve. He couldn't stand by himself. He complained of dizziness. His speech was slurred. So the decision was made to abandon the climb.

No one expected the diagnosis to be a brain tumor. An MRI scan confirmed everyone's worst fears. 'A glioblastoma multiforme,' the specialist said. 'A fancy name for a bad one, then,' Anthony had replied. And a bad one it was. Surgery tackled the basics. Radiation therapy followed. But to no avail. Everyone was devastated. The pro-gnosis wasn't good.

Anthony lived alone in a typical bachelor pad. He couldn't look after himself after the surgery, but with a combination of family, friends and home-nursing care, Anthony hung in there in his own surroundings for as long as possible. He was happy to have visitors. In fact, he encouraged it. And that's why Bobby went round to see his best mate.

Bobby hadn't seen Anthony since he and his two other climbing colleagues had seen him off in the ambulance when they'd all returned from Tanzania. Bobby was apprehensive. 'How come this hits someone who's as fit as the big man?' he'd asked his mates. No one volunteered an answer. 'What the hell am I going to say?' he enquired. No one offered any ideas. Bobby was on his own ...

When he was ushered into Anthony's front room by the care assistant, Anthony was hugely different from the man Bobby had climbed with a few weeks before. Supported by massive cushions, he was buried deep in a big armchair. He'd lost weight. His eyes were sunk into his skull. And he had a huge patch on the side of his head where his hair had been shaved round the site of the operation, and the scars were clearly visible.

Bobby shook hands with his friend. Anthony picked up his visitor's apprehension. 'Don't worry, pal,' he offered, 'it's not catching.'

Bobby took a seat on the other side of the fireplace. 'How are you?' he asked, feebly and inadequately. Anthony raised his hand slowly to the side of his head and touched the bare patch of skin. *'Is he in pain?'* Bobby wondered. *'Should I just go? Or is he going to say something deep and searching? Can I handle this? O my God ... This is too much.'*

Anthony continued to stroke the bare skin above his temple. Then, looking Bobby straight in the eye, he said, 'See the size of this bald patch?' Bobby nodded slowly. And Anthony's face broke into the biggest smile you could imagine, as he said, 'And I've still got more hair than you, you slaphead!' And Anthony guffawed with a typical, loud, all-embracing laugh, and Bobby smiled in relief and admiration.

Indeed, it was 'admiration' that became the commonest word people would use over the next few months when they talked about Anthony. When people recounted the jokes he would tell, admiration was the name of the game. When the guys shared with each other reflections on his courage, they couldn't fail to mention admiration. When Anthony was taken to the local hospice and insisted a cheque be written for £5000 as a thanks for his care, everyone spoke of admiration again. Anthony never reached his thirty-ninth birthday. But when hundreds of people turned up at his funeral, admiration was the theme.

Anthony had told his family that his ashes were to be scattered on the slopes of his favourite hill near his home. That was to be private. Everyone approved. But when Bobby got a phone call a couple of weeks later to be told that Anthony had left a letter for his mates, he wasn't sure what he was going to hear. There was no way he was going to read it alone. So, a few days later, three men gathered round the table in the corner of the local pub to do it together. Bobby read it out.

'I'll keep it simple, because you guys were never ones for fancy words. So here's the deal. You'll be given some of my ashes when I'm gone – about a big-toe's worth – and you've to take them up Kilimanjaro. I know I buggered up our trip. So do it again – for me. Raise some more money if you like. But get to the bloody top this time. I want to know I'll make it there with you. And leave the ashes on the summit. I think I'll like it there. Now, go and have a drink on me, OK?'

The three lads looked at each other. Bobby smiled first and, spontaneously, three hands were stretched into the centre of the table to hold the others, as a silent commitment to Anthony's wishes.

That's why, eighteen months later, after seven days of trekking, three elated climbers held hands again on the top of Kilimanjaro as the ashes of Anthony's big toe were scattered on the ground. 'Who would have thought that a few ashes would matter so much?' Bobby commented.

'And who would have thought we'd have such admiration for a

man with a half-shaved head who still had more hair than you?' came
the reply. And three men looked up from the ashes and admired what
they saw and knew.

### Ashes

What'll I do with the ashes,
Now that the old man has gone?
Where should I scatter the ashes?
Where does he really belong?
Down on the beach in the sand dunes?
Up on the hill where he climbed?
Or should he go down
To the bar of *The Crown*
Where the old man spent most of his time?

What'll I do with the ashes
Now that my hopes have all died?
Where to dispose of the ruins?

Why's it so hard to decide?
Leave them behind and forget them?
Pretend that I never had dreams?
Or should I explore
Being hopeful some more,
And start work on some other schemes?

What'll I do with the ashes
Now that my years have gone by –
The downfalls; the promises broken;
The suffering; the tears that I cried?
Go on being haunted by failure,
And still be cast down by despair?

Or should I let go
Of my sins, and still know
There are better days, just over there?

What'll I do with the ashes
Now that I only have dust;
Fragments of every construction
That should have been strong and robust;
Memorials marking my passing;
Towers that reach to the sky?
But who said my stuff
Was important enough
The ravage of time to defy?

What'll I do with the ashes
Now that my issues have gone?
Where should I scatter the ashes?
Where do they really belong?
Lay them aside where you want to;
Then you've a tale to relate.
But now, let's get on ...
When the scattering's done
There's more of our life that awaits.

## Ash Wednesday

*Old Testament:* Joel 2:1-2, 12-17 *or* Isaiah 58:1-12
*Epistle:* 2 Corinthians 5:20b-6:10
*Gospel:* Matthew 6:1-6, 16-21

# 17 Being bothered to notice

Geraldine was having a very bad day. Indeed, she couldn't remember having had any good days for ages. Such was the way of things. One bad day after another, no respite, no pleasure …

It hadn't always been like that. When she'd started off as a junior doctor in the teaching hospital in the city she was excited and motivated and ready for anything. But, somehow, things had changed. Medicine had become a bit of a grind – too many pressures and too few staff; too many difficulties and not enough resources; too many deaths and too few successes; too much studying and not enough satisfaction. Geraldine knew she'd get through it. Others had been that way before her. She knew it would all come right. It was part of the process. But it didn't make feeling overwhelmed any easier to cope with. She longed for a good day. But, for now at any rate, she'd just have to cope with another bad one.

It didn't get any easier on the journey home. Her head was full of what she'd have to cope with in the evening that followed. There was a tedious journey home; there was shopping to do; there was a meal to prepare; there were books to read through; there was studying to do; there was a late night ahead; there was a full working day to follow; there was on-call to cope with at the weekend.

Standing in the bus queue outside the hospital didn't help. The man in front had pushed in ahead of her to get himself tucked into the back of the bus shelter out of the rain. There was no room for Geraldine in the shelter. She had to stand in the downpour. She'd forgotten her umbrella. She was going to get very wet.

When the bus arrived, it was already busy. She was the last one allowed on board. She had to stand. The woman on the seat beside where she was standing had two kids to contend with. Geraldine could just about cope with the screaming. But the constant tugging at her coat was a major irritation. She was relieved when mother and brood disembarked and she could sit down for the rest of the journey.

The lady beside her by the window was very large, so there wasn't much of the seat for Geraldine to sit on. She was constantly bumped on the shoulder by people coming down the aisle to get off. She tried to avoid the assaults by moving further into the seat. But the large lady by the window made it clear she didn't like her space being invaded. So, with Geraldine trapped between unthinking passengers and a large lady's space, the journey home just added to an already bad day. The roadworks on the way home compounded the problem. It took ages to get through the temporary traffic lights. The rain belted down outside. The bus was packed and uncomfortable. The windows were all steamed up. The tension on board was awful.

That's when Geraldine saw the rainbow. The interminable journey towards the roadworks meant that the bus was inching its way past the park. There wasn't much that could be seen through the opaque, condensation-covered windows, and no one was taking much notice of what was outside. Geraldine only caught the change of colour out the corner of her eye, but it was clear enough that something bright outside was causing a diffused glimmer in the rain-drops running down the bus windows. Geraldine turned round to face the window to get a better look. She couldn't see properly. So, gingerly, she stretched across her large neighbour and ran a gloved hand over the window to clear away some of the condensation. The lady bristled with indignation, and grunted a 'Humpphhh …' of protest. Geraldine hardly noticed, because what she was now staring at was the biggest, fattest, brightest rainbow she'd ever seen. It spanned the whole park, and offered a complete arch from the houses on one side to the industrial estate on the other.

The bow in the sky was clear and vibrant. The depth of the brightness was astonishing. The colours were amazingly distinct from one another, in clear bands of wonder. Geraldine had never seen anything like it. She looked at the woman sitting next to her, but she was staring straight ahead, protecting her space – and missing the rainbow. Geraldine cast a quick glance over her shoulder at the other passengers, but they were absorbed with iPods, and evening papers, and books, or staring ahead – and not one of them was noticing the wonder of the rainbow.

Geraldine wanted to stand up and shout at folk, and get them to clear their windows and take in the amazing sight before they missed it. But you don't do things like that, not on a crowded bus surrounded by strangers, do you? So Geraldine satisfied herself by turning back to her festival of light and colour. She had no idea how long she gazed at the rainbow as the bus inched slowly towards the roadworks. But she stared long enough to see the rainbow begin to fade and lose its brightness and vibrancy. Soon, half of it had gone, and by the time the bus had negotiated the temporary traffic lights, the rainbow had pretty much disappeared completely.

And somehow a bad day had begun to fade away too. Oh, there was still the rest of the journey home; and shopping to do; and a meal to prepare; and books to read through; and studying to do; and a late night ahead; and a full working day to follow; and on-call to cope with at the weekend. But somehow, after being absorbed in a big, fat rainbow on a wet day, that didn't seem to matter any more. And, if anyone had bothered to notice, they would have seen that Geraldine travelled all the way home with a big smile on her face.

### Rainbows

Today, I watched the sky being transformed,
From slate-grey
And its embrace of oppression,
To a riot of colour
And the rainbow-surprise of freedom.

Today, I watched a friend being transformed,
From the blackness of suspicion
And the tyranny of rejection,
To a rainbow-awakening of brightness
And the blessing of inclusiveness.

Today, I watched a world being transformed,
From the storm-clouds of hatred
And the destruction of evil,
To a rainbow-promise of hopefulness
And the healing touch of peace.

Today, I watched my God being transformed,
From the horror of retribution
And the fear of punishment,
To a rainbow-arc of forgiveness
And the offering of grace.

Today, I watched my faith being transformed,
From a catalogue of certainties
And the assurance of truth,
To the brightness of infinite possibilities
And the rainbow-gift of growth.

### First in Lent

*Old Testament:* Genesis 9:8-17
*Epistle:* 1 Peter 3:18-22
*Gospel:* Mark 1:9-15

# 18 Up to the neck in it

'There you are. That'll do you good,' the landlady said as two bowls of steaming liquid were placed in front of David and his father. 'Eat up now. Enjoy.'

'What's this, Dad?' David whispered when the lady was out of earshot.

'Don't know,' his dad whispered in response. 'But all the other food's been good so far. So this should be OK too.'

'Looks disgusting,' David insisted.

'I'll try it first and see if it's OK,' his dad suggested, and with that dipped his spoon tentatively into the hot contents of the bowl and took the smallest sip. In an instant he was smiling broadly. 'It's OK. In fact,' he said, plunging his spoon into the thick liquid and taking a real mouthful, 'it's great, just like the soup your granny used to make. Leek and potato, I think. Come on. Get stuck in.'

It took David a few minutes of blowing and sipping, tasting and savouring before he was as bold as his dad. But his dad was right. It was *very* good, and pretty soon father and son were sitting back admiring empty bowls. The landlady of their guest house reappeared. 'Enjoy that, did you? I like empty bowls.'

'Lovely, just lovely, Mrs Morgan,' David's dad responded. 'And what do you call such a wonderful soup?'

Mrs Morgan beamed proudly. 'Oh, that's *cawl* – my special leek broth. It's a traditional recipe, see. It's been handed down through the generations. And, after all, I have to serve *cawl* on St David's Day. It's a traditional St David's Day meal. Very Welsh, so it is.' And with a flourish, their landlady had cleared their plates and had disappeared into the kitchen.

David and his dad were on a fishing trip to Bangor-Is-Y-Coed in north Wales, just south east of Wrexham, to fish on the river Dee for brown trout, grayling and – hopefully – salmon. David was now as keen a fisherman as his dad. Having started fishing off the pier at home and then progressing to fishing with his father on his boat on the reservoir, he was now well and truly hooked – as it were. And coarse fishing on good rivers was his absolute favourite.

They'd never been to Wales before. But David's dad knew someone at the angling club who'd recommended coming. *And* they'd recommended Mrs Morgan's guest house too.

The two hungry fishermen were sitting savouring the after-effects of the *cawl* when the splendid Mrs Morgan bustled into the dining room with two plates brimming with a lamb stew. 'And there's *laverbread* on the side, mind,' she proclaimed.

'What's that?' David whispered when Mrs Morgan had gone.

'Don't ask. Just eat,' his dad insisted.

And when the lamb stew and the 'seaweed pancake' *laverbread* had been duly demolished, there was a large chunk of *bara brith* – 'a traditional Welsh cake', Mrs Morgan had informed them – to follow. With lashings of butter and chunks of cheese, the *bara brith* completed the most sumptuous of meals – the best of the week by far.

'And all this for St David's Day?' David's dad had enquired of his hostess when the table was being cleared.

'Yes, indeed. Well, you have to make the effort for such a man. March the first, see, when every Welsh person feels very Welsh.'

'I'm called David too,' David offered.

'I know,' Mrs Morgan replied.

'So what makes your David so special?' the boy asked. Mrs Morgan laid her tray of plates on the table, wiped her hands on her apron and sat down with her guests by the fire.

'Well,' she began, 'it's like this. For a start, if you'd been around when St David was around, see, you would have been called *Dewi*, just as he was. That's his Welsh name. He lived in south Wales a long, long time ago. When I was in school, I was told that he was a very kind man, who lived a very simple life.' David smiled approvingly and leaned forward in his chair to make sure he didn't miss anything as Mrs Morgan continued. 'His father was a prince. And when Dewi went all around Wales, he set up churches so that people could learn how to live good, Christian lives.'

Mrs Morgan paused and smiled at her young listener. 'And here's something to think about when you and your dad are out fishing on the Dee tomorrow.'

'What's that, Mrs Morgan?' David responded eagerly.

'Well,' the storyteller continued, 'Saint David – Dewi Sant – is sometimes known in Welsh as "Dewi Ddyfrwr". That means "David the Water Drinker". It's said he drank nothing else but water, see. And sometimes, when he knew he'd been bad, to punish himself he would stand up to his neck in a lake of cold water, chanting parts of the Bible.' Mrs Morgan laughed loudly. 'Up to his neck … A bit dangerous, but what a thought … Up to his neck … Quite a man …' she chortled as she rose from the fire, picked up her tray and disappeared into the kitchen, leaving the two satisfied guests to their warming fire and musings on the life of a patron saint.

The next day, when David was up to his knees in the Dee, casting in vain for a bite as he and his dad had been doing all morning, he wondered if wading out up to his neck would have better results. He decided not to try it. But he thought he might have a go at chanting the Bible instead, it being the day after St David's day, and all. He didn't know much of the Bible. And then he remembered … that verse his granny had taught him … what was it again? … ah yes, 'The Lord's my shepherd, I'll not want; he makes me …' he said out loud.

He didn't get any further, because there was a huge tug on his line. David fought hard to bring in his catch, and when he did, he and his dad were delighted that he'd landed the biggest brown trout of his angling career thus far. He decided not to tell his dad about the Bible bit, just in case he'd be told he was silly. He would keep that to himself for now, and maybe, later on, a budding Dewi Sant might try it again.

### David

David seems such an ordinary name,
just like mine;
and yet ...
and yet, he was a saint;

So, what does that tell me?
Maybe,
just maybe,
the ordinary can become saintly.

I seem such an ordinary kind of person,
just like you,
and yet,
and yet, perhaps there's a saint in there somewhere.

So, what does that tell me?
Maybe,
just maybe,
David and I can be saints together.

Who knows?

### St David's Day

*Old Testament:* Genesis 17:1-7, 15-16
*Epistle:* Romans 4:13-25
*Gospel:* Mark 8:31-38

# 19 Stating the obvious

Jonathon had decided to paint the gate. It was the May Day Bank Holiday, and though Gail had to work – the downside of a wife who worked in retail and had to take her share of working Bank Holidays – Jonathon had a day to himself. So he'd decided to paint the little wooden gate at the bottom of the garden that led onto the lane at the back of Gray's Mill Terrace.

The gate had been in need of painting for ages, but it was one of those things that Jonathon had kept putting off. Painting gates was not his favourite pastime. Indeed, painting *anything* was to be avoided at all costs as far as Jonathon was concerned. But time and the vagaries of the local weather were beginning to take their toll on the garden gate. So Jonathon steeled himself to get it done on his day to himself. And when it *was* done, that would be that.

It was a 'first-thing-in-the-morning' job – *'So that I can have the rest of the day to myself,'* Jonathon had surmised. But 'the best laid schemes', and all that … and with Jonathon's familiar procrastination *and* his dislike of painting … well, it was four o'clock in the after-noon before he got started. *'I have to do this before Gail gets home, or I'm for it, that's for sure,'* was the final spur to getting the painting done.

So, with his overalls on, the paint stirred, the brush ready and the turpentine awaiting, Jonathon set about the hated chore. He'd only got halfway down the first spar of the gate when Mrs Whyte from number 27 came past on her way to the park with her two Yorkshire terriers. Tugging them carefully away from the prospect of getting garish green gloss on their delicate fur, she acknowledged the working Jonathon with, 'Hello, Jonathon. Painting your gate?' Jonathon grimaced, but there was no need to reply to Mrs Whyte's 'stating the obvious', for she was already off down the lane with her dogs.

Jonathon returned to his task. He finished the first spar and was so intent on his work that he didn't notice the twins from number 19 standing silently at his shoulder. He almost bumped into them as he drew back to admire the beginnings of his masterpiece. 'Goodness, don't creep up on people like that!' The twins looked at each other then back at Jonathon. 'Hello, Mr Gibson. Painting your gate?'

'What does it look like?' Jonathon snarled. 'Get to ...' And, with that, the twins were off in case a grumpy old man decided to paint them too.

Jonathon got back to the job in hand. He'd managed three spars on one side when a delivery van drew up beside the garage next door. White-van man opened the back doors of his van and pulled out a medium-sized cardboard box. He kicked both doors closed with a carefully aimed size 10, and, noticing Jonathon for the first time, greeted him with, 'Hi, mate, painting your gate?' and with a whistle was off up next-door's path, only to return a minute later with, 'Still at it? Nice day for it anyway. Oh look, I think you've missed a bit.' And he was in the van and off about his business – of delivering boxes and, no doubt, bothering other unsuspecting gate-painters – before Jonathon had the opportunity to tell him where he really *should* go.

Jonathon had had enough. Either the gate would have to stay seven-eighths unpainted, or he was going to have to find another way of sorting this out. Too many people stating the obvious was too much to bear. But Jonathon had a solution, a 'cunning plan' that would get the gate finished, take him away from any unwanted inter-ruptions, *and* please his wife into the bargain.

Within half an hour he'd unscrewed the gate from its hinges, spread newspapers all over the kitchen floor, carried the gate, the paint, the turpentine and the paintbrush indoors, and was getting stuck into the unpainted parts of his garden gate. Why hadn't he thought of this before? No passing dog-walkers ... no inquisitive kids ... no random delivery men ... no one, *no* one who would wander by, stating the obvious. At least the hated chore could be finished in peace.

It all went well, and Jonathon was just finishing the second side of the last few spars, when the back door opened and in walked Gail. 'Hello, Jonathon, painting the gate?'

Gail Gibson will never know how close she had been to hearing an uncharacteristic string of oaths, being covered in garish green gloss paint and wearing a nearly completely painted garden gate as a necklace. Well, what do you expect when someone goes about stating the obvious?

### Trouble

The trouble with asking Satan to get behind you,
Is that Satan is now behind you,
And you've no idea what he's up to.

The trouble with having Satan in front of you,
Is that Satan is in front of you,
And you know full well what he's about.

I suppose it's stating the obvious,
But 'better the devil you know
Than the devil you don't.'

Or, to put it another way,
Better to face up to the trouble that you know
Than have it sneak up on you from behind.

'Get thee behind me, Satan,' is the obvious thing to say.
But turning round and saying 'gotcha'
Might be kind of useful too.

I suppose it's stating the obvious,
But 'better knowing what the devil is up to
Than having no idea at all.'

## Second in Lent

*Old Testament:* Genesis 17:1-7, 15-16
*Epistle:* Romans 4:13-25
*Gospel:* Mark 8:31-38

# 20 Refuge

When Jack Johnston's barn went on fire no one was really surprised. Jack was a good farmer but a careless kind of man, so there was no telling what might have caused the fire – old and faulty wiring, a carelessly positioned lamp, a discarded cigarette end. And when the barn went up, no one stopped to think about the cause anyway. All anyone knew was that Jack Johnston's barn was on fire and that spelled trouble.

It was the direction of the wind that did it. The summer wind had turned south the day before, and that meant that the fire was being blown towards the village. The first things to go up were the trees in Two Acre Wood on the village edge. In the height of the summer the undergrowth was tinder dry, and when that caught fire from the sparks from the barn, the trees had no chance. Within minutes, the whole wood was ablaze, sending showers of sparks well into the air, with the wind blowing lighted debris further towards the village.

Jenny Miller was the first to raise the alarm. She'd opened the back door of her cottage to let her cat in from the garden when she smelt the smoke. And when she saw the wood begin to burn, she rushed inside to call the fire brigade. That was the start of the biggest emergency anyone in the village could remember. Even before the fire-trucks arrived, people were being roused from their sleep, homes were being evacuated, folk were rushing around to make sure their loved ones were safe, and everyone was moving as far away from the fire as possible.

'As far away from the fire' was right up at the other end of the village. The fire chief had advised everyone in close proximity to 'get the hell out of there', as he politely put it. And pretty soon a large crowd of frightened and bewildered villagers were crowded together in the chill night air wondering what to do next.

'Let's open up the church for everyone,' someone suggested. No one ever knew *who* had suggested it, but pretty soon crowds of anxious villagers were packing themselves into the little village church – and some of them, it has to be said, hadn't been inside the church for a *very* long time.

The church, of course, was cold – at least for a time till the heating began to take the chill off the air – because no one expected all of *this* to be happening in the middle of the night, did they? Some folk organised hot drinks, and soon steaming cups of warming tea were being passed around to all and sundry – and from the *best* Women's Group china cups too.

The carved wooden chairs from around the altar were made into makeshift tables, and people sat in the pews or cross-legged on the floor as they finished their tea. The purple pew-cushions from the side aisle were dragged out so that sitting on the floor could be made more comfortable. One family put two pew-cushions together in the corner and bedded down their frightened children, assuming they were settling in for a long night. The velvet, tasselled table-cover from the oak table in the vestry became makeshift bedding, and soon two little children were fast asleep.

It was like that till the wee small hours of the morning. When the all-clear came, the villagers slowly made their way into the dawning half-light of the day. They were struck by the chill of the air – the warming refuge of the church had done its job. The heavy smell of charred wood was everywhere. Two Acre Wood had gone completely, and beyond it could clearly be seen the few remaining blackened timbers of Jack Johnston's barn. Word quickly went round that no one had been hurt, that no other property had been damaged, and that everyone could safely return to their homes. The villagers had been lucky.

When a few of the congregation went back to the church after the villagers had left, their beloved church was very different from the pristine, holy place they were familiar with Sunday by Sunday. One of the purple pew-cushions was wet and stained where someone had spilled tea on it. The velvet vestry table-cover was a crumpled heap in the corner. Three of the precious Women's Group china cups had been broken. 'Frankly,' said one, 'this is a disgrace. You would think people would have enough gratitude to leave things as they found them and not get the church in this kind of state.'

So they set about putting it to rights. There were things that had happened in their church the night of the fire that no one could have expected to witness, and, to be honest, which many of them didn't like. And when it was back to normal, they were more than happy. But did they notice that the congregation was expanded somewhat on the following Sunday by several folk who hadn't been in church for a *very* long time?

## A divine clear-out

The notice says, 'It's cleaning week;
We need some volunteers
To give the church a good spring-clean,
The biggest one in years.'
Before you rush to volunteer
And contribute your part,
Perhaps you might give thought to this,
And answer from the heart ...

I wonder how we'd take it
If our Lord offered his time
And rolled his sleeves up, did his bit,
More human than divine,
To help us with the cleaning of
Our own most holy place?
And would he find it tidy, or
An absolute disgrace?

Oh, he wouldn't find us selling things,
Like pigeons, and the rest.
'*Fairtrade*'s our game,' and anyway,
We'd only sell the best.
But might he find us peddling
Ill-will and discontent,
And selling truths so different
From the Truth he really meant?

Oh, he wouldn't find us running our
Own money-changing booth.
For 'Free-will offering' is our norm;
We're honest, that's the truth!
But might he find us selling short
His openness and grace;
A love that's unconditional
That offers all a place?

Oh, we wouldn't be with those whose church
Is run by thieves in dens,
For if you measured righteousness
We'd score ten out of ten.
But might he find our holiness
More shallow than it seems,
With cant and much hypocrisy
As underlying themes?

Be careful when your invite calls
For willing volunteers,
For Christ might slip in too and find
What's lain well hid for years,

And clear the very temple that
*You* thought was just sublime.
For with the human Christ you may
Get cleansing that's divine.

### Third in Lent

*Old Testament:* Exodus 20:1-17
*Epistle:* 1 Corinthians 1:18-25
*Gospel:* John 2:13-22

# 21 Patrick

'Wi' a name like Murphy, it shouldn't take much workin' out where ah come frae, eh?'

Mona smiled and carried on with her work. She had to take great care while bathing Hetty and continued with the gentle sponging of her patient's wrinkled and sensitive skin. Hetty liked her soak in the hospice jacuzzi-bath, but got even more pleasure from the careful washing afterwards from her favourite nurse. For her part, Mona always enjoyed her times with one of her favourite patients. She knew that nurses shouldn't have favourites. Everyone should be special. But, in Hetty's case, some were more special than others.

'So, where d'ye reckon ah come frae, eh?' Hetty repeated.

'No idea,' Mona responded.

'Come oan, lassie,' Hetty insisted. 'Murphy? No? Weel, here's a clue. Today's St Patrick's day ...'

'Oh, of course, you come from Ireland,' Mona responded. 'North or south?'

'Aha! Gotcha!' Hetty announced, in as firm a voice as her feeble frame could muster. 'It's neither,' she proclaimed with triumph.

'But,' Mona protested, 'Murphy? St Patrick? I thought ...'

'Aye, a'body does. But Murphy's no ma *maiden* name, ye see? Ah was born in Cumnock in Ayrshire. Did ye no' get that frae the accent, eh?'

Hetty fell silent. Mona smiled again and continued with her personal tasks. But when she looked up at Hetty she realised that the old woman was crying. 'Hetty?' she enquired, taking the distressed woman's wet hand in hers and now kneeling beside the bath. 'What's the matter? Living in Cumnock can't have been *that* bad.'

Hetty grinned weakly through her tears. 'Ach, lassie. Yer a guid soul. But, ye ken, ah aye greet when I think o' ma hame an' ma man

– an' it being Saint Patrick's Day. He wis ca'ed Patrick. Paddy, Paddy Murphy. An' ye don't get mair Irish than that, eh?'

'You must miss Paddy a lot, Hetty,' Mona offered.

'Aye lassie, ah dae that. An' him been gone thirteen years since. He was a saint, ma man, an' ...' She stopped in mid-sentence, and her tears began to flow once more, more copiously this time.

'What is it?' Mona asked after a while.

'Ah cannae tell ye, lassie,' was all Hetty could offer. 'Ah cannae tell ye ...'

Mona waited to see whether any more would come. It didn't, and so she decided not to push it. 'Never mind, then,' she said. 'Come on. Let's get you out of this bath before you get a chill.' And it wasn't long before the thin, bony frame of Hetty Murphy was wrapped in a big, fluffy bath towel as she sat in a chair being dried by Mona's skilful and caring hands. She was just at the stage of helping Hetty dry her face when the old woman took both of Mona's hands in hers and held them to her chest. She looked her nurse straight in the eye and said, 'Ma man was a saint, so he was. But ... but ... but ah wisnae worthy o' a man like that.'

For a third time Hetty Murphy was in tears. And this time Mona felt she had to find out why. Now kneeling in front of her distressed patient, she squeezed Hetty's bony hands in hers and whispered, 'Do you want to tell me about it?'

Hetty looked up, tightened her grip on Mona's hands as strongly as she was able, and replied, 'Yes, lassie, ah dae. If ye'll but listen ...' And listen Mona did, as Hetty Murphy told her story.

'Ah was a young lassie at hame in Cumnock when ah met a laddie at the dancin'. That was Paddy Murphy. He fair swept me aff ma feet, so he did. Ah was besotted in love wi' him in nae time at a'. He was frae Dublin, ower in Scotland for work. An' a better, mair gentle, lovin' man ah've never met. My family took tae him an' a'. So we arranged tae go ower tae Dublin, tae see his ain family. An' that's where it a' went wrong.'

Hetty stopped, as if wondering whether she should continue. Mona offered no prompting, hoping the silence would be enough. It was. After a few minutes, Hetty took a deep breath and continued with her story.

'In the hoose when we got there was Paddy's mither an' faither. Ah shook their haunds. An' when ah wis done, Paddy's mither up and piped, "What religion is your woman?" Ah didnae ken why that maitered, fur it hadnae come up wi' Paddy an' me. So Paddy replied, "What do you mean, mammy?" An' his mither raised her voice an' spat oot words that sent a shudder doon ma' spine. "Well, Patrick Murphy. Is she a Catholic? Is she a Catholic?" Noo, ah kent ah wisnae, but ah wisnae shair that Paddy did. It didnae maiter. An' ah wis surprised when he said, "Naw, mammy, she isn't." Weel, that was the start o' it. His mither jumped up oot o' her chair an' shouted at Paddy, "Take that woman out of this house. I'll have no Protestant whore marrying into my family. Take that woman out of here and don't come back with her on your arm. It's her or your family. No good Catholic boy will marry the likes of that." Weel, ye can imagine the uproar. There was shoutin' an' cursin'. An' the upshot o' it a' was that Paddy took me hame, back tae Cumnock. An' we were mairit – Patrick Aloysius Murphy an' Heather Jean Jamieson – in the toon ha', nae the church, mind, nae Catholic, nae Proddy, nae nuthin'. An' that was that. Me an' Paddy settled doon, and we had oor ain family, an' gran'-weans tae, an', since Paddy deed, ah've got a wee great-gran' wean an' a'. Paddy an' masel' were mairit for fifty–fower year. He was a saint tae me. He never saw his family again. He chose me ower his ain family. Only a saint wid dae that.'

Hetty was in tears once more. Mona let go of her hands, took the corner of the towel and gently wiped the tears from Hetty's cheeks. And, as she did so, Hetty caught her gaze again. 'Tell me, lassie,' she said hoarsely, her voice barely above a whisper, 'was it ma fault? Was it me that broke up Paddy frae his family? Ah' cannae get it oot o' ma mind. Was it me that did it wrang? Was ah the sinner tae Paddy's saint?'

Mona returned Hetty's gaze. And, looking deeply into her eyes, she took a deep breath and said, 'Hetty Murphy. You caused no breakup. You caused no heartache. It was narrow-mindedness that caused that. It was bad teaching that caused that. If there is any fault, it's not yours, Hetty. You did what was good, responding to Paddy's love for you, being a good wife and mother and grandmother. You did good, Hetty. Saint Paddy might be saying even now that he had his saint too, and that's you, eh?'

Hetty sat quietly, as if taking time to absorb Mona's wisdom. Her tears had ceased, and after a while she was smiling again. Leaning forward slowly, she kissed Mona gently on the cheek. 'Thanks, lassie. You're a guid soul. An' a' that from me rememb'rin' it's Saint Patrick's Day.'

Mona smiled in response. 'Ach well, maybe we'll just have to change it to "Saint Hetty's Day" instead, eh?' The newly christened Saint Hetty furrowed her brow. 'Naw, lassie. When ah think on what Paddy Murphy did for me, then Saint Patrick'll dae jist fine.'


**All are one**

If you ever go across the sea to Ireland
And be there at the closing of the day,
You will find more saints than you could yet imagine,
And openness to help you on your way.

There are saints who challenge bigotry and hatred,
Rejecting both the orange and the green,
Condemning all sectarian division,
And evil, both exposed and still unseen.

There are saints whose story labels them as Catholic,
And Protestants who've come a different way,
Who hold the hand of those who cherish justice,
Whose flag of peace remains their sole display.

So, give thanks for saints from Erin's Isle who teach us
A hatred of the bullet, and the gun,

And the human labels that will yet divide us;
Who show us, under God, that all are one.

## St Patrick's Breastplate

*I include this hymn here for the obvious reason that it is attributed to St Patrick and, in particular, is well known for its section which begins 'Christ be with me ...' The words are a translation of a Gaelic poem called 'St Patrick's Lorica' or breastplate. (A 'lorica' was a mystical garment that was supposed to protect the wearer from danger and illness, and guarantee entry into heaven.) Cecil Alexander penned these words at the request of H.H. Dickinson, Dean of the Chapel Royal at Dublin Castle. There was a desire that a gap in the Irish Church Hymnal be filled with a metrical version of 'St Patrick's Lorica'. A carefully collated copy of the best prose translation of it was prepared. Within a week, this exquisitely beautiful as well as faithful version of St Patrick's Breastplate was completed.*

I bind unto myself today
The strong Name of the Trinity,
By invocation of the same
The Three in One and One in Three.

I bind this today to me for ever
By power of faith, Christ's Incarnation;
His baptism in Jordan river,
His death on cross for my salvation;
His bursting from the spicèd tomb,
His riding up the heavenly way,
His coming at the day of doom
I bind unto myself today.

I bind unto myself today
The virtues of the star lit heaven,

The glorious sun's life giving ray,
The whiteness of the moon at even,
The flashing of the lightning free,
The whirling wind's tempestuous shocks,
The stable earth, the deep salt sea
Around the old eternal rocks.

I bind unto myself today
The power of God to hold and lead,
His eye to watch, His might to stay,
His ear to hearken to my need.
The wisdom of my God to teach,
His hand to guide, His shield to ward;
The word of God to give me speech,
His heavenly host to be my guard.

Christ be with me, Christ within me,
Christ behind me, Christ before me,
Christ beside me, Christ to win me,
Christ to comfort and restore me.
Christ beneath me, Christ above me,
Christ in quiet, Christ in danger,
Christ in hearts of all that love me
Christ in mouth of friend and stranger.

I bind unto myself the Name,
The strong Name of the Trinity,
By invocation of the same,
The Three in One and One in Three.
By whom all nature hath creation,
Eternal Father, Spirit, Word:
Praise to the Lord of my salvation,
Salvation is of Christ the Lord.

## St Patrick's Day

*Old Testament:* Ezekiel 36:33-38
*Epistle:* 1 Thessalonians 2:2b-12
*Gospel:* Matthew 28:16-20

# 22 The Great Piano-Player

It hadn't been the best of holidays. The idea had been good, she and the wee-one booking into the small hotel by the banks of the loch. Winnie was on her own now, without John. So she and Chloe deserved a break. And the all-in package at the 'child friendly' hotel sounded ideal. After all, there was an adventure park nearby, and pony-trekking to be tried. There was childcare in the hotel – at least enough to allow a stressed mother to get the odd meal in peace – and there was a children's menu to satisfy even the fussiest of children. Yes, the idea had been good.

But it had rained! It hadn't let up for one moment since they arrived. It had already rained enough to ensure that the annual rain-fall for a lochside village was likely to be exceeded in one, miserable July school-holiday week.

Oh, how it had rained! The adventure park was 'Closed temporarily due to the inclemency of the unseasonal weather'. The pony-trekking was unavailable – because any sensible pony would be spending the week in the equine equivalent of a cosy front room watching TV. And after three days cooped up in the hotel lounge, Winnie came to the inevitable conclusion that, for her and Chloe, it hadn't been the best of holidays.

And, on top of it all, there was the piano. A bored Chloe had dis-covered the hotel piano on day two of the soggy vacation. The far-from-new upright sat in the corner of the lounge, and it was a real struggle for a mother, aware of the other residents, to keep her little girl from continually creating a discordant cacophony of horrible noise. The hotel staff didn't have a key to lock the piano lid – she'd asked. The ample supply of kiddie's colouring books on the hotel table weren't nearly as much fun – she'd tried. A mum's patience had worn very thin, and the other guests were bound to complain – they hadn't yet, but they might. (Lord preserve us from an open piano and a wee girl on a wet holiday in what used to be a quiet lochside hotel!)

Winnie was just coming back from the toilet – having warned an extremely bored and fidgety Chloe on pain of much retribution to finish colouring in the circus picture in the colouring book and to stay well clear of the by now out-of-bounds piano – when she heard the inevitable racket – the shapeless, atonal tune, battered out fortissimo by the budding infant-school concert pianist. She was mortified, and even more so when she saw a matronly type rise wearily from her leather armchair in the corner of the lounge and head sternly towards the recalcitrant child.

An embarrassed but protective mother was about to rush forward to ensure that her offspring didn't have a heavy piano-lid bashed down on her little fingers by this fearsome octogenarian, when she stopped in her tracks. For instead of remonstrating with the junior off-key piano-player, the old lady stopped behind the piano stool and stood for a while as an engrossed Chloe, unaware of the watching presence, continued with her unique solo performance. Then, leaning forward, and with bony arms stretching round the child and her own fingers now poised over the keys, she whispered, 'Keep playing, little one. You're doing just fine.' And for every note the little girl played, old, wrinkled hands played other notes around it. Here, a melodic chord; there, an arpeggio; now, an embroidered trill; then, a rising crescendo; again, a gentle phrase; at last, as a finale, a resounding flourish.

The other residents in the lounge – including a relieved but amazed Winnie – broke into spontaneous applause. Both piano-players turned to their admiring audience: one elderly lady, smiling, looking slightly embarrassed and surprised; and one beaming little girl, now standing on the piano stool with a friendly arm around her little shoulders, bowing, bowing and bowing again.

Having lifted Chloe down from the stool and with the applause dying away, the old lady returned to her leather armchair. A little girl with a huge smile ran to her mummy for a hug. And a bemused mother wiped away a big tear from her eye, as she heard, from the far side of the lounge, someone asking in an all-too-loud stage-whisper, 'Who's the Great Piano-Player?'

## Making music

I'm no great shakes as a piano-player …
my fingers are fat and stubby,
and I seem to hit the wrong keys all the time;
I know what I *want* to do …
there's a tune in my head that sounds good to me,
but I don't know how to play it right;
I try so hard,
but what I create somehow turns out
more like noise than music –
once again.

So, if there's a God out there who believes in me –
come to me now, and stand with me;
don't be distressed or annoyed by what you hear;
wrap your arms around me, and help me out;
put your notes round my notes,
so that together we can make good music;
fit my tune into your glory song
so that people might ask,
'Who's the Great Piano-Player?'
once again.

### Fourth in Lent

*Old Testament:* Numbers 21:4-9
*Epistle:* Ephesians 2:1-10
*Gospel:* John 3:14-21

# 23 Dear John

Patricia often went to sit by her husband's grave. 'Often' meant what it said – she went as often as she was able. At the start, it was every day. Her daughter would ask her how often she went to the cemetery. 'Once a week or so,' Patricia would lie, to make sure her daughter didn't worry. But Patricia knew different. Every day, it had been. And when there were no time constraints – like work, or the closing-time for the cemetery gates, or having another appointment to keep – it would be for hours on end.

There were even times when she'd lain on top of the grave to be as close as possible to her husband. She would have pitched a tent and kept a permanent vigil at the graveside. She would have been the eternal flame at the tomb of all that was her life. But you don't tell your daughter that, do you? So it was 'Once a week or so,' and that kept her happy.

It was a little different now, but not much. Most of Sunday afternoons would be spent in the graveyard. Once church was over, Patricia would make her way to the village cemetery, and the hours would blur into one another as she lost track of time. It wasn't uncommon for the cemetery attendant to remind her that the gates were about to close and she'd have to go now – and she hadn't even realised it had got dark.

She'd slip out from the office at lunchtime and tidy the flowers or remove the autumn leaves; she'd take an hour on the way home to trim the grass or polish the headstone; she liked the drawn-out summer evenings – she could stay longer at the grave.

She would speak to him, of course. 'Dear John,' she would begin, 'dearest, dearest John.' Her conversation in the early days, often through tears, would be about how she missed him; how it was agony without him; why did he have to go? Sometimes she was downright angry with a husband who would leave a wife behind, just when life close to retirement was getting easier and there was such promise of things to do and places to see. Why did he go and take all that with him? And there were times when it was all about downright despair, while she pleaded for him not to be dead.

She still did that. She'd sworn at him often enough for causing her loneliness and sorrow. Of course she knew he hadn't gone from her on purpose. Of course she knew … But you don't think rationally when you're at your husband's graveside and you miss him so very, very much, do you? But now there was a new side to her conversations. She would tell John what was happening. She would share hard decisions with him. She would sometimes ask for advice. Which was fine – apart from one major problem … she never really felt John was there.

She knew he wasn't *there,* that suddenly he'd pop out from behind a gravestone and say, 'Boo!' It wasn't *that* kind of 'there'. She knew he was dead, and that all that was left in the ground was an expensive coffin and a precious, decaying corpse. She knew *that.* But she wanted so desperately to feel he was *there* … you know, actually listening, close to her, aware of what she was on about and how she was feeling, and, most of all, responding to her rantings and pleadings, her questions and her information. But, try as she might, she never did. She talked often and long. She wasn't going to stop that. Even if her husband didn't hear her, it did Patricia good to get things off her chest. But she just longed for a day, even a second, when she would feel he was there. 'Dear John, dearest, dearest John, can you hear me? Are you with me? Where are you, my dearest John?'

Patricia was in the middle of a long peroration one Sunday afternoon, when she became conscious that an elderly lady was standing beside her. Patricia had been spending time clearing away some old flowers, arranging some fresh ones in a vase, pruning a little rose bush at the corner of the plot, and occasionally running her index finger along the gold lettering of John's name on the headstone. And all the time she'd been talking to her husband. She was kneeling down with her back to the cemetery path, so she didn't notice the stranger till she straightened up ready to get back to her feet. 'Oh, I'm sorry. I didn't see you there,' she blurted, hoping the stranger hadn't heard her ramblings. *'She'll be thinking I'm mad,'* she worried.

'I'm sorry. I didn't want to startle you. It's just that ... well ... I was wondering ...'

*'Oh my God. She does think I'm loopy. I wish I'd heard her come.'*

'You see, I heard you talking ...

*'That's it. She's clocked me. "Mad widow-woman, talking to herself." I hope she doesn't know anyone I know ...'*

'And I realised that there was no one there. So you must be talking to ... well ... is it your husband?' Patricia nodded gently.

'Oh, I'm *so* glad. You see, I do it too. I talk all the time to George. My sons think I'm absolutely doolally. But it's a comfort, isn't it?' Patricia nodded again, not sure what to say.

'I know he isn't there, of course. At the start I wanted him to speak back to me, to tell me he was OK, to give me reassurance, or even to offer advice. But he never did. So I gave up worrying. I figured out that if he never responded much to me when he was alive, how could I expect the old so-and-so to speak to me now? He always had his head buried in his newspaper. I never knew whether he'd taken in what I'd said or not. He just grunted occasionally. I should have asked him questions afterwards. But I never did. I just went on and on, and he was there to allow me to go on and on. So that's what I still do now. It's reassuring that I can talk, and, wherever he is, he just lets me go on and on. And, you know, in a strange way, that *is* his reply, isn't it? He just gives me space to talk.'

Patricia was standing now. 'Thank you,' she said, 'I know just what you mean.' She offered the elderly lady her hand, and the two widows parted with the promise to look out for each other when they were in the cemetery.

When Patricia was alone again, she felt a sense of peace that she hadn't had for a long time. It didn't include a sense of John's presence. That would have been too much to expect. But, none the less, she knelt down in front of the headstone once again, ran her index finger along the gold lettering of John's name, and whispered, 'Dear John, dearest, dearest John ... you old so-and-so ... thank you for giving me space to talk ...'

### Dear John

I don't know why I'm writing this, because I know you're never going to read it. But then ... Anyway, it'll do me good to write to you, no matter what. So what do I want to say?

I don't know, actually. I miss you. I miss you being around. I miss your whistle when you come in the front door from the shops. I miss you leaving your slippers where you stepped out of them in the middle of the bedroom floor – even though I've told you a million times not to. I miss you laughing out loud at the TV, and jumping up and down when your team scores. I miss the quietness of you when we listen to music together. I miss you being warm in bed. I miss you spending endless hours over your crossword and looking so disappointed when I fill in the last clue. I miss your touch. I miss your calm reassurance ... I miss you so, so much.

Aaarrgghhh! I hate you for leaving me like this. Why did you have to go and take all the good stuff with you, so that 'we' has gone and only 'I' am left? I miss you ... I don't hate you *really* ...Well, yes I do, a bit. I just miss you not being here, and 'me' being 'us' for ever.

Can you read this? Do you know what I'm saying? Can you understand? No ...

Well, tough. 'Cause I'm saying it anyway. And it makes me

feel better, so there! And it makes me feel … well … in a strange way, that you're closer than ever.

So, missing you makes me feel you're closer … Mmmm … I think I'll finish off now, 'cause there's some stuff I'm going to have to go and work out.

As always.

With *OOOOOODLES* of love.

P

x x x x x

## Fifth in Lent

*Old Testament:* Jeremiah 31:31-34
*Epistle:* Hebrews 5:5-10
*Gospel:* John 12:20-33

# 24 Go for it!

'Remember the Chinese proverb, boy: "The longest journey begins with the smallest step",' Mr Haggart intoned – and not for the first time either. It had been a mantra Maynard had become all too familiar with in recent times. And, right now, it didn't help one little bit. 'Come on, boy,' Mr Haggart was shouting. 'Go for it. You have to try. Come on! Make an effort! You'll get nowhere if you don't have a go.'

It was no use. Maynard had failed again. He just couldn't get started. And as he stood shaking on the little platform at the top of the rope-slide, hanging onto the bar and peering over the edge to what seemed a *long* way to the ground, Maynard simply lost any bottle he'd ever had. Thankfully, no one mocked him as he made his way down from the platform. Mr Haggart just sighed a very loud, resigned kind of sigh. That said it all. Maynard had been a disappointment once again.

He should never have come to the adventure camp with his Scout troop. Oh, he was good at other things, like knots and camp-fire songs; and he had lots of badges, like first aid and cooking; and he could recite screeds about the history of Scouting; and he was a Bob-a-Job week specialist. But Maynard just couldn't do physical stuff for toffee.

He was overweight. He was uncoordinated. He'd fallen off a swing when he was a kid, and that hadn't helped his confidence one little bit. But mostly, Maynard was just downright scared. And no amount of encouragement about 'starting with the smallest step' and 'going for it' made a blind bit of difference. So rope-slides, climbing trees, monkey-bars, assault courses were out for Maynard.

The only thing he could manage was swimming. It was probably *partly* – so his nasty brother had said – because he carried so much blubber he could float all the way across the North Sea. But Maynard wasn't going to try *that,* or anything else that required too much of an effort. He couldn't put his head under water – too scary; he always needed his feet to touch the bottom, and wouldn't swim out of his depth – too panicky; he didn't like rough-and-tumble in the pool – too unpredictable; he couldn't swim a length – well, he *could* if he tried, but there was no way … too much, too risky. So Maynard swam across the pool at the shallow end, carefully avoiding all the stronger swimmers doing their twenty lengths. Maybe he *could* do that too one day. But Maynard was scared to go for it. So the Scouts' 'Life Saving' badge was a no-no for Maynard. Other people would have to do the rescuing if someone was in trouble.

That would have been fine if someone else had been around when Digby Mathieson fell into the river. He wasn't *supposed* to fall into the river, of course, because Digby was one of the best-behaved and most ultra-careful boys in the troop. And anyway, he'd broken his shoulder and wrist the previous week when he'd fallen off his bike and he had his arm in plaster and hanging in a sling. It was touch and go whether he'd be allowed to come to the camp. But he'd promised to behave – no problem there for Digby; and Mr Haggart and the other troop leaders had promised to look after him – no problems there either.

Once Maynard had been let off trying the rope-slide, and with Digby Mathieson incapacitated down one side, the two lads were dispatched along the river bank to collect wood for the campfire. Maynard carried the big canvas sack. Digby held the small axe. And a sufficient quantity of suitable firewood was duly collected. Maynard hoisted the full sack on his back – that's what big lads are for, isn't it? – and the two pals were ambling back to the campsite when the fox came shooting out of the undergrowth. The two Scouts got such a fright that Maynard swung round in the direction the fox had run, and clobbered his unprepared companion full on his bad shoulder with the sack of firewood. Digby screamed in pain, staggered backwards to escape the menacing Maynard, and fell right off the edge of the path into the river.

Within moments he was thrashing about in the water. Completely incapacitated by his injured arm, he tried to reach for the grass on the bank with his good hand. But he was too far away. The more he tried and failed, the more he panicked. The more he panicked, the more he thrashed about. And the more he thrashed about, the more he was taking in water.

Maynard was panicking too. What was he to do? Should he run back to the camp for help? Too far, and he'd never make it anyway. Could he find a stick that was long enough for Digby to catch on to? Nothing obvious lying around. Maynard looked at his struggling friend, and he heard a voice in his head shouting, 'Come on, boy, go for it.' And in an instant, he'd leapt into the water.

He didn't know what he was supposed to do. The water would be over his head. He'd sink without trace. They'd both go down together. But … to Maynard's surprise, he found that he was standing upright, with his feet firmly on the river bed, and the water no more than up to his waist. Digby was grabbing onto his arm, and then he was gripping Maynard's waistband. 'Steady on, man. You'll have my trousers off,' was all Maynard could think of saying. But pretty soon two wet Scouts were struggling onto the tow-path, and neither was quite sure who was helping the other.

What they *were* sure of though was that they had a great story to tell round the campfire that night. And, when the truth came out, Mr Haggart called Maynard out front the following night and, with great ceremony, presented him with a new badge – which looked suspiciously like a triangle cut from an old tea-towel, and written on with felt tip pen – which proudly reminded Maynard that there might be more times like this one when he could 'GO FOR IT' – and succeed.

### Go for it

'Go for it,' you said.
'Go for what?' I asked.
'For *it* ...' you said.
'What's it?' I asked.
'Just "it",' you said.
'What help is that?' I asked.
'That's not for me to decide,' you said.
'So, is it up to me?' I asked.
'That's it,' you said.
'No more advice, then?' I asked.
'No,' you said.
'So, I have to go for it?' I asked.
'Quite right,' you said.
'Did I ask what "it" might be?' I asked.
'You did,' you said.
'Well?' I asked.
'Just go,' you said.
'Is that it?' I asked.
'That's it, that's exactly it,' you said.

### Passion/Palm Sunday

*Old Testament:* Isaiah 50:4-9a
*Epistle:* Philippians 2:5-11
*Gospel:* Mark 14:1-15:47

# 25 The women of the village

It was the women of the village who did it all, and Janet Ross who was the leader of the campaign. It was the first time the women had asserted themselves, and the village was the better for it. It was the first time Janet Ross had taken the lead in anything. But it changed her life.

Janet was seventy years old. Up till then she'd just minded her own business and got on with being Janet Ross, wife, mother and grandmother, local worthy and long-time resident of Forresthall, a bustling mining village at the head of the valley. The village had been built round the pit-head, and for generations coal-mining had been the lifeblood of Forresthall and all the other villages along the valley.

Janet had brought up a family in the village. Her father had been a miner. Her husband, Willie, had spent forty-nine years in the pit since he joined his own father at the age of sixteen. Their three sons were miners, the oldest one, Andrew, in a surface job and his brothers, Bertie and Willie Junior, at the coal-face. Andrew's son was an electrician and worked at the pit. It wouldn't be long before Bertie's two lads would follow their father into work at the mine in one form or another. Mining was in the family. Mining was Forresthall's life. Mining was Janet Ross's world.

That was – until the strikes … The strikes of the 1980s tore the village apart. The Union against the Thatcher government; management against the Union; changing practices against miners' rights; pit closures against the life of villages like Forresthall. That was what it was all about. But what it *became* to be about was village against village; family against family; brother against brother; son against father. The strikes ripped families asunder. It was sad, and it was bitter, and it was painful.

Janet's husband, retired though he was, was clear what side he was on, and Bertie stood with him in that; Andrew and Willie Junior were in opposing camps; Andrew's son sided not with his father but his grandfather; even Bertie's two sons were on opposite sides. It broke

Janet Ross's heart. But then, she was no different from any other wife and mother in the village. She talked and wept with them, while the men manned picket lines or were called scabs.

The strike moved from weeks into months. Things become more crucial still when financial hardship began to have a serious effect on village families and the welfare of the children. That's when Janet Ross decided enough was enough.

'Maggie Frobisher an' I have been talkin', she announced to Willie one teatime after he'd got back from a meeting of those who still wanted to work.

'Frobisher, wife o' yon striker, Mattie Frobisher. You shouldnae be keepin in wi' the likes o' yon, wi' a man that's nae mair than a dangerous, destructive bastard. That's the man that ca'ed oor Bertie a scab tae his face doon at the Club. Bastard!'

That was enough for Janet Ross. 'Don't you dare come in here wi' your dirty mouth, Willie Ross. Maggie Frobisher and her bairns are no involved wi' your or her man's politics. But while you an' me have oor pension tae live on, and no strike's gonna threaten that, whit have they got? Whit has ony strikin' family got. Nae wages. Nae money. Nae food. Bairns that go hungry. It's no' right.'

'*Right*, woman? Whit wid you ken aboot right. That damn Union is destroyin' oor livelihood. Let the bastards stew in their ain juice. Let them damn well starve. An' if you an' Maggie Frobisher keep up wi' ain anither, you'll get nae support frae me.'

'*Support?* A widnae come beggin' for your support. There are women in this village that have mair gumption than you'll ever have, Willie Ross. You wait and see. Where there are needs tae be dealt wi', it'll be me and the women that'll be tae the fore.'

'You? Dinnae mak' me laugh, woman. You couldnae organise a raffle.'

Janet Ross had nothing more to say. There were things to be done. It was no use wasting energy on the likes of Willie Ross. And that's just what Maggie Frobisher told Janet she'd said to her own husband as well. And it's just about what every woman said when they met in the church hall the next afternoon to get started with what needed to be done.

The result was the saving of the village – not because a strike was settled (it would be a long time before that came about) or because the pit was saved (because it wasn't) or because family members suddenly began to sink their differences (some of the divisions in families went on for years) but because caring people got mobilised, and people in need were helped, and the women did what needed to be done.

A pre-school breakfast club was organised in the church hall. A food cooperative was set up in the Miners' Welfare. Money for clothes, especially for the children, was donated by helpful charities. A soup-run was organised using the back of the priest's estate car. And the women's group even managed to get access to a holiday cottage where the most needy of families could have a break in the summer. And it was all organised by the women of the village – with Janet Ross out in front.

Janet Ross has been dead for twenty years. There's no pit now. Forresthall has become a commuter village for the big town. Bertie Ross is retired and still lives in the village. And he likes nothing better than when his two sons bring their families to stay, especially when he can tell his grandchildren stories about the pit, the times when the women of the village rescued the community from oblivion, and how much of that was owed to his very own mother, a remarkable woman called Janet Ross.

### The women

The advice was as sound as it was warm:
'Keep it simple, son.
Never bother wi' them fancy words.
Tell the fowk there's a God that loos them.
An' dae it simple.'

That advice was from a woman
who changed my life.

The meaning was as profound as it was humble:
she held the chalice in her hands,
and lifted her eyes heavenwards
in her silent, heartfelt prayer
of absolute adoration.
That meaning was from a woman
who touched me with holiness.

The courage was as strong as it was beautiful.
'I need to go now,'
her whispered words, as eyelids closed
and opened next in the glorious company
of saints and angels.
That courage was from a woman
who taught me about dying.

The compassion was as constant as it was plentiful.
'There's always someone ...'
as another brokenness found healing,
and loneliness was dispelled again,
and a crying child found comfort.
That compassion came from a woman,
who showed me what caring really was.

The advice, the meaning, the courage, the compassion,
and much more besides,
offered to such as me,
from the women who were aware enough
to see, even in me,
someone worth spending time with
so that I could listen and learn.

## Monday of Holy Week

*Old Testament:* Isaiah 42:1-9
*Epistle:* Hebrews 9:11-15
*Gospel:* John 12:1-11

# 26 Kindest affection

There were only two things that really mattered in Pauline's life – her signed photograph of Lulu, and the box of pen nibs she'd been given by her great-grandfather. There were other things that mattered too, of course – like her mum and dad, and her big sister Robyn – but parents and sisters matter to everyone, don't they? No, there was no doubt about it ... the very, *very* important things to Pauline were her Lulu picture and her box of pen nibs.

The Lulu picture? Well, that was special because she'd discovered that Lulu had been born in the same street as her gran – '1948, the Lauries' eldest ... I remember her well ...' her gran had said. And the box of pen nibs? Well ... there's a story ...

The pen nibs were in a little maroon and cream metal box, about the size of a matchbox. 'Waverly Pen' it said in bold letters on the top, and in smaller writing, '3 dozen pens, MacNiven & Cameron Ltd, Waverley Works, Edinburgh', surrounding a picture of a smart pen nib. On the other side of the box-lid was a picture of Sir Walter Scott with slogans proclaiming 'MacNiven & Cameron's pens are the best', and, in tiny writing, endorsements such as 'They are a treasure – *Standard*'; 'A luxury for the millions – *Argus*'; 'They eclipse all other pens – *Globe*'; and, most important of all, 'Pen makers to Her Majesty's Government Office'.

Inside the box there were four unused pen nibs with 'Waverley' stamped along their length, and on the bottom of the box there was the little rhyme that Pauline knew off by heart:

*They come as a boon and a blessing to men,*
*The Pickwick, the Owl, and the Waverley Pen.*

The box of pen nibs had belonged to Pauline's great-grandfather, her gran's dad – Papa Burlington. Pauline loved her papa, and it was an absolute delight to go to visit him in his care home and listen to his stories of life after World War 1, and get a great big cuddle from the old man. Best of all were stories of Papa Burlington's school days – classes of forty children; strict discipline; sitting at desks and reciting things – like tables of numbers, and parts of the Bible – all together with the teacher; learning to do numbers and letters on a black slate with a piece of white chalk; and, of course, writing with a pen with a nib.

Pauline had never used anything other than a biro-pen and so she was fascinated by tales of inkwells and pens; nibs and copperplate writing; blotting-paper and smudges; and much more besides. She loved it when Papa Burlington would take his fountain pen from his waistcoat pocket and, in a shaky but clear hand, write letters on Pauline's notepad, in a beautiful style she'd never seen before.

One day, from another pocket in his waistcoat, Papa Burlington unearthed a little metal box of Waverly Pen nibs – 'the kind of pen nibs I used to use when I was your age,' Papa Burlington had said. 'Maybe you can try them some day.' Pauline never had, and when Papa Burlington had died at the age of ninety-two when Pauline was eight years old, she'd decided she never would, because her special possession was too good to spoil.

Pauline was twenty-three when her gran died. It was a blessing, everyone had said – and Pauline had to agree – because, for a number of years, there had been no quality of life for the old lady. The ravages of living with Alzheimer's had taken their toll on her gran and the whole family. They were sad at their loss, but relieved that the suffering was over. And now there was gran's house to clear. Pauline had nothing to do with that. She'd offered to help, of course, but she'd been assured by her mum and dad that they could manage. Pauline had her final year in college to finish anyway, and she had to concentrate on her studies.

When she got home for the Easter break, she was sitting in the kitchen having a cup of tea with her parents and catching up on how things had gone, when her mum announced, 'Oh, I almost forgot. I've got something to show you.' In moments Pauline's mum had returned to the kitchen with a ragged brown envelope in her hand. 'I found this in gran's things,' she said. 'I never knew she had it. It's a letter written by Papa Burlington.'

Pauline's heart raced. *'A letter, written by my papa?'* Carefully she took the battered envelope from her mother and, opening it gingerly, drew out the contents – a single sheet of notepaper, folded in four. One of the folds was torn, but the sheet of paper was still intact. Pauline laid the notepaper on the table and gently unfolded it. And there she saw the beautiful copperplate writing that was clearly her papa's style. The paper was yellowed with age. The ink was brown and faded. But the style of the lettering and the clarity of the writing made it easy enough to read. Pauline scanned the page before her, and then, without thinking, she began to read the words aloud. 'Dear Ada,' it read, 'thank you for coming to join us for tea yesterday. Mother and father were so pleased to meet you. It was delightful. You are such charming company, my dear – and pretty too. I hope you shall call again. Indeed, I look forward to it. With my kindest affection. Yours ever, Alfred.'

'Ada was your great-grandmother,' Pauline's mum whispered, as if trying not to break the spell of the moment.

'So this must have been written to her before she and papa were married,' Pauline exclaimed.

'Probably his first love-letter,' her dad added.

'We think you should have this,' Pauline's mum suggested, after all three had sat in silence for a while. Pauline carefully refolded the precious page and returned it to the safety of its envelope. 'Thank you,' was all she could say.

There are now only *three* things that really matter in Pauline's life – her signed photograph of Lulu, the box of pen nibs she'd been given by her great-grandfather, and Papa Burlington's first love-letter. Because, every time she reads his words, his 'kindest affection' is very, *very* close.

**Listen**

Listen to me,
For I will speak to you
In words on every page
I've left behind.

Listen to me,
For I'll still have a voice
In every phrase, in every letter
I've ever penned.

Listen to me,
For I'll still talk to you
In every story
I've ever written.

Listen to me,
For I will dwell with you
In every memory
I've ever created.

Listen to me,
For I'll go on calling to you
In every statement
You ever remember.

Listen to me,
For I'll still share with you
In every conversation
You even yet can recall.

Listen to me,
For we are bound together,
And, it's just possible,
I might still have something useful to say.

## Tuesday of Holy Week

*Old Testament:* Isaiah 49:1-7
*Epistle:* 1 Corinthians 1:18-31
*Gospel:* John 12:20-36

# 27 The rumour

Ethan had heard the rumour. He was never one for gossip, and tended to shrug his shoulders when someone sought to impart some juicy piece of information to him that was no more than mere speculation. 'Listen, Ethan. You've not to tell a soul ... it's a mega secret ... but I've just heard that Johnny and Emma ...' Ethan would smile politely, promise to keep the secret, and promptly forget all about what he'd just been told. But *this* rumour wasn't going away. Indeed it hadn't been a 'one-off' like most of the others, whispered over a coffee in the canteen or shared by a colleague at the water-cooler. No, this one was different.

For a start, he'd got it from several sources, including mates who weren't in the usual 'rumour-mill' circles. And for another thing, some of these sources were people Ethan considered to be pretty reliable, not the kind prone to exaggeration or perpetrating lies. This wasn't like the usual office gossip. This one was serious and carried an air of truth that was very, very disturbing. Someone had a knife out for the boss.

The head of Ethan's section was a person he'd always admired. Ever since Isobel Harrison-Stanford had taken the reins in the part of the bank's call-centre that dealt with new accounts, Ethan's job-satisfaction had gone up tenfold. Everyone – but everyone – had been on edge when the new section-head was appointed. For a start, no one knew her. They'd expected the vacancy to be filled by an 'internal candidate'. So when they heard that the job had been given to a high-flier from across the country and with a double-barrelled moniker to boot, no one was happy.

As it turned out, the new boss's arrival had been a breath of fresh air. She was approachable – 'Call me Izzy, and if *anyone* calls me "Miss Harrison-Stanford", you're on your bike!'; she was fair – like the time

she'd stood up for Ethan when one of the callers unfairly complained
about his attitude; she was efficient – and the drop in sickness levels
and turnover of staff was ample evidence that the section was run
well; and – probably most important of all, though he'd never dare to
admit it to anyone – Ethan fancied her like mad.

But the rumour just wouldn't go away. Someone – clearly disaf-
fected by Izzy's appointment and, despite her success since she arrived,
not being prepared to let it go – was doing the dirty. The rumour
took various forms … chequered background, skeletons in the cupboard kind of thing; sleeping around, with several names in the frame
as one-night stands; political affiliations, a 'not in the best interests of
the bank' sort of issue. But, wherever the rumour originated, and
whatever form it took, clearly someone was out to get her.

Ethan didn't know what to do. *He'd* never had any cause to doubt
Izzy's background, or loyalty to the company, or whatever. She was
the best boss he'd ever had. So what was he to do with the ever-
mounting strength of the rumour that was doing the rounds? He
could ignore it, of course – he was good at that – and hope that
either there was no substance in it or that, even if there was, it
wouldn't make any difference anyway; he could challenge the
rumour-mongers – something he had *never* done before – and run
the risk of alienating himself from his colleagues, or being labelled a
'boss's toady'; he could pass on the rumours to Izzy's line-manager –
whom he'd never even spoken to in all his time in the call-centre and
probably wouldn't even recognise if he passed him in the corridor; or
he could talk to Izzy – after all, she insisted she was always approachable – and lay it all before her … and be tongue-tied, and make her
think he was currying favour, or trying it on.

Ethan was well and truly stuck. He just didn't know what to do.
Someone was trying to stab his boss in the back, and he didn't know
how to handle it.

Maybe he would just wait. It would all blow over. Yes, that's it. It
would all go away. Rumours are only rumours, after all. If nobody

acts on them, then they just die out. Pour fuel on the flames, you just make a bigger conflagration; do nothing, and the embers just fade away. *'That'll be it,'* Ethan figured. *'It'll come to nothing. Izzy's too good for this. No way she'll be brought down. No way ...'*

When Ethan turned up for his afternoon and evening shift at the call-centre, there was a letter on his desk. It was on bank notepaper. It was headed 'New Customer Accounts Section', and addressed to 'Dear colleague'. Ethan scanned the contents, and, as he did, he broke out in a cold sweat. The letter read, *'It has come to the attention of the call-centre management that there are certain matters which require investigation. Consequently, Miss Harrison-Stanford has been suspended until further notice. With immediate effect, the section will be managed by the call-centre deputy manager, Mr Joseph Ibbotson. You will be informed of the outcome of the investigation and any long-term decisions which require to be made. You may be required to be interviewed as part of the investigatory process. If you have any queries, please address these in writing to Mr Ibbotson, or myself. Yours sincerely, Mr Peter Preston, Call-Centre Manager.'*

Someone had betrayed Ethan's boss, the best boss he'd ever had, and Ethan had no idea what to do.

### Woz happenin'?

'Woz happenin', man?'

'Dunno. But it sounds bad.'

'How so, man?'

'Rumours, an' 'at ...'

'Rumours? Wot about?'

'About your man.'

'The man? Wot's goin' down?'

'Word on the streets is ...'

'C'mon, man, wot's the deal?'

'Word on the streets is ... he's for the chop.'

'No. Can't be for real, man?'

'Itz wot's out there.'
'No. Can't be happenin'. No way, man. No way.'
'But that's the story, OK?'
'Just talk, man. Stories an' 'at.'
'Sounds true …'
'Yeah, man. But it's only a rumour, right?'
'Cool. But rumours iz rumours, yeah?'
'So, woz happenin', man, an' when's this goin' down?'
'Dunno …'
'But the rumours …'
'Didn't go that far …'
'Wot we gonna do, man?'
'Dunno …'
'Any ideas, man?'
'Dunno …'
'No use you are.'
'Let's …'
'Wot, man? Let's wot …?'
'Let's go an' find the man.'
'Now, man?'
'Yeah. Let's go see …'
'Good plan, m' man. Let's go see wot's happenin' …'

## Wednesday of Holy Week

*Old Testament:* Isaiah 50:4-9a
*Epistle:* Hebrews 12:1-3
*Gospel:* John 13:21-32

# 28 Serving

Sally was *so* pleased that she was to be present for the Communion. It wasn't what she expected, as she'd had no idea that Communion was to be part of the deal. But when it was announced that the event would close with Communion, she was buzzing with anticipation.

The event itself had been pretty special. It was an education day in the Church's central offices, all about 'inclusiveness' and how to bridge the gaps between those 'inside' the church, and those 'outsiders' who felt excluded ... communication issues ... appropriate language ... facing prejudices and judgemental attitudes ... disabled access ... prejudice around homosexuality ... mental health issues. It had been an enlightening and immensely useful day.

And when Sally realised that the sharing of the Communion was itself going to be 'different', she was even more excited. The discussion groups had been round tables, about seven or eight people in each group. The groups had been with each other throughout the day and an openness had clearly been established as the day had progressed. And the groups had been set up so that they contained a variety of people. So when Communion was announced, people were asked to stay in their groups. The bread and the wine would be brought to each table. The sharing would be with people who'd come to know and trust one another. It was imaginative and, to Sally at least, a fitting end to an exceptional day.

As the small, pottery chalice and plate with a rough chunk of bread was placed on her table, Sally looked around at her group – William, a local vicar; Tommy, a teenager from a church youth club, and his mate, Sonya, who'd not said much throughout the day; Midge in her wheelchair; Mrs Chalmers – no one had got her first name – a delightful white-haired Christian lady who was 80 if she was a day; and Stephane, who suffered from Tourettes. Sally had only a scant knowledge of Tourette's Syndrome before she'd met Stephane at the training-day, but she knew a lot more about it now. She knew about the uncontrollable tic that made Stephane's movements unpredictable to say the least; she knew about the spontaneous and unexpected cursing that always took people by surprise; and she knew of the stigma and the rejection felt by a young man like Stephane.

And now it was Communion – and Sally could do her bit to help Stephane. Above all the others, she could help him feel included. She could be part of making the Communion work for *him*. She felt really good about that.

In time, the bread was shared and, as instructed, passed from person to person around the table. The bread came to Sally from Midge on one side of her, and when she had partaken she passed the sacramental bread to the twitching and cursing Stephane on her other side. 'The Body of Christ broken for you,' she said, as she steered the bread into his uncoordinated fingers.

In that moment Sally was Stephane's minister. She was facilitating the Communion for him, and feeling immensely pleased to be able to do that.

As she basked in her inner pleasure, the time came for the pottery goblet of wine to be shared. She'd worked out that, when it came time for the wine to be given to Stephane, she would hold it for him and let him drink. Yes. That would be it. She'd be doing her 'including' bit again. But Sally realised to her horror that the cup of wine was coming around the table *the other way*! The wine would be passed from Mrs Chalmers on Stephane's far side, through him, to Sally! A chalice of wine in the twitching fingers of Stephane? The Blood of Christ in such unpredictable hands?

The inevitable scene forming in her mind was one of unmitigated disaster. Communion ruined ... The wine all over the place ... The Sacrament losing its meaning ... Worship going dreadfully wrong ... Embarrassment all round, and mostly for Sally ... It seemed an age as the cup of wine made its way round the table. Then ... and then ...

it was being passed to Stephane. *'Dear God, not this, not now, not me,'* was Sally's heartfelt prayer.

On the other side of Stephane she heard Mrs Chalmers' gentle words, 'The Blood of Christ shed for you,' and watched Stephane hold his hands out to take the cup. And when his fingers closed round the goblet, his twitching stopped. He raised the chalice to his lips, and there was no muttering and cursing. He partook of the sacramental wine, and he was perfectly still. Releasing one hand, he stretched out to pick up the small cloth that had been placed in front of him. Without a tremor, he wiped the rim of the cup. Then, turning to Sally, Stephane said, in a clear voice, 'The Blood of Christ shed for you,' and let go of the chalice into her hands. As soon as his fingers left the cup, Stephane started to twitch, and curse, and mutter under his breath once more.

Sally remembers little more of the events of that Communion. But what she is left with now are lots of questions, like ... Who was the broken person at that Communion table? Who was flawed? Who needed healed? Who needed to be accepted? Who needed to learn about being included?

### The circle

Inside the circle I'm safe and secure;
Outside the circle I'm hurting once more;
Inside I'm turning my back – I just don't want to know.
Outside the circle I'm trying to get in;
Inside the circle, where I've always been;
Outside I'm breaking my heart – and I've nowhere to go.

Inside the circle I'm trying to look out;
Outside the circle, 'Can you hear my shout?'
Inside I want to break free – but it's hard to reach through.
Outside the circle I'm seeing the cracks.

Inside the circle I'm taking the flak.
Outside I'm praying we'll touch – as I reach in to you.

Inside the circle I'm no longer trapped.
Outside the circle, the walls have collapsed.
Inside I'm stepping away – and a new day can dawn.
Outside the circle, I'll welcome you home;
Inside the circle, I felt so alone;
Outside I'm happy to share – so that we can move on.

### Maundy Thursday

*Old Testament:* Exodus 12:1-14
*Epistle:* 1 Corinthians 11:23-26
*Gospel:* John 13:1-17, 31b-35

# 29 The stations of the crowd

## 1 Patsy Gallagher is condemned

There was nothing people could put their finger on. Oh yes, there had been the unwanted teenage pregnancy and getting in with a dubious crowd; there were the rumours of drug-taking and prostitution; and living in a squat in town did nothing to stop the bad-mouthing. And yet Patsy Gallagher was condemned. She was condemned by people who had once been her friends. She was ostracised by a community which cared little for her welfare. She was shunned by people who could have made a difference. There was nothing people could really put their finger on, but Patsy Gallagher was condemned, none the less.

## 2 Gerry Black receives his cross

People will tell you it was the drink that did it. Maybe Gerry Black would tell you the same. But that was only a symbol. Rejection was the cross that Gerry Black had to bear. And once he'd begun to slide into a dissolute life, the rejection just got worse. Who wanted to know a homeless man who just got in the way when you were rushing through town; a down-and-out who still felt like a real person inside but was always treated like worthless trash? It hadn't always been like that. There was once a time when Gerry Black was up there with the best of them, playing his part and feeling good about himself. But that was then, and this was now, and rejection was a heavy cross to carry.

## 3 Elvis has his first fall

Andrew Presley – aka Elvis – didn't expect to be languishing in Shortlane Remand Centre awaiting trial for the theft of the cigarettes. He'd been in the wrong place at the wrong time. The heist had been bungled and should have been well over and done with before the alarm went off. But his brother and his crew were getting cocky, and the police arrived before they could leg it. Elvis had only come along because his brother had persuaded him. But now he was in trouble, deep trouble, and he was frightened. They'd cut all his hair off since he'd been on remand, and he was wearing a denim jacket that was two sizes too big for him. He felt like shit. He was scared he'd never be able to get up from this.

### 4 Meeting a mother's love

Bessie never had any children of her own. She would have loved to have kids, and yearned sometimes for grandchildren whom she could fuss over and generally spoil rotten. It wasn't to be. But Bessie was still a mother at heart, and so she spent her life caring for people who needed caring for. She'd worked as a home carer, and there was more that she did for her clients out of working hours than her bosses ever knew. And now, in her later years, she cared for the people in her stair – like Norrie who lived across the landing. 'Ach, he's just like a wee laddie,' she would say of her neighbour who was around her own age. 'The poor soul needs motherin'. And anyway, what price do you put on a bit of love and compassion when you've got nobody?'

### 5 Chic Chandler is made to bear the cross

Chic Chandler had a passion for fundraising, for one specific purpose – to support anti-landmine charities throughout the world. It was a passion which began when the US military were in Iraq and his brother had his legs blown off in a landmine explosion. It deepened when Chic got involved with the innocent victims who'd been maimed by indiscriminate landmines during conflicts or long after the warring factions had gone. But the passion had become a campaign and the campaign had grown into an obsession and the obsession had become life-consuming. Anti-landmine work was everything for Chic. Sometimes it was an intolerable burden, but if not him, then who would take it on? It shouldn't have been *his* cross. Sometimes it was too hard to bear. But what else could he do?

## 6 Mr Symington understands gentleness

The nurse told Mr Symington that the hairy biker-man who'd accompanied him to hospital had been 'tenderness personified'. 'You'd not expect such gentleness from a "Hell's Angel" guy like that,' she told a colleague later. Mr Symington didn't expect it either, not from a man he'd never have wanted to associate with, with the studded-leather jacket and the bandana round his head. According to the nurse, hairy biker-man had even covered Mr Symington with his leather jacket while they were waiting for the ambulance. Mr Symington hardly knew the guy. Why would an almost-stranger be as caring as that? 'You'd not expect such gentleness ...' was right enough.

## 7 Mrs Bowman falls again

The first fall had been a disaster. It happens, of course. Mrs Bowman knew that. But it only happened to *other* people who were old. The long spell of ice and snow had taken its toll of more than the feisty Mrs Bowman. And now she had a fractured elbow to cope with. It just wasn't good enough. Still, it could have been worse. She could have ended up in hospital, or be languishing at death's door with pneumonia. But she wasn't. She was at home, and still able to 'do for herself'. And she had her project to keep her going ... But then she fell again. The pain was excruciating. She lay on the floor of her hallway for ages. No one came to help. It was dark outside. 'This could be it,' she thought. She prayed. She prayed hard when she fell again ...

## 8 Meeting Janet Ross and the women

If it wasn't for the women the village might have descended into all-out civil war. That was what the miners' strike almost achieved. Brother pitted against brother; father and son on opposite sides; family and village life torn apart. It was Janet Ross and the women who rescued the village from disaster. They saw the need for support for those in difficulty, and they mobilised people to help. They set up soup runs and food stores for anyone, for both the feuding sides. They convinced the Church and other groups to contribute to their cause. They did what needed to be done to help families survive and hold the village together, Janet Ross and the women, and no one expected that ...

## 9 Freddy Aitcheson falls for a third time

The coloured-glass fish still stood proudly on top of the TV in the Aitcheson household. It was Tracy's prize possession. It was a reminder of a good day when her wastrel husband, Freddy, had bought her the present of the glass fish she'd always wanted. A good day ... But that was a long time ago. Surprises like that were a distant memory for Tracy. Now the norm for Freddy was betting and drinking, and too much indulgence with both. It was the third time this week that Freddy had been carried home, much the worse for wear. Maybe it would be the last. Tracy wasn't sure she could take any more. A fourth time would be too much ...

## 10 Ahmed Kahn is stripped of everything

It was decision day at *Kahn's All-Day Store*. No matter what Ahmed and the family had tried to do, business hadn't picked up enough to keep the shop viable. The slurs, innuendo, rumours and downright abuse had persisted since the store and Ahmed's family had been linked with the terrorist arrests. Of course it was all unfounded. They knew that. But 'mud sticks' ... 'there's no smoke without fire' ... and all that. And once the integrity had gone, well, everything had been lost. They'd given themselves a time-limit. If things hadn't picked up by the end of the month ... And now that the end of the month had come, it was decision day at *Kahn's All-Day Store*.

## 11 Patricia is left hanging

It was all very well for Patricia to get reassurance about John. But she still had to deal with his death. People tried hard, of course, with their reassurances and the sharing of their own experiences. She knew their motives were good and that they were trying to be helpful. But, somehow, no matter how rational she was, or how clear she thought her mind had become, when she stood at John's graveside, all the positives disappeared. It was all just too hard, too painful. People said it would take time, and how often had she heard 'and time's a great healer …'? But she felt lost, in a kind of 'nothing' place, a strange limbo which she hated with a passion. 'How long? How long … How long will I be hanging here?' she asked John through her tears at his graveside ... and never felt she got a reply.

## 12 Bobby and his mates face another death

Bobby and his two mates couldn't understand why someone had to die so young. After all, Anthony was only thirty-eight, with more of his life ahead of him, to make the most of and share with his three best pals. But it wasn't to be. A devastating brain tumour saw to that. From the time he'd collapsed on their climb up Kilimanjaro to his death in the hospice was no time at all. They remembered his dying. They remembered his ending. They remembered his funeral. And now they were committed to following Anthony's wishes one more time – to take his ashes to the top of Kilimanjaro – to finish the climb they'd never completed. That was going to be a hard one. It felt good and bad at the same time – to deal with his wishes *and* to face another physical and emotional climb. Another mountain *and* another death to be faced?

## 13 Jamie is prepared for the end

'The Glory Leg', they had told Jamie. 'You'll be a star when it's done, that's for sure. We couldn't do it without you,' they'd reassured him.

But Jamie was still nowhere near the finish, and he was dying on his feet. 'A team of four to run the marathon,' seemed all very well in the planning, and even on the day. But no one expected it to be like this, least of all Jamie. 'Glory'? Glory was the furthest thing from his mind. For with every painful step, every aching muscle, every torturous yard, every scream in his mind to give up, 'glory' was not part of the deal. How could he prepare for the glory of the end when every moment felt like death?

## 14 Where has Murdo gone?

Ian knew that Murdo was dead. He'd seen him and touched him when he was dead, and though Ian hadn't been to the funeral, the knowledge of the death was indisputable. But where was he now? Where was the wise man who'd been gentle and kind to a little boy? Where was the fascinating man who'd fired Ian's imagination with his wonderful stories? There was a gravestone where he could read Murdo's name. He had stories to remember and even tell his own kids. He could picture the old man sitting at the door of his house smoking his pipe, chatting with his friends. But was Murdo in gravestones or stories or mind-pictures? Ian knew that Murdo was dead, but where was Murdo now?

### Stations

Stations – places of waiting …
waiting for another movement, a beginning again;
waiting for another word of explanation for the delay;
waiting for another time when the waiting will be over.

Let me be patient in my waiting place;
let me be trusting in my waiting time.

Stations – places of newness …
new things to see and know in these unfamiliar surroundings;
new people to watch in all their different styles and moods;
new things to feel and make sense of on the journey.

Let me be comfortable with this new place;
let me be understanding of this new time.

Stations – places of passing …
a passing express train, with the speed I'd like to have;
a passing crowd, rushing about in their comings and goings;
a passing thought, as I wonder what will happen next.

Let me be tolerant in this passing place;
let me be willing to learn in the passing of time.

Stations – places of angry questioning …
anger at not knowing, and no one having an explanation;
anger that my 'why?' and 'when?' and 'how?' have no answers;
anger in silence when no questions can be verbalised.

Let me find peace in this angry place;
let me know hope in this questioning time.

Stations – places of stopping and starting …
stopping to let people go and welcome others back;
starting after too long, and glad to be moving forward;
stopping and starting, as I've done many times before.

Let me be accepting of this stopping place;
let me be excited by this starting time.

Stations – places of wondering …
wondering about more stations and a final destination;

wondering about my companions and how they feel;
wondering about the whole journey making sense.

Let me find clarity in this wondering place;
let me know purpose in this wondering time.

## Good Friday

*Old Testament:* Isaiah 52:13-53:12
*Epistle:* Hebrews 4:14-16; 5:7-9
*Gospel:* John 18:1-19:42

# 30  The Phone Call

Rosemary MacAldin was waiting. She was waiting for The Phone Call that she'd been promised would come. 'Don't worry,' she'd been told, in a way that had been designed to reassure. But what did they know? *They* weren't the ones who would have to wait for The Phone Call. So she hadn't been reassured one little bit. And she knew she wouldn't be – until The Phone Call came.

Rosemary had been waiting for The Phone Call all morning and halfway into the afternoon. The phone *had* rung of course – at half past eleven. Rosemary had jumped. Well, you do when you're waiting for the phone to ring – don't you? *'This'll be it,'* she'd thought as she reached for the handset.

'Hello. Is that the MacAldin household?' the caller had enquired.

'Yes,' Rosemary had replied, conscious of the tremor in her voice.

'Mrs MacAldin, is it?' the enquirer had continued.

'Yes,' the diffident reply.

'Well,' the voice had gone on, brightening as it did so.

*'Could that mean good news?'* Rosemary had wondered.

'Well ... that's good, because we're in your area doing a survey on home improvements. Now, don't worry, we're not selling anything. We're just ...'

Rosemary hadn't waited for the rest of the sales' pitch, and had never found out what the anonymous caller wasn't going to sell her. The handset had been slammed back in its cradle with purpose. It hadn't been the first time she'd done that, but this time there was more purpose in it than usual. 'Why do they phone when you're always waiting for something else?' she'd muttered out loud – and had gone back to the waiting.

Her sister had phoned just after lunchtime. Rosemary had jumped again and, grabbing the phone, was all ready to give a telesales operative a piece of her mind.

'Hi, Rosie, it's me,' her sister had said. Rosemary was half relieved it was her sister, and completely frustrated that it wasn't The Phone Call after all. She hoped she could conceal her irritation from her sister. She probably wouldn't.

'Hello,' had been her limp response.

'Any news?' her sister had asked.

'No. No news,' the brief reply.

'When did they say they'd phone?'

'As soon as they knew.'

'But when?'

'How do I know?'

Well, I don't think it's fair.'

'Well, what can I do?'

'Are you sure your phone's working?'

'For goodness' sake, woman. It must be working if you got through.' Rosemary wasn't trying to conceal anything any more.

'I suppose ...'

'So you can suppose yourself off the phone and not tie up the line in case they can't get through with The Phone Call.'

'OK. OK. Keep your hair on. I was only trying to help. Will you call me if there's any news?'

'I will.

'Promise?

'Oh, get off the phone ...'

Rosemary had never hung up on her sister before. But there was always going to be a first time. So she had waited for The Phone Call, praying that no cold-caller or stupid sister would get in first.

Rosemary was no good at waiting. She'd had half a mind to phone herself to ask how things were going. But she didn't. *'They'd just tell me there's no news yet, and then go off the phone and talk about a neurotic woman who had no patience and wouldn't believe that they would only phone when they had something to say.'*

The waiting was *so* hard, especially when the news was going to be so important. Even someone with the patience of Job would struggle to wait for something as life-changing as this. And Rosemary MacAldin was no Job.

Rosemary MacAldin had been waiting for The Phone Call all morning and half the afternoon. She'd got past the stage of analysing what she'd do with the news – whatever it was. One way or another, she'd just have to handle it. It was the waiting that was the worst. She just wanted to be put out of her misery. She just wanted to know.

She jumped when the phone rang at thirteen minutes to five. Somehow she knew this was going to be it. She was shaking when she reached for the handset. She could hardly get the words out when she spoke. *'One way or another,'* she thought.

'Hello?' she croaked.

'Mrs MacAldin?' the voice enquired.

*'Reassuring? Could it be reassuring?* Yes. Rosemary MacAldin here ...' she'd mumbled, handset in one hand and reaching for the box of tissues on the hall table with the other.

'Oh, Mrs MacAldin. Good. I'm glad I've got you. It's the hospital here ...'

### Waiting

'It's the waiting that's the hardest bit,' she'd said,
weeping in her frustration.
'I know,' I said,
not knowing, really ...
because I'd never had to wait like that.
So I waited with her;
it was all I could do.

'It's not knowing that's the worst thing of all,' he'd said,
holding out his enquiring hands.

'I know,' I said,
not knowing, really …
because I'd never been in the unknown like that.
So I waited with him;
it was all I could do.

'It's not being clear what's happening,' they'd said,
and other things along similar lines.
'I know,' I said,
not knowing, really …
because I'd never struggled with a lack of clarity like that.
So I waited with them;
it was all I could do.

I waited with her for some news;
I waited with him for the knowledge;
I waited with them for this clarity.
It was all I could do …

And I knew a little more what waiting was like,
really …

### Holy Saturday

*Old Testament:* Job 14:1–14
*Epistle:* 1 Peter 4:1–8
*Gospel:* Matthew 27:57–66

# 31 A bit of a resurrection

Murray had been waiting for the mail to come for seven days straight. Oh, the mail had come, right enough, on each of the past six days. But not the mail he wanted, not the message that mattered.

He'd been told it would be this week. He'd been told he'd hear with the rest of them, all at the same time. So every day this week he'd been up at the crack of dawn; every day this week he'd been waiting, and wondering, and hoping; every day ... But nothing, apart from bills, and circulars, and his monthly bank statement – nothing ... not the letter he'd been promised; not the good news he'd hoped for.

There was no point in phoning, of course. That would have seemed like impatience. And anyway, if everyone phoned, there would be chaos. So every day he'd waited – and nothing came. And now it was Sunday. And there was no mail on a Sunday, no chance of word coming today. And it wouldn't come by private courier, would it? No, not that. Couriers didn't work on Sundays. But Murray was up at the crack of dawn on the Sunday anyway. No reason to be up this early today – no mail to wait for, was there? But he'd been so used to it all week, and he couldn't sleep on. So he was up and about when he didn't need to be, and he was steeling himself to wait for the Monday.

Being 'up and about' was an exaggeration for Murray since the accident. It was one of the risks that went with the job. Being a soldier in Afghanistan was a dangerous business. He'd been lucky. Others had died. Some would never be able to walk again. But Murray had been lucky – if you call a ten-ton army truck falling on your legs being lucky, that is.

It was an accident. Not friendly fire, or a sniper bullet, or a roadside mine, or a suicide attack. Just an accident. The jack holding up the back of the truck had collapsed. Murray was underneath. He'd been lucky. He could have died. It had been a kind of a death. Losing both legs is a kind of a death, isn't it? A large part of Murray had died that day – his army career; the camaraderie of friends; his passion for basketball; his ability to pull the girls.

Rehabilitation was slow, painful and frustrating. Good people did good things for Murray. They'd helped him get some of his life back. They'd seen the restoration of some of the old spirit. 'A bit of a resurrection,' one of them had said. It didn't *feel* like a resurrection to Murray. A resurrection would have been coming back from the dead. And that would have been standing up and running about; dispensing with crutches and his stair-lift; and burning his bloody wheelchair in a back-garden, resurrection bonfire. But it had been a kind of starting again, if you like. And discovering wheelchair basketball had been a big part of that.

It was the guys in the hospital who had suggested it. Sports were always part of the rehab process. It was all about motivation, team-building and reaching goals. Murray had never thought basketball would stimulate him again. It was too upsetting to think of what might have been. But the first time he'd thrown a three-pointer clean and sweet, and watched the ball slip into the basket without touching the rim, he was hooked again.

It had progressed from uncertainty to enjoyment; from a bounce-game in the rehab gym to a proper competitive match; from using a borrowed wheelchair to having his own, custom-built, sports' version; from playing with a city team in the Super League to being picked for the national squad; and when Murray had wheeled himself out for his first international appearance – against a crack *Team Italia* – he was on a high. 'A bit of a resurrection', right enough.

And now? It had all been worth it when he'd been told he'd been included in the provisional squad for the Paralympics – the provisional squad, 50% more than would actually be picked for the final number. And after further training and more competition, conditioning and fitness-coaching, the final group was to be announced this week.

So Murray had been waiting for the mail to come for seven days solid. Oh, the mail had come, right enough, on each of the past six days. But not the mail he wanted, not the message that mattered. And now it was Sunday – and what a long, drawn-out, hopeless Sunday it was going to be.

Murray was just wheeling himself into the kitchen to rustle up some breakfast when the phone rang. 'Damn,' said Murray, realising he'd not picked up the handset from the hall on his way past. So, swinging his chair round, he headed back the way he'd come. He got there just as the answering-machine was kicking in.

'Hello,' he said.

'Hello, is that Murray Lindsay?' the voice enquired.

'Yes, that's right. Who is this please?'

'Oh, sorry, it's General De Villiers here, from Battalion HQ.'

Murray's instant reaction was to stand up and salute – an army reflex that was still with him, obviously. So he saluted in his mind and hoped the General would be OK with that. Murray knew General De Villiers well. He'd been his commander in the field. And now that the General had a desk-job back in HQ, he was regularly in touch with the men and women who were recovering from their battle scars.

'General ... thank you ... yes ... good morning, sir ... what can I do for you?'

'Sorry to bother you first thing. But I wanted to offer you my congratulations.'

'Congratulations? What do you mean?'

'You're in the squad, man. The Olympic bods have been in touch. The letters have gone out. But they phoned here late yesterday to give us the news. Good PR for the Battalion, and all that. And bloody good news for you too. Well done, man. You've done us proud.'

'Thank you,' was all that Murray could think of saying.

'Well, I'll let you get on. Great stuff, man. Great stuff. You're a marvel. Bloody well done. Have a good day.'

And, with that, the General had hung up, leaving Murray with the phone in his hand and the message still ringing in his ears ... and beginning to wonder if 'a bit of a resurrection' had just turned out to be an awful lot bigger than he could ever have imagined.

### Glory

On Easter morn, watch glory rise;
See radiant light transform the skies
From brooding black to coloured form
On Easter morn.

On Easter Day, hear praises ring,
As all rejoice, and angels sing
Their songs of hope to guide our way
On Easter Day.

On Easter Eve; the day has run
From breaking dawn to setting sun;
We know what truly we believe
On Easter Eve.

On every morn, see glory rise.
Look! New light drifts across our eyes
As our day breaks, old darkness gone
On every morn.

Through every day hear songs they sing –
Majestic anthems angels bring,
Or whispered melodies that stay
Through every day.

Each restful eve, when time has gone,
From early dawn to passing sun,
Review the glory we've received
Each restful eve.

On Easter morn, our Glory rose;
Our Light returned ... but don't suppose
That Life and Love are only born
On Easter morn.

On every morn, see glory come;
'This is the day' for everyone
To seize the moment and be born
Anew each morn.

### Easter Day

*Old Testament:* Isaiah 25:6-9
*Epistle:* 1 Corinthians 15:1-11
*Gospel:* John 20:1-18

# 32 More of a team game

Scottish Country Dancing was Calum Fisher's life. Ever since he could remember, he had got a buzz out of the music, the twists and the turns, the steps and the intricacies. His mother reckoned it was Mrs Campbell, Calum's P5 teacher in primary school, who'd got him hooked. Most weeks, she introduced her enthusiastic class to another move or a simple dance as part of their PE activity. And when Calum wore his first kilt, and when the *whole* of the senior Christmas dance when he was eleven was Scottish Country Dancing, well ...

He'd progressed, of course, from familiar 'couple dances' – *The Gay Gordons, The St Bernard's Waltz,* and – Calum's favourite – *The Highland Schottische* – to proper 'set dances' for skilled and experienced practitioners. *The Duke of Perth* was the beginning. *The Haymakers* quickly followed, and soon *Hamilton House, Postie's Jig, Speed the Plough,* and many others were mastered with skill.

Calum didn't dance on his own, of course, but was a valued member of the town's Scottish Country Dance Display Team. Eight couples – usually forming two 'sets' of four couples each – practised every Tuesday in the church hall close to the town centre, and for displays, teaching events, and hosting the annual 'Country Dance Festival', one set would be selected, made up of those who were available on the necessary day. With the women in their white dresses and tartan sashes, and the men in their white shirts, tartan ties and appropriate clan kilts, it was a colourful spectacle. Indeed, for Calum it was a great social life as well as a useful keep-fit exercise. There was no doubt about it, Scottish Country Dancing was Calum Fisher's life.

That was until Carol emigrated to the USA ... It wasn't her choice, she told the others when she broke the news one Tuesday night in the church hall. 'Husband's job', 'chance of a lifetime', 'before we have kids', 'not for ever', 'would take you all with me if I could' were all expressed and explored as the group chewed things over with Carol at the end of their practice. Carol explained that she'd not be able to be part of the Festival in a month's time. They'd have to manage without her. 'No one's indispensable,' she assured them.

That's not how Calum saw it. Carol had been his partner for three years. She was the best thing that had ever happened to him. She was, in his eyes, absolutely indispensable, no matter what she might say. It just wouldn't be the same without her.

Calum was gay. He wasn't pushy or strident about it. He just was what he was, and among those to whom he had come out, he simply wanted to be accepted. The Scottish Country Dance Team gave him that. Carol gave it to him 'in spades'. He was able to be close with her without anything being misconstrued. He could walk her home without her husband being suspicious. He could buy her gifts and not feel he was going too far. Carol made him feel totally alive, more himself than he could be in most other places or with most other people. *'No one's indispensable?'* Calum queried. *'How little people know …'*

The first practice in the church hall after Carol had gone was purgatory. People were very nice, of course, and he knew they were all feeling the loss. But it just wasn't right when he danced with Patricia. It was OK, but no more than that. His heart wasn't really in it. And when he stood on Patricia's toe halfway through their first try at *The Wind that Shakes the Barley,* he felt such a fool. Dancing with Yvette was better, but still not right. It was that kind of evening – OK mostly, but just not complete.

It was no different on the following Tuesday, or the next. Calum was struggling big time. Maybe he'd invested too much in Carol. Maybe he'd just pack it all in. *'How long should I give it?'* he asked himself. *'How long before it comes right? Is it worth it at all?'*

The postcard from Carol was as unexpected as it was welcome. *'Great American Ball Park, home of the Cincinnati Reds'* the logo informed him, though Calum had no knowledge of or interest in baseball whatsoever. He was *much* more interested in what Carol had to say. It wasn't much, but it was enough.

Settling in OK, *she wrote.* Better than expected. Missing the dancing, though. May start a team out here, who knows? Went to baseball with neighbours last night. Interesting. More of a team-game than you'd think. Hope the team's going well and ready for the Festival. Miss you all. Say hi to the rest. Love. Carol. x x

The team danced in the Festival as usual. Calum chose not to put himself forward to be one of the selected ones. It was great to watch the rest, though, and despite everything they did pretty well – or at least a blind man running for a bus wouldn't have noticed any drop in standards. And Calum had made a decision. He'd get back to practices on a Tuesday night after the post-Festival break. Carol would never know it, but from a long way away her words had made a difference. *'It's more of a team-game than you'd think,'* she kept saying, over and over again, to her ex-dancing-partner.

### I looked

I looked for you in every face I saw;
I searched for you in crowded street;
I yearned to see you in my open door
To make my life complete.

But all I see are strangers' faces there,
No one to recognise as you.
And when I look, you do not come to me
As I would want you to.

I longed for you to fill your fireside chair;
I dreamed that you still shared my bed;

I listened for your footstep in the hall,
Familiar gentle tread.

But all I gaze upon is emptiness,
And every day I wake alone.
I hear no welcome sound to comfort me,
No gentle, soothing tone.

I prayed that I would feel your presence when
I cried for love to make me whole.
I craved for peace to ease my aching heart,
For healing in my soul.

But prayers are never answered in the way
I hoped. Does God not hear my plea?
I find no stillness for my raging thoughts,
No word to comfort me.

And yet, and yet I know it will be so,
Until that day will dawn, when I
Will know your presence does not then depend
On ache or painful sigh;

When I will know you in my life, my heart,
My soul, and all I'm yet to be;
When I will find you in that secret place
Where you will come to me;

When I will need no fireside chair to hold
Your spirit's presence in this place;
When gentle steps are not required to bear
Your love and blessèd grace.

When prayers need not be said to bring you back
From heaven, to walk this lonely earth;

When rage has done its worst and I've survived,
And found again my worth;

When you and I are one in love again,
In letting go and holding on;
When time has bid us glimpse eternity,
And aching days are gone.

I know that day will come when I will see
Your face, and smile again. So I
Will love you, and I'll wait with patience till
I need no longer cry –

But laugh and sing, and share our lives once more
In love that death cannot destroy.
My love, my life, my hope, my one, my all,
My everlasting joy.

Amended from a piece first published as 'I looked for you in every face' in *New Journeys Now Begin* by Tom Gordon, Wild Goose Publications, ISBN 978-1-905010-08-0

### First after Easter

*Old Testament:* Psalm 133
*Epistle:* Acts 4:32–35
*Gospel:* John 20:19–31

# 33 The Shop

No one ever believed the charity shop could be rescued after the fire. 'An electrical fault' was the best the Fire Service could come up with. And now all that remained was ashes, charred beams and ruined stock. No one ever believed the charity shop could be rescued after this.

'Disasters come in threes, you know,' Mrs Sinclair from across the road had pronounced as she'd stood with the others watching the blaze at its height. 'Well, there was yon break-in, three weekends ago, when the place was done over. And then there was Lizzie's death. And now this. I just said to ma man the other day, "Something else bad'll happen, mark my words ..." and there you are, eh?' And there, indeed, they were, standing watching their precious charity shop go up in flames.

The charity shop had been a key part of the upswing in the fortunes of the local community. With the commitment of the local churches, political parties, community associations and the local schools, an empty shell had quickly developed into a shop that was nothing short of a godsend for the area. They'd tried to give it a clever name, but locally it was simply known as *The Shop*.

*The Shop* did the usual nearly-new things. But it also developed a 'school exchange' section, where outgrown school clothes could be passed on and educational toys and books made good use of. A 'Christmas Club' was organised so that people could save up for the expense of Christmas. There was talk of a debt-advice worker having regular sessions in the back office. And the funds raised by *The Shop* were ploughed back into the community. The Playgroup got new equipment. The Pensioners' Club got an outing. The railings round the church were painted. Everyone benefited in one way or another.

Lizzie Carrington had been one of the leading lights. It was Lizzie who'd persuaded the Co-op superstore to supply the shop's fittings and fixtures. It was Lizzie who'd done the appeal on the local radio station and had spoken straight from the heart. It was Lizzie who had held the purse-strings, and paid out the shop's profits twice a year. Not alone, of course, as she would tell you often. But Lizzie was special.

The news that Lizzie Carrington had dropped dead from a heart attack when she was on holiday with her daughter was the worst news anyone could have imagined. How would *The Shop* survive without her? No one knew. But now it didn't matter anyway, because the fire meant that *The Shop*, too, just like Lizzie Carrington, had gone for good. 'Disasters come in threes,' Mrs Sinclair from across the road never tired of saying. And this disaster was the end of it all.

But Betty Grant was having none of that, thank you very much. Betty was relatively new to the area. She'd got a house locally after her divorce and she worked in the local library. She was a quiet kind of person, well suited to the library's peaceful surroundings. She liked the area and admired the guts of the local activists. And the one she'd admired the most had been Lizzie Carrington. She'd been in awe of the woman, and couldn't believe how much she'd achieved for the local folk. Lizzie was Betty's inspiration ... and, not surprisingly, she'd been drawn in by Lizzie to work in *The Shop*. 'Well, lassie. Are you up for it?' Lizzie had asked Betty one day. And 'up for it' Betty certainly was.

Betty hadn't been helping for long. She wasn't entirely sure about how it all worked. She was learning to work the cash-register, and that was complicated enough. Most of the rest of it was beyond her. But she was committed, and she was excited about it all. And as Betty Grant stood outside the charred remnants of the shop the day after the fire, she was faced with a choice: She could walk away, and retreat into her quiet, library-based life. Or she could do something about it. But how could she, or anyone else, for that matter, do *anything* useful without Lizzie's inspiration, Lizzie's reassurance, Lizzie's forceful presence. How could she ...?

As Betty stood and stared at the ruins of everything she'd come to believe in, she became conscious that she wasn't alone. Turning round, she saw a small girl standing beside her, also staring at *The*

*Shop*. The little girl was holding a battered bike with one hand, with the other gripped round a red ice-lolly which she was slurping eagerly.

'You sad?' the girl enquired.

'Yes, I am,' Betty replied.

'This is my nana's shop,' the girl continued.

'Oh,' responded Betty. 'And who's your nana?'

'Nana Lizzie,' came the answer.

'Lizzie!' exclaimed Betty. 'Lizzie Carrington! Is that your nana?'

'Uh huh. But she's dead now,' the little girl offered factually, and without emotion.

'I know,' said Betty.

'You sad?' the girl persisted.

'Yes I am,' Betty stated firmly. 'I'm sad that *The Shop*'s been burned, and I'm sad that all Lizzie – your nana – worked for has gone. I'm sad that it's all finished. And I'm sad that Lizzie isn't here any more.' Betty was conscious of a break in her voice. The two companions lapsed into a thoughtful silence.

'My nana says you should never give up.' the girl affirmed after a time.

'Oh?' said Betty.

'She says that it's what you do when bad things happen that makes you a real person. She says that you have to keep going, no matter what. She says …'

'*Says*,' Betty responded. 'But she's …'

'I know,' the girl replied, picking up on Betty's hesitation. 'My nana's gone now. But I can still hear her, because she's my nana, and she says we should try and be "up for it" when things go bad. She says … and I always listen to my nana.' And with that, the ice-lolly long-since finished, the little girl hopped on her bike and was gone.

But not so Lizzie Carrington, it would seem, who at that very moment was standing outside the ruins of *The Shop* asking Betty Grant, 'Well, lassie, are you up for it?'

**Voices**

Sometimes, just sometimes,
When the time is right,
And I'm tuned in properly,
I can hear my granny's voice.

Sometimes, just sometimes,
When I can be bothered to listen,
And I'm in a receptive mood,
Her voice is as clear as a bell.

It's always the same, every time.
'Keep it simple, son,' she's saying.
'Tell them that love matters.'
That's my granny's voice for me.

Sometimes, just sometimes,
When my mood is right,
And I need to be reminded about something,
I can hear my granny's voice.

Sometimes, just sometimes,
When I've forgotten the truth
And I need to start again,
Her voice is ringing true for me.

And the message hits home, as it should;
And I keep it simple, as she said;
And love matters above all else.
That's my granny's voice for me.

Sometimes, just sometimes,
When the time is right,
And I'm tuned in properly,
I can hear ...

Sometimes, just sometimes,
When I can be bothered ...

It's always the same ...

Sometimes, just sometimes,
When my mood is right,
And I need to be reminded about something,
I can hear ...

Sometimes, just sometimes,
When I've forgotten the truth,
And I need to start again ...

And the message hits home, as it should;
And I ...

## Second after Easter

*Old Testament:* Psalm 4
*Epistle:* Acts 3:12-19
*Gospel:* Luke 24: 36b-48

# 34 Tagged

Melody first met Mr Thompson when she went to visit her aunt. Melody's aunt lived in a little village in the country, and at the end of her row of quaint terraced houses was Mr Thompson's farm. It wasn't a very big farm. But when you're little, everything seems big. And when you come from the town, everything on a farm seems wonderful. So, Mr Thompson's farm was always huge and amazingly wonderful to a little girl.

At first Melody was only allowed to go to the farm with her mum and dad or her aunt. 'Too dangerous …'; 'Farmer's too busy to be interrupted …'; 'You'll get in the way …' were the grown-up excuses. But, in time, Melody was allowed to go along on her own. 'Just to watch, mind …'; 'Don't be cheeky …'; 'Not for too long …' were the grown-up injunctions ringing in her ears.

So Melody would watch intently, for she became fascinated by the farm. She would climb on the wooden gate at one corner of the yard and watch the tractors come and go. She would sit on the stile at the corner of the field and watch Mr Thompson take feed out to his cattle in the meadow. She would watch as the farmer took his two dogs up on to the hill to gather the sheep. She would watch when the lambs and ewes were separated, and ewes were dipped, and sheep were sheared. She watched when the lambs were marked with a slap of red paint on their backs so that Mr Thompson knew which lambs belonged to him.

One day, Melody was leaning on the wooden fence that formed one side of the pen at the corner of the field which Mr Thompson and his two sons were using for their sheep-sorting. Melody was fascinated by all the goings-on – the milling around of the animals; the plaintive bleating of the lambs; the skill of the men in grabbing the beasts; the occasional panic of a ewe as she tried to jump the fence.

Mr Thompson was busy – but not so busy as to be unaware of the watcher by the fence.

'Wanna help, young lady?' the farmer asked as he was wrestling with a recalcitrant ewe close to where Melody was standing.

'Me?' Melody replied.

'Yes, you, little un'. You've been watchin' long enough to know what's to do. So, if you want to help, come now.'

Melody was over the fence as quickly as her little legs and limited climbing ability would allow her. As first she was scared, especially with all the sheep milling about her in the pen. Mr Thompson and his two sons smiled knowingly at the girl's apprehension.

'Here, lass, you can hold this, 'cause it's warm work, this is.' And with that, Mr Thompson had stripped off his jacket and had thrown it into Melody's arms. Melody felt she was doing her bit, and Mr Thompson seemed happy enough that his jacket was in a safe pair of little hands.

Pretty soon, all the lambs were in one pen and the ewes were in another. Then Mr Thompson took the lambs one by one, held them securely between his legs, took a big set of pliers which he'd asked Melody to unearth from the pocket of the jacket she was holding and nipped a hole out of the lamb's right ear. It seemed cruel, and Melody was sure that the bleating of each lamb was because they were sore. After all, she wouldn't like that done to *her* ear – no way! But Mr Thompson wasn't finished. For, after he'd punched the hole with his pliers, he fitted a yellow tag into the hole and squeezed it tight so that it was securely fitted in place, before releasing the lamb from his grip.

One by one, the lambs were tagged, till the whole of the pen was filled with bleating lambs, all with a splash of red on their back and a big yellow plastic tag in their ear.

Melody had never seen anything like it. She stood quietly in the corner of the pen, clearly reluctant to be involved with such cruelty. Mr Thompson didn't bother. He just got on with his work till it was done. And only then did he appear to notice that Melody had stepped back from the action.

'Too much goin' on for thee, little un'?' Mr Thompson enquired.

'No,' Melody replied hesitatingly. 'I just wasn't sure …' She didn't know whether to continue with her enquiry in case she was being cheeky. But the farmer picked up her uncertainty in any event.

'You're not sure about the taggin', eh?' he suggested. Melody nodded. Mr Thompson put his big hands round Melody's waist, hoisted her up and sat her on top of the gate post till she was at eye level with him.

'Well, young un',' he continued, 'it has to be done. It doesn't hurt the lambies. And if it does, it's only for a second or two. But it's necessary, for their protection – and ours.'

'But why?' asked Melody, finding her voice again.

'Well, it's like this. When the sheep and the lambs are in the field or on the hill, the lambs know which sheep they belong to, just by the sounds of their call.' Melody knew that well enough, having been fascinated from a very early age how the lambs knew which mother to go back to in a whole field of sheep that all looked the same. She nodded. 'But you see,' Mr Thompson continued, 'we don't know which lamb is which and which ewe is which. So we have to tag them, to tell one from the other. The red mark on their back shows that they belong to my farm. They've all got that. But the tag tells me which one is which, so that one lamb is distinct from another.'

Melody smiled. 'You mean, like having a name,' she said eagerly.

'Yes, indeed. Just like having a name.' And turning round and pointing to a random lamb in the corner of the pen, he offered, 'Look. That one could be Allan. And there's Danny. And John. And Nigel. And Ruth …

'And that one's Sally. And there's Liam. And Jack. And Tom …' Melody continued. And, pretty soon, a farmer and his little helper had names for every lamb in the pen, as they tried to outdo each other and the names became more and more obscure. Melody was sure several of the lambs had been named twice. But she didn't care. Now she knew that every lamb mattered – by a tag or a name, every lamb was an individual.

With triumph in her voice, she announced that the final lamb should be called Mr Thompson. And Mr Thompson laughed, and suggested that Melody would be a much better name, as a farmer and his helper went back to the farmhouse for a well earned afternoon snack.

## My old, familiar name

So 'Call me by my old, familiar name'
I once heard said; and rightly did exclaim,
'That's mine to own!' So, will you do the same,
And call my name?

Don't call me to control my life, and claim
With all that goes with this, your power game,
That I am yours to own, direct and tame;
Just call my name.

With tenderness of tone and style proclaim
That this, my humble life, brought down with shame,
Is yet redeemed, recalled, renewed, reclaimed –
So, call my name.

Familiar, old, unique – this is my name;
It's known, so now we need no guessing game;
I'm waiting for the beckoning voice again –
Where is my name?

I will arise, though stumbling, weak and lame,
To heed your call, and firmer ground regain;
Yes I'll respond, my heart with love enflamed,
And call Your name.'

## Third after Easter

*Old Testament:* Psalm 23
*Epistle:* Acts 4:5–12
*Gospel:* John 10:11–18

# 35 The button

The first funeral Michael attended was his uncle Danny's. Uncle Danny had been a familiar figure through all the eight years of Michael's life. The fact that he was Michael's mother's only brother, and lived across the street, and was a single man, and didn't keep too well, and had a sister who fussed a lot … meant that uncle Danny was a regular visitor at Michael's house.

There was always something new to learn or an old game to play when Uncle Danny was around. Snakes & ladders was always an option. Checkers was mastered when Michael was very small. The two companions would play endless games of cribbage on a wet afternoon. And Michael had just started enjoying Uncle Danny teaching him the intricacies of chess.

So, when Uncle Danny upped and died, Michael didn't know what was going on. *'Pretty inconvenient,'* he thought. After all, Uncle Danny had *always* been around, hadn't he? So why had he gone now, when Michael was just about to master the opening moves of the Sicilian Defence from his chess professor?

There was a lot of fuss in Michael's house over the next two days. Because Uncle Danny had died on a Friday, and the Registry Office was closed on a Saturday, and nothing much happened on a Sunday anyway, the funeral was to be at the end of the following week. So the weekend was full of … Michael's mother crying a lot; visitors coming to the house, most of whom Michael had never seen before; and an old man with white hair and dressed all in black, apart from a white collar, being the most regular visitor of all.

Michael knew he was Roman Catholic. The whole family were Catholics. Not that it mattered much, as going to Mass was a rare occurrence. But in the days before Uncle Danny's funeral, the family seemed to be much more Catholic than usual. Apart from the man-in-black being around a lot, mother took to carrying a set of rosary beads; a candle was lit and placed in the living room window – Michael had never seen a candle in his house before, apart from birthdays; and all the family, dressed in black, went to the church the night before the funeral, and Michael had to stay home to be looked after by a neighbour. *'Why can't I be there?'* he queried.

But the most confusing thing of all happened in the church on the day of the funeral. Michael didn't understand much of what was going on. He tried to take it all in, of course. Most of all he was conscious of his mum crying. But the *strangest* thing happened when they were all leaving the church to go to the cemetery.

Michael was walking behind his mum, holding his dad's hand, when suddenly his mum thrust out her hand behind her towards Michael, half turned towards him, and whispered, 'Hold this!' Michael thought he was being given a sweetie, but when he opened his hand he found to his surprise that he'd been given a large, black button. And as his mum continued out of the church and Michael trailed along behind, he closed his fingers very tightly round the button, because it was obviously *very* special indeed, and *he* was the one who had been entrusted with its care.

All the way to the cemetery in the big, black limousine, Michael gripped his precious possession ever so tightly. *'What do I do now? Does everyone else have a button?'* he wondered, though no one in the car was saying anything, and he didn't think it was right to ask. *'What am I supposed to do with it?'* he worried anxiously as more words and rituals round the grave were dealt with. *'Should I toss it into the grave?'* he pondered as, one by one, the mourners threw earth on top of Uncle Danny's coffin. But nobody encouraged him to do anything with his button. So he just kept holding it tightly till everything was done.

*'What's this button for?'* stayed with him as people hugged and kissed when the funeral was over and the family headed back home. Nobody explained. Nobody seemed bothered. The button was obvi-

ously important, something that was designed to initiate a little boy into the adult world of funerals and dying. So he stuffed the big, black button deep into his trouser pocket, and decided that, one day, he would have to ask …

It took a few weeks before Michael plucked up the courage to raise the subject. His mum was sometimes very busy, often quite upset, and always fussing. But in a quiet moment at breakfast before school one morning, Michael decided now was the time. 'Mum,' he asked tentatively. 'Can I ask you something about Uncle Danny's funeral?' There was a long pause before his mother answered.

'Yes?'

'Well, you know, at the church …'

'Yes …'

'Well, there's something I didn't understand.'

'Yes …'

'You know, when we were all coming out …'

'Yes?'

'Well … you gave me a button and told me to hold it … and I did … and I've kept it ever so safe … and I was wondering what mattered about the button … where it fitted in to being Catholic and all that … or was it about Uncle Danny … and did everyone have a button … 'cause … I just don't understand …'

Michael's words tumbled out one after another and, as they did, he thrust his hand deep into his trouser pocket and retrieved the precious big black button from his ever so safe place and held it in the palm of his hand. He wondered if his mother would be upset again. He was surprised, therefore, when she let out a burst of laughter.

'The button, son,' she chortled, 'that button is not about being Catholic or even about your Uncle Danny. He didn't even *have* a button to leave as a legacy. It's got nothing to do with the funeral at all.' She giggled, and came over to put her arm round Michael's shoulder. 'You see, the button came off my coat when I stood up in the church, and I didn't want it to get lost. I was going to sew it back on when I got home. And I had to hold my coat shut all the time I was at the graveside.' She laughed again. 'The button, Michael, the button just came off my coat. And you were the nearest one to look after it. Give it here, and I'll sew it on right away.'

As Michael handed the precious button over to his mother he felt a little silly, but a whole lot clearer. The button *was* precious and important. Because, after all, it had helped his mother have a laugh for the first time in ages.

### Legacies

'And to my best friend,
the sum of £100,
in recognition of her kindness
over many years …'

A legacy –
a gift of money to spend as I choose,
a legacy from a grateful friend.

But what about those legacies I already have,
worth more than any amount of money can measure?
Legacies as the gift of friendship –
of goodness and depth,
of meaning and purpose;
legacies that will last
when all my money is spent.

'And to my grandson
my own grandfather's gold pocket-watch,
a gift from the past
to be used well in the future …'

A legacy –
a gift of an old timepiece,
a legacy from a generation past.

But what about those legacies I already have
that can't be measured by the passing of time?
Legacies as a gift from a grandfather –
of wisdom and teaching,
of stories and examples;
legacies that will last
when minutes of time give way to eons of eternity.

'And to my sister,
the Georgian dresser in the lounge
which she's always admired,
and the contents to go with it …'

A legacy –
a gift of cupboards and drawers,
a legacy in which to keep more things.

But what about those legacies I already have
that contain more than can fill any Georgian dresser?
Legacies of all a family has shared –
of sorrow and joy,
of events and celebrations;
legacies that can't be confined
to a mere piece of furniture.

'And to my minister,
the contents of my library,
in recognition of the many books
we've talked about together …'

A legacy –
more books than could ever be read,
a legacy from a trusted colleague.

But what about those legacies I already have
of all the insights that were never contained in books?
Legacies as the gift of common interest –
of ideas and concepts,
of truth and clarity;
legacies that will last
when no clever words are left.

'And to the town museum,
my collection of paintings,
in recognition of their beauty
that can still give people pleasure ...'

A legacy –
a gift of pictures from all kind of places,
a legacy from a loving collector.

But what about those legacies I already have,
of things seen and admired that no one ever painted?
Legacies of the wonder of the world –
of skies and hills,
of people and scenes;
legacies that will last
when there are no more canvases to cover.

And to you ...
legacies worth more than money;
legacies that will outlast time;
legacies unconfined;

legacies words can't explain;
legacies beyond visual portrayal.

How rich I have become
with legacies such as these.

Now, what legacies am I going to leave to others
after I've gone?

Legacies … I wonder …

### Fourth after Easter

*Old Testament:* Psalm 22:25-31
*Epistle:* Acts 8:26-40
*Gospel:* John 15:1-8

# 36 Subtraction

The vet said that Dougal had to take tablets. Not that Dougal was suffering from anything especially serious. He'd been a bit 'off colour' – *an odd phrase to use for a dog who wasn't well*, Brian thought when he explained to the vet that Dougal hadn't been himself for a few days. But the vet had understood, and after a blood test had diagnosed a mild hormone deficiency – for Dougal, that is, not Brian. 'Two tablets a day, three if he's over twenty kilos, and come back to see me in three weeks – and don't forget to bring the dog.' And, having weighed the dog and pronounced that 'two tablets should do for an eighteen-kilo dog ...' the vet dispatched Dougal and Brian to get on with taking the tablets – Dougal, that is, not Brian.

Dougal and Brian were inseparable. Dougal was named after the shaggy-dog character in the 1960s' kiddies' TV show *The Magic Roundabout*, though he was the *least* shaggy dog Brian had ever known. Brian himself had been called after the Magic Roundabout's snail (or so his mother had told him). So, when he'd had a rabbit it had to be called 'Dylan', and his pet mouse was 'Ermintrude', and he'd once had a hamster called 'Florence' ... So when he'd got a dog, it *had* to be called Dougal. There was *no* choice in the matter whatsoever.

And now Dougal had to take tablets because the vet had diagnosed a mild hormone deficiency. That left Brian with a bit of a problem when he got home. The vet had explained the *reason* for the tablets, and the *effect* of the tablets. He'd gone into great detail about the *content* of the tablets and *when* they should be given. He'd given instructions about *how* the tablets should be administered, hidden in Dougal's food, and so on. In fact, the vet had given Brian *so* much information, Brian couldn't remember what weight he'd said Dougal was, and therefore *how many* tablets Dougal was to get.

For some reason Brian remembered that twenty kilos was the cut-off point, three tablets if you're above, two tablets if you're below. But, for the life of him, he couldn't remember Dougal's actual weight. The vet's was closed for the weekend. So there was nothing else for it. Brian was going to have to weigh Dougal himself.

That's where the fun began – fun for Dougal, that is, but certainly *not* for Brian. It would have been simple enough if Dougal could have been persuaded to sit for more than a nanosecond on Brian's bathroom scales in the begging-for-a-biscuit position. But Dougal and sitting were seldom compatible. And when a desirable dog-biscuit was on offer, why would any self-respecting dog want to sit on a scales contraption for any length of time anyway? Dougal was rapidly taking on the Magic Roundabout 'Zebedee' role in his bouncing up and down trying to get the biscuit, and Brian was beginning to metamorphose into a grumpy 'Mr McHenry' in his frustration. All in all, weighing Dougal was turning into a bit of a disaster.

Then Brian had a brainwave. If he weighed *himself* first, and then, with Dougal in his arms, weighed the two of them together, then subtracted one from the other ... hey presto, he would have the weight of a hyperactive, hormone-deficient dog.

Brian was first. Weighing himself was easy. He'd done it before. 10 st 1lb – 64 Kg. Then it was Dougal's turn – or, at least, Brian and Dougal together. It was surprising enough to a medium-sized mongrel that he was picked up in the first place, and even more that he was expected to keep still while his master fiddled about with things. But with the element of surprise, a moderately soothing voice, and a timeously offered dog-biscuit, Brian managed the task, and pronounced himself satisfied that master and dog had a combined weight of 82 Kg.

Dougal went off about his stuff. And Brian sat down with his figures. It was subtraction time – 82 less 64. Dougal was an eighteen kilogram dog – two tablets would suffice!

Later that day, with Dougal having had his quota of hormone tablets and now curled in a ball in front of the fire, Brian pondered the subtraction thing. What would it be like if Dougal wasn't there? It would be much more than the subtraction of eighteen kilograms of fidgety, disobedient dog from Brian's life. It would be the loss of companionship, fun, wonder, unconditional affection, worry, exercise, vet's bills, and much more besides. Subtraction couldn't really be measured by weights from bathroom scales and simple arithmetic on a scrap of paper, could it? Subtraction, in Dougal's case anyway, would be a calculation that could never, ever be worked out.

### According to your love

According to your love
I am your lover true.
For this you say –
'You are the one for me'
and I – 'I love you too.'
For I can do no less -
according to your love.

According to your love
I am the only one.
For this you say –
'I love no one but you';
and I – 'You're my love too.'
Even though it's not enough -
according to your love.

According to your love
I am your soul-mate now.
For this you say –
'Yes, you and I are one';
and I – 'I'm one with you.'

For that is how it feels –
according to your love.

According to your love
there is no life alone.
For this you say –
'In death I'll die with you';
and I – 'You'll never know.'
For I'm not sure I do –
according to your love.

According to your love
we glimpse eternity.
For this you say –
'Even time means nothing now';
and –, 'Eternally.'
For I know that is true –
according to your love.

According to your love,
I am alive once more.
For this you say –
'Our loving gives us life';
and I – 'A life of love
for ever shared with you' –
according to your love.

### Fifth after Easter

*Old Testament:* Psalm 98
*Epistle:* Acts 10:44–48
*Gospel:* John 15:9–17

# 37 The discovery

Mike didn't do death. So the thing Judith regretted most about his dying was that they hadn't had a chance to talk. No, that wasn't strictly accurate ... They'd had the *chance* to talk, indeed there had been many opportunities. But none of them had been taken. Mike didn't want to go there. And it didn't seem right for Judith to force the issue. It was too hard for them both to get into. So they hadn't talked at all about Mike's death.

She'd known, of course, that she would regret it. But, at the time, loyalty to Mike's wishes was more important than anything else. They'd been told together by the oncology consultant that time was limited. Neither of them had asked the obvious, 'How long, Doctor?' And the doctor didn't volunteer a time frame. There had been hugs when they got home. There had been tears. But no talking – just a silent acknowledgement of the inevitable.

Judith once had a sneaky look at the internet and worked out that Mike's prognosis would be about six months. In actual fact, he got four, and she even thought she would lose him before that. She'd *hoped* Mike might open up as he got more ill and he realised himself that time was running out. But he didn't – well, a leopard doesn't change its spots, does it?

Mike didn't do death. So the thing Judith regretted most about his dying was that they hadn't talked. Maybe it was his protection of her, and he didn't want to make her upset. Mike could never cope with tears. So maybe he couldn't cope with the inevitable tears that would be a result of talking about things. Or maybe it was because he wouldn't be able to find the words. He was never a sentimentalist, was Mike. No soppy stuff; few words of endearment; a solid, dependable, trustworthy, faithful presence; a big, strong, silent support.

Judith had hoped – a long time ago – that he might change. But he didn't. So she went on loving him as he was – the strong silent type. And she knew she'd never find a better man.

But now he was gone, how she wished they'd taken time to talk. Mike had left no instructions about the funeral, so she had to guess at his wishes. That had been stressful, and she hoped she'd got it right for him. It would have been easier if they'd talked … Then there was the stuff in the house – who was to get what, and the like. And how did he organise the bank accounts? And how do you renew the car tax? And where was the house insurance policy? And what should she do with his golf clubs? There was so much to think about, with no preparation – and no guidance from talking things through.

But mostly, and increasingly, Judith wondered how Mike had felt through it all … and what he felt about her … and how he coped with leaving … and did she let him down by not forcing the issue … and should she have taken the initiative … and did he love her? Did he love her? How was she to know? Mike didn't do death. So the thing Judith regretted most about his dying was that they hadn't taken the opportunity to talk.

Judith didn't expect to find the diary. She's not sure to this day whether she was expected to find it in the first place. But she must have been. In any event, she almost missed it. If she hadn't checked the inside pockets of Mike's old blazer, then the diary might have ended up in the charity shop with the jacket. Mike had never been a diary kind of person, so this 'freebee' diary from the local newspaper had obviously found its way into the blazer pocket without a lot of thought. Judith idly flicked through the blank pages. Mike had been less of a writer than he was a talker, so it was no surprise to Judith that the pages were pristine and unspoiled. She looked up Mike's birthday – nothing. She casually glanced at her own birthday – nothing; wedding anniversary – nothing; date of their engagement – nothing; opening of the golf season – nothing; date of his admission to the hospice – nothing. No secrets. No final messages. No revelations. 'Typical,' thought Judith, unsurprised by her findings.

Why she turned to the date of Mike's final diagnosis, she doesn't know. But when she did, she almost dropped on the spot. For there, in Mike's unmistakable, spidery scrawl were the words, 'Judith. The best ever.' She read it again, not believing it the first time. She read it again – through tears – and again – as she sat down on the bed – and again and again and again. Judith. The best ever. The best ever. Judith. Judith. The best ... Judith ...

Judith has no recollection of how long she sat on the bed with the diary in her hands. She has no memory of how much she sobbed, and smiled, and kissed the diary, and told Mike she loved him, and sobbed, and kissed the diary, and spoke to her man ... She has no recollection ...

Mike didn't do death. So the thing Judith regretted most about his dying was that they hadn't taken the chance to talk. But what she does know now is that, in four short words, planted in a diary, and stuffed in the inside pocket of an old blazer, a big, strong, silent man had sown a seed for a grieving wife that, in time, would be the single most important thing she would draw upon in all the coming years.

It's twenty-two years since Mike died. Judith has carried his diary in her handbag all that time. One of her friends asked her recently if they'd had a chance to talk much before Mike died all those years ago. 'Oh, yes,' Judith had replied, 'indeed we did. Me and Mike, we talked – an awful lot ...'

## The letter

I once wrote a letter to my dad.
I didn't write my dad many letters,
Well, you don't, do you?
The odd postcard from holiday ...
But mostly we talked on the phone.

But, when my mother died,
I wrote my dad a letter.

I wanted to say things to him
That I'd never had the chance
To say to my mum.

So I wrote a letter to my dad ...
It wasn't over the top at all,
In fact, it was quite gentle,
Telling him he'd been a good dad to me
Over all the years.

I was anxious when I sent it.
Maybe I was pushing things too much.
I was scared I'd gone too far.
What would he make of this boy of his
Writing him a letter like that?

He never mentioned it when I phoned him –
Did it get there?
Was he upset with me?
Couldn't he bring himself to mention it?
Had I blown it altogether?

It was six months before he mentioned it.
'Oh, and thanks for your letter, son,'
Was as much as it was.
But it was enough for me –
And we kept on talking on the phone.

Nearly twenty years later
When my dad died,
I had his stuff to go through ...
And I found my letter in his wallet,
In the pocket of his favourite jacket.

I once wrote a letter to my dad.
I'm glad I did, now.
He'd carried a piece of me for twenty years,
Something that really mattered,
Just as I carry him close to my heart – all the time.

### Ascension Day

*Old Testament:* Daniel 7:9-14
*Epistle:* Ephesians 1:15-23
*Gospel:* Luke 24:44-53

# 38 Safe

Jenny always held her mother's hand when she was crossing the road, even when the 'green man' was showing that traffic had stopped. Her mother insisted, 'Hold my hand, poppet. It's a busy road. Come now! Take my hand. Then you'll be safe.' Well, it's what grown-ups do, isn't it? So, for every busy road, and even for the quieter ones near her house, it was the same. 'Hold my hand, Jenny. There's a road to cross.' So Jenny dutifully held her mother's hand when she was crossing the road.

It almost went disastrously wrong on the crossing outside the supermarket. Jenny had been helping her mum with the shopping – something she always enjoyed. And so a careful mother, with a full shopping bag in one hand and the other hand available for a dutiful child to hold on to, stood at the crossing waiting for the lights to change so that she and Jenny could pop into the newsagents on the way home. Jenny had a ball in her other hand. Nothing unusual about that, as Jenny and her favourite ball were largely inseparable. And so you had to hold your mother's hand *and* grip your ball tightly as you crossed the road.

The lights changed. The traffic stopped. The 'bleeper' on the crossing sounded and the 'red man' changed to green. And Jenny and her mum set off to cross the road. And that's when Jenny dropped her ball. In an instant, the ball was out of her fingers and was running under the wheels of a stationary car. Jenny's precious ball ... And in a split second, Jenny had let go of her mother's hand and was off after the ball. 'Jenny!' her mother screamed, and turned to catch her daughter.

Just at that moment, a cyclist came careering down the road. Assuming there was no one on the crossing, and unable to see the developing crisis, the cyclist jumped the lights, saw Jenny, braked suddenly to avoid hitting her, swerved violently, and ran straight over the bag of shopping that Jenny's mum had dropped in the middle of the crossing in her attempt to rescue her child.

Thankfully, no one was hurt. The cyclist just managed to stay upright. Jenny was whisked across the road by a scared and relieved mother. And there were broken eggs, squashed tomatoes, slices of bread, and the remains of a day's shopping scattered all over the street. As angry pedestrians and drivers alike remonstrated with the shaking cyclist, an angry mother remonstrated with a bewildered Jenny. 'I *told* you that you always have to hold my hand. You're more important than a silly ball. It's too dangerous to cross over by yourself. *You have to hold my hand,* right?' Jenny nodded through her tears. A lesson had been learned. Holding your mother's hand would always keep you safe.

When Granny Robertson from next door invited Jenny to come to the shops with her – with Jenny's mother's approval, of course – Jenny told Granny Robertson the whole story of the crossing and the cyclist – including how she'd rescued her precious ball at the end of it all which was, of course, *very* important. 'I have to hold your hand when I'm crossing the road, Mrs Robertson,' she insisted on their way to the shops, 'because that way I'll always be safe.'

Granny Robertson just said 'Oh,' as the conversation went on to other things. That is, until they were approaching the crossing in front of the supermarket, and Granny Robertson insisted, 'Now, young Jenny. Here we are, about to cross the road. You want to be safe from danger? Then, come, and I'll hold *your* hand while we cross.' Jenny paused. It *sounded* the same as her mum had said, but … then … it was kind of different. Dutifully, Jenny held out her hand to take hold of Granny Robertson's, just as she did with her mum. But as their fingers touched, before Jenny could grip on to Granny's Robertson's hand, the old lady took Jenny's hand firmly in hers. Now, not only didn't it *sound* right, but it didn't *feel* right either.

'But …' Jenny began.

'What's the matter?' Granny Robertson enquired, the flicker of a smile appearing on her face.

'But …' Jenny stammered on, 'when we cross the road, I hold on to my mum's hand. *She* doesn't hold on to *mine*.'

'Ah. I know that. But you see, if you hold on to mine, no matter how hard you try and grip tight, you'll always be distracted, and your attention will wander …'

'Like dropping my ball, you mean.'

'Exactly. Like dropping your ball. And you'll let go, and then you'll be in danger …'

'From cyclists …'

'From cyclists, and cars, and much more besides. But, you see, when I hold on to *your* hand, I'll not let go. Because my hand is bigger than yours. No matter how much you get distracted and chase after silly balls, I'll hold on tight. Because that's *my* job, you see. And if *I* hold *your* hand, you'll be safer than ever.'

Sure enough, Jenny felt very secure *indeed* as Granny Robertson held her hand tightly as they crossed the road. Even though there was no ball to drop to test its effectiveness, Jenny felt very safe indeed.

The next time Jenny and her mum stopped at the crossing in front of the supermarket, Jenny's mum said, 'Now, hold my hand while we cross the road, so that you'll be safe.'

'Don't want to,' Jenny replied. But before her mother had time to scold her for her cheekiness, Jenny concluded, 'Because I want you to hold *my* hand, because Granny Robertson says that way I'll be safer than ever.'

### Safe

A hand held out for me to hold;
A hand stretched forth; and now I'm told
To reach and grasp, to touch and know
This hand that's offered now.
A hand held out with tender touch;

A hand to heal; that offers much
To comfort me; new strength to show ...
This hand is offered now.

A hand held out; a sign of grace;
A hand that offers love's embrace;
To draw me close; hope's hold to find ...
This hand still offered now.
A hand held out, admonishing;
A hand to warn; an offering
Of learning's growth for soul and mind ...
This hand yet offered now.

A hand held out – this hand I seek;
A hand stretched out when I am weak;
That lifts me up when I would fall ...
This hand I'm offered now.
A hand that's yours; a hand that's mine;
A hand that's human, and divine;
That brings what's needed, giving all ...
This hand ... look ... offered now.

### Sixth after Easter

*Old Testament:* Psalm 1
*Epistle:* Acts 1:15-26
*Gospel:* John 17:6-19

# 39 Ah, sweet mystery of life

'One of the great mysteries of life,' remarked Freda as she and her husband were sitting at breakfast one morning, 'is why a man would wear a hat while he's driving.' Jim never responded. He seldom did, especially when Freda was expounding on one of her 'great mysteries of life'.

'After all,' Freda continued, clearly undeterred by her husband's typical lack of interest and his unremitting concentration on the front page of his morning newspaper, 'a man doesn't *need* to wear a hat while he's driving. A hat's for keeping his head dry when it's raining, or keeping him warm in the winter, and *neither* of those is a problem *inside* a car. So why?'

Jim, now studiously taking in the contents of page two, remained unresponsive. Freda remained undeterred. 'You see it all the time – trilbies, flat caps, and those ubiquitous baseball things. But why? Now women, on the other hand – well, they're different.' Jim was now on page three. 'When *we* wear hats, they have to stay on all the time. After all, if you're off to a wedding or the like, you don't want to have to take your hat off and on all day. Just *think* the state your hair would be in. But men? Wearing a hat in the car? One of the great mysteries of life …'

Jim nodded imperceptibly. He'd heard Freda explore many 'great mysteries of life' at the breakfast table over the years – from 'Why does wearing black make your bum look smaller?' through 'How come there's only one "Monopolies Commission"?' to 'How does the man who drives the snowplough get to work in the winter?' and 'Why doesn't glue stick to the inside of the bottle?' And he'd stopped listening a long time ago. The 'great mysteries of life' could remain mysteries for as long as they liked, he reckoned. It wasn't worth wasting brain power on such stuff.

All of that changed, however, one Sunday morning. The day had begun with a storm raging round the house, and a strong wind agitating the trees at the bottom of the garden and bringing heavy rain lashing against the kitchen window. 'It's one of the great mysteries of life that you know where the wind goes but you don't know where it comes from,' was Freda's conversation opener.

'Whit,' Jim replied, already engrossed in the Sunday Supplement.

'What?' responded Freda.

'Whit!' Jim repeated.

'What are you talking about, man?' enquired Freda, surprised that her husband had even acknowledged that the conversation was happening.

'Whit. I'm talking about "Whit".'

'Whit?'

'What?'

'What's "Whit" got to do with anything?'

'Listen, woman,' said the exasperated Jim, tossing his paper on the table. 'Not all mysteries need to be explained. Life is full of questions – as you so regularly prove. So learn to live with the questions for once.'

Freda was stunned into silence by this unexpected outburst. Jim took that as a signal that the floor was his. So he grabbed his chance. 'See the wind, eh? No? 'Cause you can't see it, can you? So does it matter where it comes from? Do we have to understand it? Why not just accept that it comes from *somewhere* and let that be the end of it. Marvel at its effect. Know what it does. See the rain it brings. Be amazed that those trees wave about with nobody moving them.' He pointed to the bottom of the garden. 'I don't know where the wind comes from, and I'm not in the least bothered ... but I can see what it does. Isn't that enough? Let it be, woman. Live with the mystery ...'

A loquacious wife was struck dumb. His lesson in the mysteries of life complete, Jim returned to his paper. The silence continued for a while. Freda was the first to speak. 'But ...' she offered diffidently.

'But what?' Jim replied.

'But what about "Whit"? Where does that come in?'

'Och woman, this is Whit Weekend, isn't it?'

'Uh huh. So …?'

'So … Whit Sunday, Pentecost, the coming of the Spirit, "the breath of God", and all that; the wind of the Spirit that changed everything. You know, a bunch of frightened folk, not knowing which way to turn, and, hey presto, they're up and out there, full of life, ready for anything. I'll bet *they* didn't know where the wind began, but they were bloomin' sure they could see its effect. So they showed the difference it made, and didn't worry about where it came from.'

'Oh,' said Freda. 'And the "Whit" bit?'

'Well, this Spirit thing – this Spirit thing's been celebrated ever since. Pentecost Sunday and stuff. And when lots of believers were baptised they would all wear white robes. Hence, 'white' … whit … Whitsun … OK?'

Freda nodded, hoping that would indicate that it was 'OK' enough, even though it was largely still a mystery. She rose from the table and moved over to the kitchen sink to wash the breakfast dishes. 'One of the great mysteries of life,' she began, 'is … why is there always a teaspoon in the bottom of the washing-up bowl when all the dishes are done?'

'Because you need a teaspoon to stir that cup of tea you're just about to make me,' Jim replied.

'But I *never* make you a cup of tea in the morning,' Freda retorted.

'I know,' said Jim. 'It's always puzzled me, that. Ah, sweet mystery of life …'

### Mysteries

'What's a mystery?' I asked.

'I've got no idea,' you said.

'That's no help at all,' I replied.

'So why the question, then?' you asked.

'Because you always have the answers,' I said.

'Well, usually, right enough,' you replied.

'So why not now?' I asked.

'I dunno,' you said.

'So no insights on mysteries, then,' I replied.

'Why do you want to know?' you asked

'I dunno,' I replied.

'It's a mystery, then,' you said.

'Looks like it,' I replied

'You want to find out about everything, don't you?' you asked.

'Yes,' I said.

'Well, you can't,' you replied.

'Don't you?' I asked.

'No', you said.

'Why not?' I asked.

'Dunno,' you replied.

'That'll be a mystery, then,' I said.

'Could be,' you replied.

'So we're no further forward,' I said.

'We are a bit,' you said.

'Why?' I asked.

'It's a mystery,' you said.

### Pentecost

*Old Testament:* Psalm 104:24-35b
*Epistle:* Acts 2:1-21
*Gospel:* John 15:26-27, 16:4b-15

# 40 Starting over

'The swiftest horse cannot overtake a word once spoken.' So pro-nounced Proverb Professor as Georgina's English teacher was coming to the conclusion of a long lecture about the demerits of gossiping. It was all because Daren Chalmers had said something nasty about Veronica's hairstyle, and she was upset, and Proverb Professor had got to know, and Daren had apologised, and the whole class had got a long peroration about thinking first before you speak because once a word is out there, it can't be taken back. 'The swiftest horse ...' and all that.

'A Chinese saying,' Proverb Professor intoned. 'Take it to heart. Think before you speak.'

Proverb Professor was Mr Bannerman, head of English in Georgina's school. Mr Bannerman had been known as Proverb Pro-fessor for as long as anyone could remember. Proverbs were Mr Ban-nerman's stock-in-trade. He had one for every conceivable occasion.

'One volunteer is worth two pressed men,' he would offer as a thank-you for someone offering to help with something. 'English naval derivation – from forcible enlisting by press-gangs – 18th century.'

'All roads lead to Rome,' he would suggest as a number of the class reached a similar conclusion from different directions. 'Common in English usage in the 14th century – originally Latin. A reward is possible for someone who brings me the Latin version.' Georgina never bothered.

'There is one thing stronger than all the armies of the world; and that is an idea whose time has come,' he would suggest, as a new topic of monumental importance to the syllabus was being introduced. 'From the writings of Victor Hugo in the 19th century. Anyone tell me from where? No? Well, I suggest you find out.' And Georgina never did.

Most of Proverb Professor's proverbs went in one ear and out the other for most of the class most of the time – Georgina included. Until, that is, she came down badly in her English Literature A-Level prelim.

There were always prelims a couple of months before the main exams. They helped assess a pupil's progress, allowed a subject-teacher to see what a class needed to brush up on, and gave grounds for appeal if someone had done well in the prelims and badly in the actual exam. Well … Georgina did badly in the prelim. Oh, there were plenty of excuses – her mother had been poorly and had recently been admitted to hospital; Georgina had been off school herself at a crucial stage of the year with some dodgy stomach business; and, the week before the prelims, her gran had died. But excuses didn't help Georgina's sense of devastation and failure.

Her whole world had come crashing down around her ears. She was almost inconsolable. And, worst of all, she dreaded having to explain herself to Proverb Professor. No doubt she would get some trite proverb thrown at her, with a suggestion that '"You've made your bed, so you can lie in it" … English – 16th century, girl …' ; or '"Sow much, reap much; sow little, reap little" … Chinese' – you understand what I'm getting at?

So it was with some trepidation that Georgina found herself being beckoned into Proverb Professor's class at the end of the school day. She needn't have worried. Mr Bannerman was neither trite nor uncaring. He was sympathetic, sensitive and supportive – not attributes Georgina had seen in her English teacher before.

He reassured her there was still time; that she had what it took to do well; that he had faith in her; that next time she'd do better. And, before she left, Mr Bannerman looked his young pupil in the eye, and said, 'There was once a man who came to a very wise teacher. The man was an OK kind of guy, who, on the surface at least, seemed to be doing pretty well. But inside there was failure. So he asked the teacher, "How can I get it right?" And the teacher said, "You have to be born again." Now, the man was an intelligent kind of guy, and he knew that he couldn't be born again, because he was a grown man. So he said so, and laughed at the teacher's apparent stupidity. But the teacher was very wise. And he said to the man, "No. I don't mean being born again like a baby. Now that would be silly. But I mean being born again on the *inside*. Your spirit needs to start again. You need to begin all over – *from the inside out*." Now, the very wise teacher said a lot more besides, and he wasn't ever sure that the guy had a clue what he was on about. So the guy had to go away and work it out. So, Georgina, you have to do the same. You have to start again. From the inside … If you get that right, you'll know you have another chance.'

Georgina wasn't sure she understood it, any more than the guy in the story did. But she knew she'd been appropriately reassured. Her consultation with Mr Bannerman was over. She stood up to leave. 'Thank you,' she offered. 'And who was the wise man,' she asked tentatively. 'A reward if you can find out,' was the reply.

But before Georgina turned to go, Mr Bannerman continued. 'Now I know you and the rest of the school call me Proverb Professor. I don't mind that. In fact, I'm quite delighted.' Georgina could feel her face reddening. 'So, in case you were expecting the stereotype, I'll leave you with a quotation rather than a proverb. OK?'

Georgina could only offer a slightly embarrassed smile in response. 'When I was your age,' Mr Bannerman said, 'one of the trendy people was Mary Quant. And, yes, I once knew about trendy things too … And Mary Quant once said, "Being young is greatly overestimated … Any failure seems so total. Later on you realise you can have another go." It's the kind of thing our very wise man could have suggested to the guy who was struggling to start over, don't you think? Now off home – and maybe this is the time you've learned that you can have another go …

'And in case you forget, "Fall seven times, stand up eight …" Japanese – 7th century … Or "Go and get stuck in …" Professor Proverb, English Classroom, January 2011 …'

## To fall

To fall
and to rise again
when falling was hard
and the ending was almost total,
and the rising was well-nigh impossible.

To rise
and to fall again
when the rising was great
and a new beginning was on the cards
and I'd never fall, or even stumble, ever again.

To fall
and to rise again
when the falling's been done
but the pain stays in the memory
when the rising should have made it disappear.

To rise
and to rise again,
maybe better prepared to fall,
knowing that rising is always a possibility,
even when I thought falling was the end of everything.

## Trinity

*Old Testament:* Isaiah 6:1-8
*Epistle:* Romans 8:12-17
*Gospel:* John 3:1-17

# 41 A knowledge of form

It wasn't Emma's fault that she had disturbed Jimmy McNally. The resident of Flat 2/3 Dunlop Street wasn't on the list of pastoral visits for the deaconess of St Peter's Parish Church. He never had been and was never likely to be. Jimmy McNally didn't do church.

Emma knew nothing of this as she stood outside the door of Flat 2/1. She had been ringing the doorbell for some time, but knowing that Miss Amelia Simkins, the occupier of 2/1, was absolutely stone deaf, Emma reckoned that it would be some time before Miss Simkins would answer the door.

Emma knew her elderly parishioner was at home. Everyone in the stair and halfway along Dunlop Street knew that there was someone at home in 2/1, for Emma had never heard a television turned up so loud in her whole life. The BBC lunchtime news was being broadcast to the whole neighbourhood, courtesy of Miss Amelia Simkins' TV. No wonder she couldn't hear the doorbell!

An experienced deaconess, however, had developed some tricks of the trade. On this occasion, all Emma's ingenuity would be required. The doorbell alone being no competition for the news-casters of the BBC, Emma decided that rattling the letterbox should be added – but to no avail. So, as her *pièce de résistance* – and feeling that she could now audition for any vacant one-man-band slot at the Edinburgh Fringe – Emma gave it her all. She lifted up the flap of the letterbox and jammed it open with her mobile phone. The decibel level of the TV was incredible. Undeterred, Emma bent down with her ear close to the open letterbox and listened for a pause in the newscast. And in that moment of relative stillness, she went for it big-time – ringing the doorbell with one hand, banging the door knocker with the other, and kicking the bottom of the door with her right foot as hard as she could.

That's when Emma met Jimmy McNally. The door of Flat 2/3 swung open, and a clearly unhappy man stood in the doorway. 'What the hell's goin' on? Ah cannae hear masel' think wi' a' this racket.' It was hard for Emma to explain. She apologised for the disturbance, and excused her insensitivity on the grounds of Miss Simkins' deafness. Thankfully, the owner of Flat 2/3 was quickly placated. Introductions were made, and a considerably more amenable Jimmy McNally invited Emma inside. Emma protested, saying that she'd made enough of a nuisance of herself. But Jimmy insisted. 'The old stick's deaf as a post,' he confirmed, 'so we've got an arrangement. If ah discover someone who cannae get an answer, ah come inside an' ah phone her. She's got a flashin' light fixed up tae her phone so she can see when it's ringin'. Sit doon, lassie. Just gie's a minute.'

Jimmy McNally busied himself with the phone. It took a while, but eventually he got through. 'It's Jimmy … Aye, Jimmy … JIMMY. Aye, FRAE NEXT DOOR … AYE … There's a lassie at yer door … A LASSIE … FRAE THE CHURCH … A LASSIE … DEACONESS … FRAE THE CHURCH …. COME TAE SEE YOU … Aye … AYE … Frae St Peter's … ST PETER'S … DOON THE ROAD … AYE … OH AYE … OK THEN … Tomorrow … TOMORROW AFTERNOON … AYE … AH'LL TELL HER … AYE … … … JIMMY … FRAE NEXT DOOR … ST PETER'S AYE … BYE, THEN.'

'She's no' feelin' that great, she says,' Jimmy reported. 'You'd be better common' back tomorrow. Ah think she got that. Ye can try onyway.'

Emma thanked Amelia Simkins' helpful neighbour and turned to leave. 'I'm sorry to bother you,' she offered, 'but thanks for your help. If I can do anything to help you at any time, you only have to ask.'

Jimmy McNally smiled broadly. 'Thanks, lassie. But what ah need help wi', you couldnae handle.'

Emma was not a little intrigued. 'Mmmm. Sounds like a bit of a challenge.' She returned Jimmy's broad smile with one of her own. 'Why don't you try me?'

Jimmy turned round and retrieved a newspaper from the table at the side of the room. 'There you are,' he proclaimed. 'Pick me a winner at the 3.30 at Kempton Park.'

'What?' Emma stammered.

'You said "If I can do anything …" Well, ah need help wi' ma bettin' line. Ah was just about to phone ma bookies. So, c'moan, lassie. Gie's some help, eh?'

'But I've never picked a horse in my life,' Emma protested.

'So noo's the time tae start. See, there's the runners. Pick wan oot o' them …'

Emma knew she was trapped. So, taking the newspaper in her hand she looked with mock-studiousness at the list in front of her. She didn't know where to start, but she had to do something. So she closed her eyes and poked the paper with her finger. When she opened her eyes, she said boldly, 'There you are. Number 7. "Go Lightly".' Jimmy McNally retrieved the newspaper, looked at the list, and let out a guffaw nearly as loud as his neighbour's TV.

'Och, awa' wi' ye lassie. That wan's only got three legs an' runs backwards. "Go Lightly"? It cannae go at a'. Awa hame wi ye, lassie. Stick tae yer prayin' an' yer guid works. Ye'll dae nothin' wi' the horses.'

Emma was back outside Flat 2/1 Dunlop Street at three o'clock the following afternoon, hoping that Miss Amelia Simkins remembered that the deaconess from St Peter's was due to call. She was just about to start her percussion practice on Miss Simkins' door when, to her surprise, the door of Flat 2/3 swung open, and there, once again, stood Jimmy McNally in the doorway. 'Ah've been waitin' for you, lassie. Where huv you been a' ma life, eh?'

'What do you mean, Mr McNally?' a bemused deaconess responded.

Jimmy beamed even more widely than he'd done the day before. He had a newspaper in his hand and, poking it fiercely with a stubby finger, he announced, 'See yon horse you picked yesterday?' Emma nodded. 'Well … WELL,' Jimmy proclaimed with obvious glee, 'it only came in at twenty-five tae one. TWENTY-FIVE TAE ONE,' he repeated. 'So where huv you been a' ma life? Me wi' ma knowledge o' form, an' you wi' a direct line tae the Almighty … Eh? We could hae cleaned up a lang time since.'

Just then, Miss Amelia Simkins opened the door of Flat 2/1, and Emma didn't know which of her two friends she should visit first.

### Which way?

Which way to go?
'The road less travelled'
or treading a familiar pathway?
I know which one I'd choose …
But who knows …?

Which prompting to follow?
Doing the new thing
or reverting to familiar patterns?
I know which one I'd choose …
But what if …?

Which attitude to adopt?
Taking a different point of view
or sticking to my familiar position?
I know which one I'd choose …
But, then again …

Which option to take?
Taking the risk,

or playing safe with the familiar?
I know which one I'd choose …
But, maybe …

What way to live?
Taking the unpopular way,
or going with the familiar crowd?
I know which one I'd choose …
But would I be right?

What truth to believe?
Taking the spirit's way,
or being familiar with evil?
I know which one I'd choose …
But why don't I?

### Ninth after Easter

*Old Testament:* 1 Samuel 8:4-11, 16-20
*Epistle:* 2 Corinthians 4:13-5:1
*Gospel:* Mark 3:20-25

# 42 Ryan's tree

Ryan was a tree warden, and he had the responsibility for looking after *one* tree. Ryan was the best warden the tree ever had. The fact that he was the *only* warden who bothered about this particular horticultural specimen was neither here nor there. Ryan was a tree warden, and his *one* tree was very, very important.

The tree in question was a silver birch on the strip of grass between the main road and the service road outside Ryan's new house – number ninety-nine Kilmartin Avenue. All the houses in the estate were new. The estate itself was a new beginning for many families from the clearance programme in the run-down areas of the inner city. The sprawling conglomeration of terraces, semis and flats wasn't fully complete when the families moved in. The houses were up, but there was still a lot to do to sort out the green spaces, pathways and play-areas before the estate was what it was meant to be. And the silver birch tree was part of that development.

It wasn't the only tree, of course, but part of an extensive programme called 'greening the estate'. This was a joint venture between the Council and the builders, and, most importantly, with the enthusiasm of Mrs Alice Hobson, the wife of Joe Hobson, owner and Chief Executive of Hobson Construction who were the estate's principal contractors. Alice Hobson was a flamboyant character, whose wealth and lifestyle appeared to place her in a different league from the people on the estate. But she had a passion for the environment and a deep concern for the welfare of the local people. And she had influence … and money …

Alice Hobson had personally chosen every sapling for planting in the estate. And when the planting was done, every house had a direct view of one or more of the trees. Oaks, horse chestnuts, elms and a scattering of silver birches – like the one outside ninety-nine Kilmartin Avenue – had been carefully distributed in every street.

But filling a new estate with sapling trees was one thing. Taking care of them was quite another. The Council would continue to do the environmental bit – staking, straightening, watering, and the like. But who was to do the 'caring' bit, watching and protecting the trees from damage or vandalism? That's why Alice Hobson came up with the idea of 'tree wardens'. If every tree could have a warden, someone who had the responsibility for looking after it, then every tree would have a protector, someone who would look out for its welfare. That's why Ryan had become the tree warden for the silver birch on the strip of grass between the main road and the service road outside number ninety-nine Kilmartin Avenue.

The ceremony for the announcement of the tree-planting scheme and the investiture of the tree wardens took place in Ryan's school one Friday afternoon. Each tree warden was presented with a large, round badge with a tree printed on it and the words 'Tree Warden' emblazoned across it. Every child between the ages of eight and eleven had a badge. Each tree warden was allocated their tree within sight of their own house. Ryan felt ten feet tall when he got his badge from Mrs Hobson. And Ryan Scott, tree warden *extraordinaire,* set about being warden of his silver birch tree with enthusiasm and commitment.

That's why he fell foul of Mrs Graham from number ninety-one when he told her that she shouldn't let her dog lift its leg against his sapling tree. 'Your dog should do that somewhere else,' Ryan had insisted in his best tree-warden voice. 'It'll spoil the tree.' Ryan had got a bigger row from his mother than he'd had from Mrs Graham for his 'cheek'. But he was still determined that he was going to do his best for his tree, even if he was to stand beside it to warn off Mrs Graham's tree-threatening pooch every time it came close. It never happened. The silver birch survived.

Ryan had to look out for the local lads playing football too. The tree and its protective container couldn't *possibly* be used as a goalpost for the makeshift football pitch on the narrow grass strip. It would be too vulnerable to a strong kick or a bashing from a mistimed tackle. Of course Ryan played football with the rest of the kids, but he always tried to kick the ball further up the street to keep the game away from the tree. Any tree warden worth his salt had to be constantly vigilant. And the tree survived.

No one really slept much on the night of 'the great storm', and Ryan was up and down to his bedroom window all through the long night. The noise of the wind was frightening, and the rain battering on the roof was *very* loud. If he could have built a protective shelter round his precious tree, he would have done … But as that was beyond the capacity of even the best of tree wardens, he just worried instead. In the morning, the devastation was awesome. The storm had torn slates from roofs. Panes of glass were broken in Mr Graham's greenhouse. The flagpole beside Hobson Construction's show house was snapped in two. But … the saplings were OK. Their youthful flexibility had allowed them to ride out the great storm. And Ryan's tree survived.

The first winter was a problem too. The infant tree was two feet, eight-and-a-half inches tall. (Well, good tree wardens have to know *everything* about their trees, don't they?) But the snow that fell in the January was two feet, ten inches deep. It was the biggest snowfall anyone could remember for years and years. All a tree warden knew was that the tree in his care had disappeared completely under the snow. Gone! But when the thaw came, Ryan watched with fascination as the tip of his silver birch appeared above the greying snow. And when the snow had all melted, a little tree was back in its warden's diligent care. And the tree survived.

Ryan doesn't live in Kilmartin Avenue any more. He moved away from the estate when he got married. He works for the Forestry Commission now. He has responsibility for vast forests in the north of Scotland. He has millions of trees in his care. But every now and again he goes back to have a look at the silver birch on the strip of grass between the main road and the service road outside number ninety-nine Kilmartin Avenue, just to make sure it's still OK. After all, the work of a tree warden is never done, is it?

## Hope

The ground was cold and bare; the seeds, so small and dull,
With hope were buried there, as autumn came.
My life had lost its light; my love was laid to rest;
I wept, in endless nights, and called your name.

The days grew long and sad; unseen, the seeds lay dead,
Like any hope I'd had, in winter days,
My life, now routine hours; my grind, mere lifeless tasks;
My home, devoid of flowers and sunshine rays.

Old year gives birth to new; old blooms have gone for good;
More days of missing you, that's my New Year.
Old life is left behind. New life? I don't yet know
When peace might fill my mind and banish fear.

It's too soon to believe that life will bring again
A healing in my grief, a hope that's mine …
My prayer, my endless plea, my cry, my one desire
Is that I yet might see a rainbow sign.

Green shoots through dark earth rise as seeds are breaking free
And upwards turn their eyes towards the sun.
Are hopeful signs being given? Will light defeat the dark?
As hands reach up to heaven, can hell be shunned?

Green shoots of hope appear; a smile; a moment free
Of pain and dull despair; a glimpse of spring …
Can hope bring life again? Will purpose come from hope?
Might healing come from pain and let me sing?

A seed can hold no more the glory it contains,
The colour in its store, its treasure trove;
When hope its chains will snap, it must burst free and show
That death no victory gains o'er life and love.

O grave, where is your sting when seeds burst forth with life,
And hope with triumph brings New Life again?
Let me not doubt the growth that hope will recreate
In barren, lifeless earth, for me. Amen!

*Revised version of 'Hope', first published in* New Journeys Now Begin *by Tom Gordon, published by Wild Goose Publications, 2006. ISBN 978-1-905010-08-0*

## Tenth Sunday of the Year

*Old Testament:* 1 Samuel 15:34–16:13
*Epistle:* 2 Corinthians 5:6–17
*Gospel:* Mark 4:26–34

# 43 Keep calm, and carry on

Sandy just loved his granddad. He loved his granddad's big, droopy white moustache and his wispy hair… the smell of pipe-tobacco … his funny stories and his even funnier laugh … It was just terrific when Granddad Archie was around. But, best of all – Granddad Archie was *always* calm. He only had to *be* there to create a calmness which everyone could benefit from. When Sandy was in a strop, Granddad Archie never raised his voice. He didn't need to. One look was enough to take the heat out of things. When Sandy was panicking about his exams, Granddad Archie's gentle advice seemed to be just what Sandy needed to calm him down. When there were worries at home, well, Granddad Archie just seemed to make them easier to cope with.

'Keep calm, and carry on,' he was fond of saying. 'We learned that in the war, you know,' he would intone, 'and it would be useful if more people took it to heart these days.' Sandy took it to heart, at least most of the time, because Granddad Archie's influence really mattered.

And it was that kind of influence and that kind of calmness in the face of a storm that Sandy needed right now. Today of all days, Sandy needed to 'keep calm and carry on'. For, today of all days, *this* storm was going to be the biggest one of all. But, today of all days, Sandy was more conscious than ever that Granddad Archie's death ten years before was as real as if it had happened only yesterday.

Sandy was sitting quietly at the side of the green waiting for the match to start. The match in question was the long-awaited final of the Bowling Club's open singles tournament, and Sandy was expected to be the runaway winner. This had been his season. He was the club champion. He was one half of the mixed-pairs winning partnership. He had just been selected for the national team for the Commonwealth Games. And here he was, on the brink of winning the most prestigious open singles championship in the country. He was, so the bookies told him, an odds-on certainty.

All of this was on Sandy's mind as he pondered things at the side of the green. And he was far from certain that he could keep calm enough to do it justice. He wished his old granddad could have been there. That would be the calmness he really needed.

The championship had gone well. Sandy had raced through his games as expected, heavily defeating a former champion in the semi-final. The final of the competition used a 'set' scoring system, with the first player to score seven points being awarded a set in the best-of-five set match. Sandy's opponent was an Australian who'd carried all before him since he'd come across to the UK earlier in the year. This was Sandy's first head-to-head with the Aussie master, and the final turned out to be a battle of the titans.

The Aussie threw the first jack, keeping the end long, and took the first set by taking a single on the final end. Sandy responded by taking the second and third sets, with a whitewash in the second after only three ends, scoring a four with some masterly drawing on his favourite backhand. He narrowly lost set four, his opponent scattering a tight head with a superbly positioned drive, setting the match up beautifully for the fifth and deciding set.

After seven ends of the final set, the scores were tied – six apiece. It was down to the final four bowls. It was Sandy's jack. His hands were shaking. He'd already mopped the perspiration from his brow, but in no time at all he was running with sweat again. Sandy had a raging storm going on inside his head. And it was then he heard it: 'Keep calm, and carry on.' It was *so* clear that Sandy stopped and looked around, only to be greeted by the puzzled faces of the onlookers. He bent down to position the mat. 'Keep calm, and carry on.' There it was again, as if Granddad Archie was right there beside him. Sandy straightened up and looked around again. The spectators were getting restless. But Sandy just smiled to himself and mouthed a silent 'thank you' as he felt an overwhelming sense of calmness descend.

Positioning the mat carefully, he threw the jack gently, believing he had a better chance of winning if the end was short. The jack ran straight and true. Sandy's first wood grazed the jack, settling two inches past. The crowd clapped as the marker chalked Sandy's bowl as a 'toucher'. His opponent drew on the forehand, but slipped two feet past. Sandy left his next bowl short, pleased that it could be a blocker as the end unfolded. The Aussie hit the jack with his next wood – another 'toucher', but moved the jack so that it was resting against Sandy's first bowl. It was tight, but Sandy's was a fraction closer. Sandy let his next delivery run long, as a safeguard if his opponent chose to drive. The Australian countered by leaving his penultimate wood just beside Sandy's at the back of the head.

It was Sandy's final delivery. He was beginning to tense up. But the voice came again: 'Keep calm, and carry on.' Sandy chose the backhand. But his bowl never disturbed the head. He was still lying 'one'. It would have to be enough. The Aussie stood by the mat for his final wood. He was upright. He was going to drive. There was a collective intake of breath. The crowd was on its feet. The bowl was on its way. Straight as a die it ran. It missed Sandy's blocker by a whisker. It demolished the head, scattering the bowls everywhere. The jack was sprung, and everyone watched with bated breath as the little white ball rolled gently and settled beside … the Australian's bowl at the very back of the green.

The crowd erupted. The new open singles champion was ecstatic. He leapt about and hugged everyone in sight. Sandy couldn't contain his disappointment. He felt a new storm, of anger and self-doubt, emotion and resentment, begin to build in his head. He was fit to explode. Until, one more time, the voice … Sandy smiled as he watched someone else claim the trophy he'd been expected to win. He'd just have to live with it. There was always next year. And there was always the calmness Granddad Archie could bring. 'Keep calm, and carry on.'

## When storms will rage

*(Sung to the tune 'Epiphany')*

When storms will rage and the dark clouds are gathering;
When lightning flashes and thunder-claps roll;
Grant me a peace in your presence abiding;
Offer your blessedness, peace for my soul.

When courage fails and new fears are attacking me;
When doubts o'erwhelm me and faith might depart;
Grant me your calmness, my purpose restoring;
Offer your healing and peace for my heart.

When many foes with their power are threatening;
When failed resolve makes it hardest to stand;
Grant me a hope in your blessed assurance;
Offer your comfort to strengthen my hand.

When storms are calmed and the winds have ceased bellowing;
When seas are tranquil and sunshine breaks through;
Grant me humility to pause and be grateful,
Offering true thanks in my praises to you.

When storms return, with the skies ever altering;
When waves crash o'er me and winds tear my sail;
Grant me the faith to know you will stay with me,
Offering the promise your peace will prevail.

### Eleventh Sunday of the Year

*Old Testament:* 1 Samuel 17:1-49
*Epistle:* 2 Corinthians 6:1-13
*Gospel:* Mark 4:35-41

# 44 A kind of healing

It had been a very long day for Dr Len Whyte. Busy clinics, house-calls to depressing homes, breaking the news of a suicide to a hysterical family … There were some days when it was just too much. Len was glad he was going home.

It was only a short walk from the back door of the surgery to his car. But even a short walk can be interrupted. And this time it was Mo Atwood who did the interrupting. Len almost fell over her in the gathering darkness. And once he'd regained his composure and was about to complete his short, car-bound journey, he realised that Mo was in tears.

'I'm sorry,' the apologetic doctor blurted. 'I didn't see you there. Did I hurt you?' Mo's only reply was a loud wail.

Len knew Mo and all the Atwood clan extremely well. Mo was clearly distressed, but no gentle bump from a rushing doctor at the end of a stressful day could have caused her to be *that* upset. She was in a terrible state, red-eyed, obviously distraught, and unable to speak coherently through her tears. One of Mo's children was standing nearby. From his memory, Len reckoned this must be the youngest of the eight Atwood kids, a little mite with a runny nose and a cheeky grin, who was, it appeared, as bemused by her mother's state as Len was.

'Mo,' Len exclaimed, 'what on earth's the matter? What's wrong?' Mo struggled for words through her tears, and all Len could make out through the wailing was, 'Ma laddie …', 'Bobo …', 'disaster …' and 'bike …' Piecing it together quickly, Len came to the conclusion that the ten-year-old Bobo, the only boy in the Atwood family, had clearly met with some dreadful accident … knocked from his bike on the busy main road, perhaps, and now languishing in the A&E department of the local hospital, fighting for his life. Mo had come because she needed comfort, a lift to the hospital, emergency childcare for the rest of the kids or simply because she didn't know what to do or who else to turn to. Len surmised that this was a disaster of no small magnitude.

Putting his tiredness to one side, and now kneeling in front of the distressed Mo, Len tried to get the whole story so that he could begin to work out what he could do to help. It took ages, but when Mo was composed enough to speak, she expressed her troubles in a heart-rending fashion … 'It's ma laddie …' *Yes, Mo, got that bit* … 'an' it's his bike …' *Fine, yes, got that bit too, and some time back … So what's the rest?* Len was amazed at the story. The truth tumbled out in a veritable torrent of words and emotion … 'See, his bike's broke. The mudguard's gone an' fell aff, and it's rubbin' on the wheel, and he cannae go it ony mair … Look, there it is …' and Mo pointed to a heap of bike-shaped metal leaning against the back wall of the surgery. 'There it is! See, like ah telt ye, the mudguard's got stuck on the tyre, and wee Bobo cannae go his bike, and he's that upset …' and Mo was off into another wail.

'Is Bobo all right?' Len enquired, trying to make sense of this unexpected twist in the plot.

'Aye, he's fine. He's just that upset aboot his bike …' with another snot-inducing wail.

Len looked at Mo. He looked at the bike. He looked at the youngest Atwood, still clearly bemused. 'But Mo, why did you come *here*? The surgery's closed for the day. What can *I* do to help?'

'Ah, yer a nice man, Doctor Whyte, and Davy, ma man, said ye'd ken whit to dae.'

*Ye'd ken whit to dae … Nice man …* What choice did a weary GP have with such affirmation from Mo's husband ringing in his ears? 'OK, Mo, give me a minute.' Len slipped over to his car, snapped the remote to open the boot, and returned with a small box of tools. Within moments he was back on his knees again, only this time not before a wailing Mo, but beside a broken bike. There he was, binding a piece of wire round the offending mudguard, knotting it tightly with his pliers, and fixing the mudguard securely to the ancient bike's rear frame. He was running with sweat. His hands were covered in a mixture of rust, oil and mud. He had wet patches on the knees of his suit trousers. But, in time, the job was done. The bike was mended. Another satisfied customer!

'Oh, good on ye, Doctor Whyte. Davy wis right. You kent whit to dae, right enough. Bobo'll be that pleased. C'mon you ...' And off went a by now dry-eyed Mo, with a snotty-nosed kid in one hand and mended bike trailing in the other, with the final accolade uttered from mother to child – not for Len's ears but certainly food for his soul – 'See that Doctor Whyte, hen, he's just magic!' And there was a diligent GP, filthy and completely bemused, picking up his toolbox and making his way back to his car, thinking, *Six years of university, two degrees, eight years' worth of training, and here I am fixing bikes at the back of my surgery. What ...?*

Len told the story to his medical colleagues the following morning. Only some of them thought it moderately funny. One colleague actually suggested he was mad. But the story of 'Mo and Bobo's Bike' was what kept Len going throughout that day, and for several tough days thereafter. 'Doctor Whyte'll ken whit to dae ...' Now, that's another kind of healing, isn't it?'

### Healing

Healing's what happens
When you're waiting for a cure
And don't expect much.

### Twelfth Sunday

*Old Testament:* 2 Samuel 1:1, 17-27
*Epistle:* 2 Corinthians 8:7-15
*Gospel:* Mark 5:21-43

# 45 Sent out

'Michael Lewis. MICHAEL LEWIS. Come here this minute.' A cowed eight-year-old wove his way through the tables from the back corner of the room to face the wrath of a clearly distressed Mrs Garrity.

'She's lost it,' a voice whispered to her neighbour at the table by the door.

'One more word from you, Gillian Prentice, and you'll be next.' A suitably admonished Gillian Prentice joined the rest of Class 5C in an all-embracing silence as they watched Michael Lewis complete his lonely walk to the front of the room. Mrs Garrity had been fit to explode. But by the time the object of her particular attention had reached his intended destination, his teacher had regained her composure and a more typical calmness had returned to her voice. She looked down on her recalcitrant eight-year-old.

'Michael Lewis. I have told you, and I have told you, and I have told you again, till I am blue in the face. I am fed up with your chatter, your disturbances, and your distraction of the others. I will have no more of this. You will go, and you will stand outside that door so that you have time to think about the error of your ways. You will not come back into this room until you are ready to behave. And when you do, you will apologise to me and to this class. Do you understand? DO YOU UNDERSTAND?'

An apparently contrite Michael Lewis was studiously examining his shoes. But he must have nodded sufficiently for Mrs Garrity to be assured that he'd got the message. 'So, go. Stand outside that door. And do it NOW!' And with that, Michael Lewis walked slowly to the classroom door, half opened it, slipped through it without turning round, and disappeared into the corridor. With the door closed behind him, Mrs Garrity returned to the rest of Class 5C. 'Now, children, where were we when we were so *rudely* interrupted?'

Meanwhile, in a draughty corridor, Michael Lewis was dutifully giving thought to the error of his ways. He didn't *like* being sent out. He tried *hard* not to chatter and interrupt. But sometimes ... well ... he just couldn't help himself. He *would* try harder to behave, he really, *really* would ...

His reverie was interrupted by the approach of the school janitor who was coming down the corridor carrying two classroom chairs. The janitor wasn't unused to seeing Michael Lewis pondering his behaviour in the corridor outside Classroom 5C. 'Good mornin', me lad. Sent out again?' Michael nodded, and a grinning janitor passed on his way.

It wasn't so easy when Miss McCulloch arrived. Well, it's never easy when the head teacher appears and you've been put outside the room – again ... 'Ah, the young Michael Lewis,' she said sternly. 'Sent out once more, it seems ... Eh? Cat got your tongue, child?' Michael didn't know whether to nod or shake his head. So he decided it would be better if he said nothing, and continued studying the state of his shoes. Miss McCulloch shook her head. 'What are we going to do with you, Michael? I despair, I really do despair. I shall have a word with Mrs Garrity later, mark my words.' And, with the head teacher's words duly marked, Michael Lewis was grateful when she too moved on, and he could continue to ponder the meaning of life.

★ ★ ★

'Michael. MICHAEL. Come over here. Quick as you can.' A tired and bedraggled twenty-eight-year-old wove his way through crowded chaos from the back corner of the hut in response to the anxious call from his colleague.

'We've lost her,' a voice whispered to the other medic by her side at the table by the door.

'You're right. That's another one gone.' A suitably saddened couple joined the rest of the medics in their section of the hut in an all-embracing silence of respect as Michael Lewis completed his lonely walk to their position. Michael was fit to explode. But by the time he'd walked the short journey to his intended destination, he had regained his composure and his more typical calmness. He looked down on the frail body of the eight-year-old on the table.

'Michael Lewis,' a voice was shouting in his head. 'I have told you, and I have told you, and I have told you again, till I am blue in the face. I am fed up with this, all the destruction, all this waste. I want no more of this. So you will go, and you will stand in the midst of it, and you will do what you can to help people see the error of their ways. You will come back, again and again, as I call you. And when you do, you will be doing it for me and for the others. Do you understand? DO YOU UNDERSTAND?'

An apparently composed Michael Lewis was studiously examining his desert boots. He nodded sufficiently for the others to be assured that he'd got the message. 'Let us pray,' he whispered. And with that, Michael Lewis slowly took his prayer book from his tunic pocket, half opened it, shut it again, and spoke without the need for written words. 'Dear God, it is so hard when death interrupts the preciousness of life …'

Meanwhile, in a turbulent mind, Michael Lewis was dutifully giving thought to the error of humanity's ways. He didn't *like* being sent out on another tour of duty. He tried *hard* to make sense of it all. But sometimes he just couldn't help himself feeling hopeless. He would try harder to believe, he really, *really* would …

His reverie was interrupted by the approach of two stretcher-bearers. They'd been summoned to take a dead child away. They weren't unused to seeing Michael Lewis praying beside an operating table in the corner of the hut. They smiled in recognition, did their business, and went on their way.

It wasn't so easy when Colonel Ainsworth arrived. Well, it's never easy when your CO appears and you're struggling with a dead child – yet again … 'Captain Lewis,' the colonel said calmly. 'I'm glad you're here. Like all of us, sent out to this hell-hole once more, it seems …' Michael didn't know whether to nod or shake his head. So he decided it would be better if he said nothing, and continued studying the state of his desert boots and the empty table. Colonel Ainsworth shook his head anyway. 'What are we going to do with all of this, Captain? I despair, I really do despair.'

The CO moved on. As Michael Lewis took his leave of his two colleagues, he shook them both by the hand, and went to weave his way back through the chaos that still filled the hut. But he was gratified to hear one medic say to another, 'Good Padre, that. Great that he's been sent out again,' and Michael Lewis was right back in the corridor outside Classroom 5C pondering the meaning of life.

**Sent**

> I'm old enough to remember
> in the discothèques of the 1960s,
> that when you 'felt the beat, man'
> and were 'a cool cat'
> and 'in the groove' as you were dancing,
> you could legitimately describe yourself
> as being 'sent'.
> 'Cool, man. I'm sent … gone, man …'
> And off you would go,
> transformed,
> existing in a parallel state,
> where all was well with the world –
> at least for a moment …
>
> I wonder if being 'sent'
> to do a job, or following a calling,
> is kind of the same?
>
> 'I'm gone, man.
> Sent …

and all is well with the world —
at least for a moment ...'

Well, I hope so ...

### Thirteenth Sunday

*Old Testament:* 2 Samuel 5:1-10
*Epistle:* 2 Corinthians 12:2-10
*Gospel:* Mark 6:1-13

# 46 Open the box!

First Lieutenant Reginald Pickering, known to his subordinates as Mr Pickering and to his equals as Reg, was in line for promotion. It had been no great surprise, therefore, when the company directors had called him up to head office on his recent shore leave and told him he was to take command of *The Lydia* when she next came into dry-dock. Reginald Pickering was absolutely delighted.

First Lieutenant Pickering had been second-in-command of *The Lydia* for three years. Like all the ferries in the company fleet, *The Lydia* was named after a fictional ship, and Reg took great delight in knowing the vessel he loved from the writing of CS Forester in *The Happy Return* had achieved many 'happy returns' as she plied her trade across the Channel. *The Lydia* was one of the key links between the south coast of England and continental Europe. First Lieutenant Reginald Pickering loved his job, and he loved his ship.

*The Lydia* had a good crew, and the camaraderie was of the highest order. So Reg was more than happy to lay aside his cherished rank of First Lieutenant and reach the pinnacle of his merchant naval career, Captain of his own ship, and such a happy one at that.

The promotion was, however, a mixed blessing. Reg had no doubts about his ability to command his own vessel. He had been well prepared, and the grooming and mentorship by his superior officer, the indomitable Captain Marcus Fisher, for the past three years had been vitally important. Everything his Captain knew, he'd passed on to his First Lieutenant. Reg could not have had a better teacher. And more than that, he looked up to his friend Marcus as a standard to aspire to – in leadership; in integrity; in efficiency; in appearance. There was no better role model than Captain Marcus Fisher. But that was the downside to Reg's promotion. His Captain would no longer be there to lean on. Reg would be on his own.

But there was something Reg knew he needed to clarify before he took over *The Lydia's* command, something that had intrigued *The Lydia's* First Lieutenant from the very first time he'd come on board and had his first briefing in the Captain's wardroom. Before every briefing, in preparation for the departure of *The Lydia* on every voyage, Captain Marcus Fisher, in full view of his officers, would go to the corner of the wardroom, unlock a ceiling-to-deck oak cupboard, and take out a large wooden box. Neither the First Lieutenant nor his officer colleagues ever saw what was in the box. Their Captain always had his back to them when the box was opened. All they could see was a polished wooden box with brass corners and inlays. The lid would be opened with a brass key the Captain took from the inside pocket of his uniform jacket, and carefully he would lift something from inside the box. He would study it intently for a while, and then, when it had been returned to the box, the lid would be closed and the precious box carefully locked and returned to the oak cupboard. Nothing was said. The Captain then gave his officers his undivided attention. But no one ever dared ask, 'What's in the box?'

They'd *thought* about it, of course, and there was occasional speculation when the conversation turned to the Captain's secretive behaviour with his brass-cornered box. 'Photo of his wife,' was one suggestion, knowing that the Captain had been widowed as a young naval officer. 'Old naval artefact – one of Nelson's uniform buttons, or the like,' was another, knowing the Captain's admiration for the traditions of the sea. 'Commendation from the war,' was an idea, knowing the Captain's distinguished service in the merchant navy's convoys in the 1940s. Plenty of ideas, but no one knew for sure ...

So when *The Lydia* was safely docked after the final 'happy return' the Captain and First Lieutenant would share together, Reg was determined to deal with the enigma. Alone with Captain Marcus Fisher in his wardroom when *The Lydia* had been berthed, Reg decided it was now or never. 'Captain,' he began, 'I want to thank you for all you've done for me, and for making me the man I am.'

The Captain smiled and replied, 'Reg, you were always going to be a good officer anyway. I just helped a little on the way.'

'But,' Reg continued, 'there's one last thing.' He hesitated, not at all sure he should continue.

'What is it, man?' the Captain prompted.

'Well, sir, I was wondering ...'

'Sir, is it? Well, Mr Pickering, if we are to be formal, what is your request?'

Reg knew he had to go for it. 'I was wondering, Captain ... The box ... in the wardroom cupboard ... every time ...' He never got to finish his sentence, for Captain Marcus Fisher let out the loudest guffaw the First Lieutenant had ever heard from the old sailor. Then, still chortling, the Captain rose from the table and strode purposefully to the ceiling-to-deck cupboard in the corner of the room. Within moments he had returned, holding the oak box with the brass corners before him, and was placing it carefully on the table between them. Retrieving the brass key from the inside pocket of his uniform jacket, he unlocked the box.

'This,' the Captain announced, 'is my trophy box. This box, Mr Pickering, contains the most important thing for me in all my naval career. Without it, I could not be the man you see before you today because I could not captain this ship. So, what would you have me do, Mr Pickering? Keep the secret sealed and take it with me to my retirement, or open the box and reveal all? It's up to you.'

Reg was astounded. *The secret*? And it could now be his? The special box, and it could now be opened for him? The key to his own future naval career ...? 'Captain Marcus Fisher,' he announced, 'it would be a privilege, sir, if for me, just this one time, you were to open the box.'

The Captain smiled, and with one hand slowly lifted the lid. With the other, he reached inside and took out a small, folded, yellowed piece of paper. With great ceremony he handed the precious secret to his enraptured colleague. With shaking fingers, First Lieutenant

Reginald Pickering unfolded the paper, and was astounded as he gazed on the secret of Captain Marcus Fisher's naval success. In quivering tones he read aloud something he would never, ever forget:

*Remember, because it's very important*

Port is on the left
and
Starboard is on the right.

### The treasure chest

I have my treasure chest, my mix
Of private things, my box of tricks,
The cherished bits and pieces I hold dear.
I keep them safe, and ponder them;
I pick them up, and wonder when
I'll ever tire of those I most revere.

There's nothing there that's magical,
Or tangible, or wonderful,
Or better than the artefacts that lie
In every other cherished box
That you may have; the private stocks
Of what *you'll* hold so dear in your mind's eye.

Some sage advice from years gone by
On which I constantly rely;
A standard set by someone I admire;
A kindly word; a service given;
A hurt consoled; a wrong forgiven;
A way of life to which I still aspire.

True uprightness and honesty;
Real thoughtfulness; integrity;
A truthfulness; and going the second mile;
Great courage in adversity;
Being open to diversity;
Inclusiveness of those some would revile.

And being the Good Samaritan
By showing respect, when others can
Destroy a life with prejudice and hate;
To love your neighbour as you should;
In face of harm, to do some good;
To offer love to those some would berate.

So now, this box, which hitherto
Has been concealed ... I show to you,
Not so you'll think that *I'm* the very best ...
But so that you can now look for
What matters in *your* private store –
The cherished things in your own treasure chest.

### Fourteenth Sunday

*Old Testament:* 2 Samuel 6:1-19
*Epistle:* Ephesians 1:3-14
*Gospel:* Mark 6:14-29

# 47 Crowds

'I hate crowds.' Tony Nelson furrowed his brow and gritted his teeth as the taxi swung into the Infirmary car park.

'Now he tells me,' the woman beside him exclaimed. 'Who ever heard of a politician who hates crowds? It's what gets people into politics – the buzz, the accolades, being the centre of attention. Isn't that what got *you* into it?'

'It certainly was not,' Tony rejoined. The conversation came to an abrupt end as the taxi stopped at the hospital's main entrance. Tony could see the crowds round the door – photographers jostling for position; a couple of camera crews approaching the taxi; men in suits forming what seemed to be a reception line; members of the public drawn in just because something was happening. It was always the same.

'That'll be eight pounds sixty,' the taxi driver was saying. Tony's companion was brandishing a tenner. 'Keep the change,' she insisted.

'Thanks, doll,' the driver responded. The woman cringed, but offered no reply. 'It's no' every day ah've got Tony Nelson in the back o' ma' cab. Awrra best, pal.'

By now Tony and his minder were standing in the paved area in front of a big sign that proclaimed "Welcome to your local hospital". The woman by his side surreptitiously placed her hand on Tony's elbow and squeezed it encouragingly. 'Come on, Tony, let's do it.'

'OK, Tonto. Hi ho, Silver …' and the two of them headed for the crowded hospital entrance.

'Well, that went off OK,' Alicia da Silva pronounced as she and her charge were being taxied home. Alicia da Silva was a journalist from the local paper, processing an 'exclusive day-in-the-life' of Tony Nelson, through his first public engagement since his surprise victory in the local Westminster by-election. Tony Nelson was hot news. The past two weeks had been a positive blur for the retired doctor-cum-politician-cum-media-star. Indeed, the three weeks running up to the election itself had been a bewildering roller-coaster of public engagements and TV interviews, local hustings and photocalls, sleepless nights and early mornings. It had not been what Tony had expected. He wasn't sure *what* he'd expected, really. And, in his heart of hearts, he'd *never* expected to win. But here he was, Tony Nelson MP, and having to face the crowds.

'That went OK.' Alicia da Silva might have been right. Indeed, Tony felt that he'd carried off the engagement reasonably well. But if he could have slipped into the hospital unnoticed and done what he had to do, he would have been much happier with that. 'You'll get used to it,' Alicia was saying. Tony wondered. 'But I still hate crowds,' was all he could reply.

Tony Nelson, retired consultant obstetrician, never considered himself to be a political animal. But he was incensed when he learned that the Obstetrics Department which had been his workplace for twenty years was to close and be 'relocated' to a bigger hospital forty miles away. The local people were up in arms too. A 'Save our Maternity Department' campaign was launched – or as the press had dubbed it, 'Militant Mothers on the March'. Tony Nelson was the obvious choice as chairman. He liked working in the background, organising things. He had a passion for good maternity care being close to the local people. He loved the contact with his patients and took great pleasure in being part of the high standards of care his unit offered. But, as time went on, he had been forced to take a more and more public role. And then, when the local MP had died suddenly, and a by-election was called in the midst of all the campaigning, Tony was pre-vailed on to stand as an independent candidate and front a single-issue campaign – the 'Save our Maternity Department' candidate.

It was intended to be no more or less than an adjunct to the cam-paign, one strand of the wider cause. No one, least of all a shy Tony Nelson, ever expected him to win.

It was going to be an eight-pound-sixty taxi journey back to

Tony's home. Alicia da Silva had some 'tidying up' to do for her story before her involvement with 'a-day-in-the-life' was over. She took out her notepad one last time. 'Do you really hate crowds?' she asked. Tony looked dreamily out of the cab window for a while before he responded.

'Ever since I was small, I never liked fuss and bother. I preferred being on my own, or in the company of family and friends. That's why I liked my job. Every person, every mother, every child, every consultation, really mattered. I could make a difference to that woman or that family or that situation. I'm a one-to-one person. But when a crowd comes at you, how can you separate out what really matters? How can you know who has the real needs?'

Alicia scribbled furiously, and then, looking up, she said, 'But didn't Mandela, Martin Luther King, Gandhi, and all the great reformers and peace campaigners, do the crowd bit *because* they had a passion for the rights of the individual?'

Tony smiled. 'I suppose you're right. So when I'm doing the crowd bit, as you call it, I just have to think of Mrs A with her miscarriages, and Miss B with her ectopic pregnancy, and Baby C who's a Downs Syndrome child, yes?' He paused, turned to the reporter, and smiled again. 'If every individual in the crowd matters, then the crowd is made up of individual needs, and everyone is helped – even though they're in the crowd? Yes?'

'Something like that,' Alicia responded, slipping her notebook into her bag. 'But then, I'm not the politician – or the philosopher, come to that.'

The taxi was stopping at Tony's front door. 'Thanks, driver,' Alicia was saying to the cabbie. 'We'll just drop Dr Nelson off here and you can take me up to the office.'

'Would you like to come in for a coffee,' Tony asked as he was leaving the cab. 'It's been a long day, and you'll need a break.'

'No thanks, Tony,' Alicia da Silva replied. 'You need to be alone, I suspect. And some of us have a very crowded schedule to deal with.'

## Crowds

Can you feel alone in a crowd?
Of course you can –
too many people,
and too little eye-contact;
too much to think about,
and too little time.

Then a man looks up from his newspaper,
and you catch him mouthing the words
of the song on his iPod;
and he looks embarrassed,
and smiles;
And, in an instant,
the crowd isn't there any more.

Can you feel alone in a crowd?
Of course you can –
on a wet day,
walking along a busy pavement,
avoiding umbrellas,
and puddles.

Then you stop at a crossing,
and the woman next to you bumps your arm,
and says, 'Sorry, love. I'm always doing that,'
and her clumsy apology is added to
with a smile;
and, in an instant,
the jostling crowd has moved on.

Can you feel alone in a crowd?
Of course you can –
when your team's playing badly,

and, like everyone else,
you're all wrapped up
in your own displeasure.

Then your team scores out of nothing,
and the whole crowd rises as one;
the cheers are deafening;
a stranger grabs you in a bear-hug
and smiles;
and, in an instant,
everyone in the crowd is your friend.

### Fifteenth Sunday

*Old Testament:* 2 Samuel 7:1-14a
*Epistle:* Ephesians 2:11-22
*Gospel:* Mark 6:30-34, 53-56

# 48 The Big Idea

Kenneth was struggling for the Big Idea. Not usually being the kind of person who was short of imagination or creativity, he just couldn't get a handle on what he needed, and that made Kenneth very frustrated indeed. As the youth worker in the group of churches on the north side of the town, Kenneth was more than familiar with what worked for young people of different ages, in small-group settings or big events. In the two years he'd been around, he'd become a valuable asset for advice, ideas, methodologies, resources – anything indeed – that improved the quality of the churches' engagement with the young people of the district. Kenneth was good at his job.

So when a joint worship service was planned for one of the local congregations as the high point of that year's Christian Aid fundraising, it wasn't surprising that the church leaders turned to Kenneth with the request that he coordinate the part of the worship that was aimed at the kids – 'to get the pitch right', one of the clergy put it.

'No problem,' Kenneth had replied. But the closer the service got, the more the 'no problem' became a 'big problem' as the Big Idea he was searching for was still 'no idea at all'.

Christian Aid fundraising was important. But somehow, despite the wealth of material Kenneth had to hand, nothing seemed to spark his imagination, and Kenneth knew that if *his* imagination wasn't stimulated, then he wouldn't be able to get the kids excited one little bit. He was looking for the Big Idea. And it wasn't forthcoming.

The Bible reading designated for the service was 'The feeding of the five thousand'. So what was Kenneth's pitch to be? 'Give us your money and five thousand people will be fed ...'? 'Give your gifts to Jesus and a miracle will happen ...'? 'Imagine what it's like to live in abject poverty, and not even have bread and fish ...'? But nothing seemed to be quite right.

The Big Idea came to him an hour before the service was due to start. All he needed were a few small wicker baskets. The congregation and the kids would do the rest ...

That's why, during the first part of the service, Kenneth was silently counting the number of people in the church. He figured it was two hundred and thirteen – give or take. *'Fine,'* he thought. And, just after the reading of the Bible lesson, Kenneth moved to the front of the church, faced the young people gathered in the front rows and the serried ranks of the church folk behind, and boldly announced, 'Today, guys, for Christian Aid, we are going to perform "The miracle of the feeding of the two hundred and thirteen".' There was a stony silence and many quizzical looks. Kenneth was not deterred. 'No? You don't think so? Well, let's see. I need four volunteers, four would-be disciples, to be miracle-workers.' A forest of enthusiastic hands shot up, and once four appropriate helpers had been recruited, Kenneth provided each of them with a small wicker basket and told them to 'go out and perform the miracle'. None of them moved. One of the helpers giggled nervously. Another shuffled from foot to foot. All four wore quizzical frowns.

'Don't you know what to do? No? Well, let me help,' Kenneth suggested. 'You see, I know something you don't know. When the adults are here on their own and you're not around, there's something goes on in this church that they don't want you to know.' More deep frowns and embarrassed smiles ... Kenneth knew he had them. 'D'you want to know what it is?' Four vigorous nods ...' Well, let me tell you ... It happens in all churches. The grown-ups try to keep it a secret. But today I will tell you ...' His voice dropped to a conspiratorial whisper. 'You see ... when adults come to church ... they ... they ... eat sweets!'

There was a burst of laughter from the whole congregation *and* knowing nods all round. But Kenneth had only begun. 'So,' he announced triumphantly, 'the miracle of the feeding of the two hundred and thirteen begins with you four going out ... and ... collecting the sweets.' More laughter and knowing looks. And as four miracle-workers began to move among the congregation, people were shamed into parting with their stash. Within minutes, four baskets were filled with all sorts of goodies. Packets of mints ... a handful of Roses chocolates ... several toffees ... pan drops ... boilings ... random Liquorice Allsorts ... One elderly lady was so embarrassed that she'd eaten all her sweets already, she put two pound coins in the basket!

When the collection was completed – to the accompaniment of much hilarity and enthusiastic banter – Kenneth called his four helpers back to the front of the church. The overflowing baskets were examined. 'Well, now,' he announced to his bemused but delighted volunteers, 'that's the first part of the miracle – you've got people to share what they have when they didn't really expect to – or want to. But here's the next part. Let's share what we've gathered with *everyone* here. Go back out there and share these sweets all round. We can't keep all this for ourselves, now can we? So go and invite people to take one, a sweet of their choice, and if they want two, that's fine. On you go. Share what you've gathered. There's two hundred and thirteen sweetless people waiting for a miracle.' So off went the almost-convinced disciples and, with even more laughter and chatter, pretty soon every worshipper had a sweet to enjoy.

'OK,' said Kenneth when the exercise was completed, 'back you come to the front. Now, that's the second bit of the miracle – everyone's been fed.'

There wasn't one of the four helpers who wasn't beaming from ear to ear – and that went for most of the congregation too. But Kenneth was ready to deliver the *coup de grâce* of the Big Idea. 'Now, d'you want to know the third part of the miracle? Look into the baskets, and tell me what's there.'

'There are still some sweets left,' piped up one of the miracle-workers.

'There are sweets left over,' offered another.

'Lots …' chirped a third.

244 With an open eye

'So, there you have it, guys,' Kenneth concluded. 'The miracle of the feeding of the two hundred and thirteen — when people are encouraged to share, there's enough to go round so that everyone gets fed, and there's still plenty left over.'

Kenneth paused. The congregation was silent. 'That's what Christian Aid's about, folks. *You* can be miracle workers too, every one of you, for when you start to share, everyone gets fed, and there's more than enough to go around. Today, two hundred and thirteen; tomorrow, five thousand. The next day … It's up to you …'

It was the first time anyone could recall there being applause in the church. No one minded — especially when they heard that the Christian Aid collection that year had broken all records ...

## 5000

I can't feed five thousand.
I can't even feed two hundred and thirteen.
But I can offer what I have,
and share what I can.
It would be a minor miracle …
And if everyone else did the same,
who knows what kind of miracles
might result?
Is that the Big Idea,
or what?

### Sixteenth Sunday

*Old Testament:* 2 Samuel 11:1-15
*Epistle:* Ephesians 3:14-21
*Gospel:* John 6:1-21

# 49 Miraculous, or what?

When they realised they'd run out of wine, no one was best pleased. Not that they'd run out of wine altogether. There were still the remains of a couple of the bottles which had been opened the previous evening, as well as a bottle of *Lambrusco* in the fridge that no one liked very much. But as the six of them waited for their meal in the rustic kitchen of the Tuscan farmhouse, there was a sudden realisation that such meagre rations on the wine front were never going to be enough.

It was no one's fault, but everyone seemed to be looking at Gregor. He wasn't at all convinced that it had been his turn to make sure the wine supply had been replenished. It might have been, for the arrangements for dividing up the tasks for the week's Italian holiday were usually pretty sound and properly followed. If it had been his turn, he'd forgotten. If it hadn't, then he didn't mind the ribbing.

It had been that kind of holiday – lots of sharing and lots of fun. The three couples had holidayed together often enough that the odd slip in the arrangements wasn't going to threaten friendships or spoil a vacation. Gregor and Sally, Peter and May, Tubby and Meredith were best friends. Holidays together over the years had deepened that friendship. Running out of wine wasn't going to ruin that.

'No worries, guys. I'll skip down to *Ivano's* and pick up a bottle. In fact, give me over that empty two-litre bottle and I'll get some of their house wine. Where else can you get a good quality wine at one and a half euros a litre, eh?' May, busy at the cooker putting the final touches to the meal – thank goodness she'd remembered it was her turn to do the cooking – tossed over the empty plastic water bottle from the draining-board by the sink.

'There you go,' she chirped. 'You've got ten minutes. Don't be late!'

'I'll chum you,' Meredith suggested, and in an instant the two friends were off on their wine-hunt, leaving the others to chat before supper.

*Ivano's* was the *bottega* in the village. It was a favourite haunt, and there was always the guarantee of good local wines on tap. It would only take Gregor and Meredith a few minutes to complete their task. No sweat ...

The sign outside *Ivano's* read

---

### VINI LOCALI
### LA VOSTRA BOTTIGLIA RIEMPITO
### €1.50 PER LITRO
*Local wines. Your own bottle filled. €1.50 a litre*

---

and it beckoned them in as it had done many times before. Inside, greetings were exchanged; the bottle was presented, rinsed and filled; the €3 payment was duly made; animated farewells were offered. And Gregor and Meredith headed home. Job done ...

They were just turning out of the village street onto the path to their farmhouse when Meredith noticed the mistake. 'Gregor,' she exclaimed. 'You've done it wrong!'

'How come?' was the indignant reply.

'You've only gone and got white wine. And you know it's red we need.'

Gregor realised his friend was right. 'Blast,' he muttered, 'I was too bothered getting my Italian right with Ivano. How did I know the *vino della casa* would turn out to be white? Well, I'm blooming sure I'm not going to chuck good wine away when I don't have to. We'll just have to have white tonight and be done with it ...' Just then Gregor noticed they were standing outside the village petrol station which had a little shop attached. He smiled broadly.

'Unless ...' he murmured, more to himself than to his companion, 'unless there's a possibility ...' Meredith was about to ask what he was up to, when Gregor thrust the bottle of white wine into her hands, instructed her to 'hold that' and 'wait there', turned on his heel and headed for the shop. In a couple of minutes he was back, grinning even more broadly, and carrying a two-litre bottle of *acqua naturale,* the local brand of spring water. 'Now watch closely, Meredith, you sceptic, and behold a miracle!'

With a flourish Gregor unscrewed the cap of the plastic bottle, tipped the bottle upside down and spilled its contents into the gutter. Before the last drop dripped, he was off back to *Ivano's.* In an instant, it seemed, he'd returned, triumphantly carrying a two-litre bottle of *vino rosso,* the *bottega's* red wine. 'See?' Gregor proclaimed in triumph. 'Water into wine, before your very eyes. Miraculous, or what?' And he was highly amused when the lady who'd been behind him in the queue for his *acqua naturale* did a dramatic double-take as she ambled past him. Gregor *knew* what she was thinking. *But ... only a moment ago ... that tourist-man had mineral water in his bottle ... and now it's red wine ...What kind of miracle ...?* As if to confirm her thoughts, Gregor held his bottle of red wine above his head, shouted '*Un miracolo!*' to the passer-by, and roared loudly at his own joke.

'What are you like?' Meredith exclaimed, and two laughing friends headed back to the farmhouse for their awaiting supper. There was much teasing when they returned. 'Aye, aye! So what were you two up to that took you so long, eh?' Sally enquired.

'Well, it's a kind of long story ...' Meredith responded, winking at Gregor.

'It's a miracle, really,' Gregor announced. 'Meredith is my witness – and so is a bemused local lady down in the village. For your delectation and delight I have, this very evening, turned water into wine. It's a sign, I tell you, a sign!'

Much hilarity ensued as six friends settled down to enjoy their evening meal. 'A toast,' Tubby announced before they began, 'to Gregor, the man who performed *il miracolo.*'

'Well, that's as maybe,' Peter responded. 'But what I want to know is ... how come miracle-man can leave the house on a wine-hunt with *one* bottle and come back with *two*, one red and one white, eh? A 100% increase! Now, that's the kind of miracle-worker I'm more than happy to have around ...'

And Sally, reaching for the last slice of garlic bread, added, 'And if you're *that* good, we could do with another plateful of this. I'm still starving ...'

### Life

Here's *'usquebaugh,'* the poet said,
The water that's enough
For thirsty folk to draw upon for life;
So, drink your fill; forget your woes;
Draw hard on every draught,
And leave behind your worries and your strife.

But we know well, when thirsts are quenched
From shallow pools and wells,
Our yearnings will continue deeper still;
For thirsts that look to worldly things
Will never be assuaged,
And we will never yet find life fulfilled.

Here's bread for you to feast upon
From your own treasure store.
Come, eat your fill from all the world displays.
For there are riches, even more
Than you will ever need;
A plentiful supply for all your days.

But we know well that food alone
Will never be our fill;
So lift your eyes from glass and plate and bowl,
And feast on what the spirit needs,
Beyond the world's supply;
Here's bread and wine – and nurture for the soul.

## Seventeenth Sunday

*Old Testament:* 2 Samuel 11:26-12:13a
*Epistle:* Ephesians 4:1-16
*Gospel:* John 6:24-35

# 50 The magic giveaway

'The trouble with a Chinese takeaway,' Ewan complained, 'is that you've only just finished one when you have a craving for another.'

'It's not just your Chinese takeaway,' Liam added. 'It's your Indian as well. You can get right into your nan and chapattis, and your chicken vindaloo, and half an hour later, you could go it all again.'

'That'll be the beer giving you an appetite,' Gregory suggested.

'Or because you're a guts,' offered Peter.

'No, they're right. It happens with your pizza too,' Ken assured the assembled company. 'You don't feel you can eat those last two slices, so you leave them in the box, and ten minutes later you're at them again, and they're stone cold, but you get them right down like you haven't eaten in weeks.'

'Kebabs are the same,' affirmed Charlie, 'and your chips in sauce. Now, enough of the chat, and pass me over that box of chicken-wings.' And the six friends who'd gathered in the flat for an evening in of beer, takeaways and DVDs continued demolishing their sumptuous repast.

'My kid brother had a storybook once about a family that had food for ever and ever because they had a magic porridge-pot that never went empty,' Liam reported during a lull in the conversation.

'Porridge-pot? Who would want to live on porridge all the time?' asked Ewan.

'You'd live on beer, given half a chance,' Charlie suggested.

'Now, there's a good idea. A barrel of beer that never runs out,' Ken laughed.

'Ah, "The amazing tale of the magic beer-barrel", eh? Now there's a book I'd like to read,' added Gregory. And the six friends returned to their carry-outs and their beer and their chat.

When the detritus of the evening's meal was being cleared away and another round of beer-cans was being distributed, Charlie surprised the others by saying, 'But, you know, there are some people who've had their food run out a long time ago. No magic porridge-pot for them, anyway.'

'No magic beer-barrel, then,' chirped Liam.

'Nor takeaways,' added Ewan.

'No, guys, I'm being serious,' Charlie continued, clearly irritated that his friends weren't responding with appropriate gravity.

'Oooohhh,' Gregory offered, sarcastically. Charlie threw him a look.

'C'mon guys, let him finish,' Peter suggested. 'Go for it, Charlie. The floor's yours.'

'It will be for me if I have any more beer,' Liam whispered.

'Shut up, you,' Peter insisted. 'OK Charlie, what's your story?'

'Well, I was just thinking …' Charlie continued.

'There's a surprise,' Liam cackled. But Charlie was undeterred.

'Well, here we are getting stuck into our huge weekly takeaway and another case of beer – because we can afford it. And how many takeaways and pints of beer have we demolished over the years, eh, and never given a thought for people who have no chance, eh?'

The group fell into a deep-thinking silence. Even the usually sceptical Liam was reduced to saying nothing, struck dumb by this unexpected turn in the conversation.

'It's not our fault,' Gregory suggested after a while.

'Global economics,' added Ken.

'Survival of the fattest,' offered Liam

'Or the greediest,' said Peter. And the discussion went this way and that, sometimes serious, sometimes silly, occasionally ill-informed and, now and again, poignant and deep. No one had any answers to the imbalance of the world's resources. Ken suggested giving up beer for Lent, only to be shouted down by a chorus of "No"s. A collective silence embraced the group after a time. No DVD had been viewed, but the beer was just about done, and the evening was drawing to its natural conclusion when Charlie took the floor one last time. 'OK, guys. I know we can't change the world, and it may be a futile gesture. We can't offer a magic porridge-pot …'

'Or a magic takeaway, for that matter,' Liam chimed in.

'Or a magic anything, come to that,' Charlie continued. 'But surely we can do *something.*'

'Like what?' Peter asked.

'Like … well, why not, once a month, chip in for the cost of another takeaway each and our share of a case of beer. What's that? Twenty quid each, tops. We can afford it, guys. Why can't other people benefit from our nights in, eh?' He looked round at his five companions. There were imperceptible nods and the beginning of smiles of agreement. 'Deal, guys?' And, with one voice, the five friends replied, 'Deal!' and six half-empty beer-cans were clinked to seal the agreement.

'Could be we've just started the magic beer-barrel after all,' the not-so-sceptical Liam suggested as jackets were being retrieved from the hallway.

'Or the magic takeaway,' Ken offered.

'No, we'd have to call it "The magic giveaway" if we're to prise any extra dosh out of *you,* you tight so-and-so,' Charlie suggested, to be greeted with howls of protest from five friends, because everyone assumed he was talking to them.

### Giving

> To give and not to take for once;
> To allocate without regard to cost;
> To tender what we can right now;
> To offer when it matters most.

To share when times are plentiful;
To dedicate a fitting part;
To contribute even when we're poor;
To show that heart still speaks to heart.

To sacrifice something that's ours;
To rid ourselves of vain desires;
To undergo a change of heart;
To do what selflessness requires.

The 'giveaway''s the path to take,
While 'takeaway''s the selfish way.
So think, for once; the time is now!
Come on, make this a giving-day!

### Eighteenth Sunday

*Old Testament:* 2 Samuel 18:5-33
*Epistle:* Ephesians 4:25-5:2
*Gospel:* John 6:35-51

# 51 Password protected

Peter always did his banking online. In fact, he'd become so adept at surfing the web that he used the internet for lots of things. He bought books, kept up to date with the associations he was a member of, contributed to online forums, dipped in and out of various social networking sites, and even participated in a weekly football league, where you had to predict the next's weekend's scores and pit yourself against your mates. Booting up his PC, spending time online, making use of the internet … well, it was no problem for the PC-literate Peter. And internet banking was just *so* easy and convenient …

Until, that is, Peter had a problem. When he went into his online banking site one evening to tidy up his finances, he was completely thrown when he discovered he'd forgotten his password. He got the user name right – well, after all, remembering he was Peter Palmer was fairly easy, and the banking website had recognised that OK. But when he typed in what he *thought* was the password, it told him, in big, red letters, 'PASSWORD NOT RECOGNISED. TRY AGAIN'.

*Funny*, Peter thought. So he did as he'd been instructed – *very* carefully this time. For a second time, the error message told him to try again.

Now, Peter's password had always been easy to remember. He'd been using it for years for pretty well everything. It consisted of the initial letters of the names of his wife and three children, and the year his grandmother had been born – and that made it 'tjaw1892'. Easy … But then he remembered that a site he'd used recently to buy a plane ticket had asked him to register as a new user and to choose a password, and when he offered 'tjaw1982' it wasn't accepted. So he'd changed it. And then he'd read something about changing your passwords regularly in any event, to combat internet fraud. And he'd chosen a new password in his head … But had he changed it as he'd intended?

So, completely confused between his old password, the new one for his airline site, and the one he'd made up in his head, he didn't know where he was. 'tjaw1982' hadn't been accepted – twice. So he tried the new one. But 'celtic1967' didn't work either. 'PASSWORD NOT RECOGNISED. TRY AGAIN' was now shouting at him from the screen. So he tried the one he'd thought of in his head. What was it again? The name of his primary school and the date of the Battle of Bannockburn? The initial letters of his cats' names and the year of his marriage? The street-name of his first house and the year the Beatles split up? What on *earth* was it? He tried 'coleford1314', but, again, the error message – 'PASSWORD NOT RECOGNISED. TRY AGAIN'. But this time there was more, for written in bold letters on the screen he was being informed that he was allowed ONE FINAL ATTEMPT OR ACCOUNT WILL BE DISABLED AND YOU WILL BE LOCKED OUT.

What was he to do? He needed to do his finances. He *had* to check his account details. He *must* get into the site. And if he was locked out, it would be *ages* before it got sorted – phone calls to the helpline; a new user name in the mail; another password to enter *and* remember. Peter was distraught. 'Why do things have to be password-protected?' he sighed out loud – as if venting his frustration was going to make a lot of difference.

So he steeled himself ... 'One final attempt,' he announced, just as the screen had informed him. He decided to go down the 'cats' names' route. Now, there was Whitey – and, very carefully, he entered a 'w' as his first letter; then there was Socks – 's'; then Hannibal – 'h'; and Posh – 'p'. Having entered 'wshp' with the utmost care, it was time for the numbers. But was it the year of his marriage or the year the Beatles split up? He had to decide. There was no avoiding it. Now or never it had to be. He went for his marriage – 1981 – and, with his eyes closed and praying a *very* fervent prayer, pressed the 'return' key on his keyboard. And there it was, in big, bold letters on the screen – HELLO PETER PALMER. WELCOME TO INTERNET BANKING.

Peter almost wept with joy. The sense of relief was overwhelming. He was in! No more being locked out. So, quickly, before he forgot, he scribbled the new password down on a post-it note, pulled an obscure book down from the shelf behind him, stuck the note in a random page, and noted where the book was for further reference – and reassurance that he would always have his password to hand.

The following Sunday, Peter Palmer went to church. It wasn't a regular occurrence. He'd been invited to the baptism of his neighbour's granddaughter. The church was on the other side of the town. He'd never been there before. When he arrived and went to sit down, he was tapped on the shoulder and whispered to by the lady behind. 'You can't sit there,' she insisted, 'that's where the Cunninghams sit.'

'Thank you,' said Peter. 'I've obviously got the password wrong. Can you let me know what it is so that I don't get locked out again?'

### Wisdom

The Wisdom of Solomon's there to admire;
Its value can clearly be seen;
A standard to which we'd do well to aspire,
Beyond the mundane and routine.

But what if the meaning is missed or deferred,
And words have no basis in deed?
Remember that 'actions speak louder than words'.
Perhaps that's the wisdom we need.

### Nineteenth Sunday

*Old Testament:* 1 Kings 2:10-12, 3:3-14
*Epistle:* Ephesians 5:15-20
*Gospel:* John 6:51-58

# 52 This is me!

'Is that Alf?' Liz asked, moving in a little closer to her companion to make sure they weren't disturbed. These moments with the folk were precious. There was seldom enough time in a busy geriatric unit to spend quality time with the patients. So opportunities like this were important. 'There, in the photo. Is that Alf?'

Doreen was one of Liz's favourite people. Although she was in the early stages of dementia, there was still enough of a spark in Doreen's life and brightness in her eyes for Liz to know that there was more than a woman with dementia in her care. Doreen had been in the unit for some weeks. She was waiting on an assessment for a place in a long-term care facility. And, in the meantime, she was one of the patients who kept Liz going and made the unrewarding parts of the job moderately bearable. Liz knew little of Doreen. She knew she was a widow and had no family of her own. She had a niece who lived on the other side of the country and a nephew who was abroad some-where. She seldom had visitors. And her prize possession was a bat-tered cardboard chocolate box with roses on the lid, which social services had brought in when Doreen came to the unit.

Doreen had never revealed all the contents of the box to anyone, not even to a caring nurse. But today she was sitting with an old photo-graph in her bony fingers when Liz came over to see her. It was a stab in the dark from Liz, but a calculated one.

'Is that Alf?' she enquired again. Doreen held the photograph in front of her and studied it intently. Then, laying it on her lap, she proudly announced,

'Aye, hen. That's Alf. That's ma man. Aye, that's Alf, right enough.' Doreen smiled, pointing lovingly at the picture of the handsome young man in the double-breasted suit. She paused, then moved her finger across the photograph until it rested on the picture of Alf's

companion. 'And that's me,' she whispered, wistfully. 'That's me …
that's me.' She started to tap the photograph in rhythm with her
words. 'That's me. That's me. That's me. That's me.'

Her voice was rising, still frail, but unmistakably louder. And then
she stopped, turned her head and looked at Liz. Slowly she lifted her
hand from the photograph and, with a bony finger, pointed to her
own chest. And, with passion in her eyes, and a voice louder than Liz
had ever heard before, Doreen announced firmly, 'This isn't me. *This*
isn't me.' The finger poked her chest again. 'This isn't me,' she
repeated. Her finger pointed again at the female figure beside Alf in
the photograph, '*That's* me,' and returned to pointing at herself, 'but
this *isn't* me. This isn't me any more.'

There were no tears and no anger in the old voice. But the passion was there and the meaning was clear. There was a *real* Doreen, a
different Doreen from the demented lady in the geriatric unit that
Liz knew she just *had* to get to know.

Liz spent as much time with Doreen as she could. Sometimes, the
old woman would make sense, and Liz would glean a little more information about the real Doreen. At other times, the conversations made
no sense at all, and Liz wondered if she would ever get any further.

The breakthrough came, however, with the contents of the battered cardboard chocolate box with roses on the lid. It began when
there was an outbreak of MRSA. As if it wasn't bad enough that the
patients and staff had to cope with isolation procedures, the whole
place, bit by bit, had to be 'deep cleaned'. And *that* meant, when they
came to Doreen's bay, everything, but *everything* had to be catered for.
It was a clumsy domestic who dropped the battered cardboard
chocolate box with roses on the lid when she was cleaning Doreen's
locker. The contents ended up all over the floor. It was Liz's job to
sort things out. And she was fascinated by what she found. For the
whole box was full of nothing but old photographs, obviously prized
possessions of Doreen's – and, Liz surmised, more of the story of
Doreen's life than Liz was ever going to find out.

There were pictures of Alf, of course, and some of a bunch of young women. Children were there too, though Liz wondered where they figured in the story. And as she lovingly thumbed through the box of precious memories, she was sure she'd manage to use them to tease out some more information from Doreen about the *real* Doreen they portrayed.

She never got the chance. Doreen contracted MRSA and it floored her completely. She never recovered. She died before a place in the care facility became available. Doreen's niece came to take away her things. She didn't stay to chat. Liz didn't attend the funeral. It would have been too much. But she still wondered about the 'me' that Doreen was pointing to on the day they looked at the photo of her and Alf. And she wondered what Doreen *would* have said if they'd had more time together to go through the old photos in the battered cardboard chocolate box with roses on the lid.

### Photos

You come to me, and you sit and listen.
I like that.
I like your company, your interest, your ready smile.
It breaks my day.
It fills my time, my room, my mind
with youth and newness
and – well – even things you tell me about
that I'll never understand.
You come to me, and give me time,
and make me feel I matter again.

But do you know, can you ever understand
that what you see of me,
and what you know of me,
and what you learn of me,

is not the me I am, the me I know I am,
but just the part of me that's here and now?

Do you know, can I make you understand
that what you see – and like, it seems –
is but the final picture,
the most recent image from the photographs of my life?

Because, you see, you've started with the last one.
For that's the photo of my life
that was lying here when you came along,
clear and visible, for you to gaze upon.
I'm glad you like that one.

But do you know, can I make you understand
that this is not it all?
There's more than this to see,
and know and learn about.

So, take some time to rummage through
some other photos of my life.
Thumb through them now with me.
Gaze upon the images you didn't know were there,
and look and learn.

Look there – that teenager in the mini-skirt is me,
yes, me!
Would you believe I wore a skirt as short as that?
These skinny, wrinkled legs you see today
where not always thus!
Look there.
See!
Legs were worth the showing then.
That's part of me!

Ah, and that one too,
that pretty woman,
a child on either knee – that's me!
My niece and nephew,
one four, one two,
both still for just a moment when the camera clicked,
and never still again!
How good I look, how happy then!
That's part of me.

And this, this band of happy people,
there's me – and Alf behind –
Alf – how I miss him so,
those twenty years since he passed on.
But then, a different story,
with friends *en masse*
on a summer trip to Rothesay.
Oh happy days!
That's part of me.

Look there, on Christmas Day,
in the church hall,
three years ago, I think,
(or was it four, or maybe longer since?),
with paper hat, and rosy cheeks –
the Christmas sherry can be blamed for that –
and so much fun, and not so long ago.
That's part of me.

Enough for now? Perhaps … for now …

So go, and come again another day,
and take your time with me,
to find some more photographs.

You'll see me there, in all of them,
with smiles and tears,
so slim, too fat,
alone, with friends, with Alf,
you'll see and know and understand
that this, and this, and this, and this …
is me.

Not simply now;
not just this part;
not just this final photograph,
of an ancient, wrinkled me.
There's more I need to show
if you can take the time with me.

These photos of my life,
just waiting to be looked at again.

Adapted from 'The photo-album of my life' by Tom Gordon; first published in *Holy Ground*, ed Neil Paynter & Helen Boothroyd, Wild Goose Publications; 978-1-901557-88-6

## Twentieth Sunday

*Old Testament:* 1 Kings 8:1-43
*Epistle:* Ephesians 6:10-20
*Gospel:* John 6:56-69

# 53 Love, a many-splendoured thing

John Verity was in love. The object of his affection was the perfect Jenny Hutchins. He'd only just found out her first name. Jenny; fantastic Jenny; perfect in every way … John Verity was besotted.

Jenny Hutchins could play the piano. Had anyone ever played a piano like this angel? His heart leapt as she sat down at the keyboard. She never needed any music. She could play anything, it seemed to John. She was able to caress the ivories like an angel who could coax music from golden harp strings. John was head-over-heels …

And she could sing. Oh, what rapture! Her singing was clear, delicate, tender and always encouraging of others to join her. For here was no diva. Here was someone who would offer their gift of music so that others could share the joy. John tried to sing with her, of course. How could he not? But he never felt he was good enough and always seemed to stumble over his words or go off the tune. But the object of his desire never seemed to bother. She just sang like a bird, and that was enough for John. For John was completely smitten …

And her clothes … He'd never seen anyone dress like this before. Every day Jenny was perfection itself. She always seemed to wear the most fantastic clothes, bright and colourful dresses that flowed gracefully as she walked, blouses that shimmered in the sunshine. Why could everyone not dress like this? But then, Jenny Hutchins was perfect, wasn't she, and no one else was. John was starry-eyed …

And how she danced … She seemed to float over the ground. One moment she was there, the next she was here, having moved silently and gently from one place to the other. Oh, John was on cloud nine …

Could any other woman transform a room when she entered it like this beautiful creature? Not that John ever knew. Did his heart not race faster when she came into the room? Did he not think of being alone with her when all the others had gone so that he could have her for himself? Quite certainly, John was head-over-heels, madly in love like he had never been before.

Did Jenny Hutchins love John with all her heart, the way he loved her? It *seemed* so, though she had never demonstrably shown it in such a way that John might be convinced. He *thought* she did, once anyway, when she smiled at him when he was with his mates. John felt the smile was just for him. He *hoped* it was. But it had never been followed up. If John ever knew what 'reciprocated' meant, then their love was never that. Maybe one day it would be different. But, for now, John would just have to be content with gazing in wonder at the beautiful object of his desire.

For that was what John was doing now, as Jenny Hutchins sat in her chair in the corner of the room. John just couldn't keep his eyes off her. She wasn't looking at him, not yet anyway. So John could just stare and stare and hope that the moment would last for ever. He never minded other people being around. So what if they saw him staring? What if they knew he was in love? Hadn't they ever been smitten? Didn't they know what it was like never to be able to get someone out of their mind? Had none of them been besotted like this?

John wasn't bothered. He knew he was in love. And he knew he was in love with Jenny Hutchins. That was enough.

Just then, Jenny Hutchins rose from her seat and glided in John's direction. His heart pounded. He hoped she hadn't been too disturbed by his staring. He just wanted her close, closer, closer now … And there she was, the object of his desire, right in front of him.

And Jenny Hutchins smiled and said, 'Right Class 2. Time to pack up now. The bell's about to ring. John, you've been daydreaming all day, so come and help me with the books.'

'Can I be first in the line, Miss Hutchins. *Please* Miss?' someone asked.

'Oh Miss, it's my turn,' said another.

'Goodness me!' Jenny Hutchins responded, smiling at her class. 'For six-year-olds you can really be infants sometimes.'

A bell rang in the distance. 'Go on then. Home with you. No time for a line. Bye, children.'

'Bye, Miss Hutchins.'

'John, come on now, off with you.' And John Verity smiled too. But only he knew why. For John was madly, undeniably, totally, unstoppably in love. And the object of his desire was the wonderful, beautiful, adorable, fantastic Jenny Hutchins – who had just spoken directly to *him* ...

### My lover

*(Inspired by Song of Songs 1:10 – 'My lover spoke ...';*
*and the love I have for my wife, Mary.)*

I love you
as the angels love their song,
and sing with rapturous joy
of all that yet belongs
to what is good, and right and true
in time and all eternity.

I love you
as the swallows love their flight
and dance with careful step
upon the rising air
a sweet gavotte or minuet,
in time with mystic melody.

I love you
as the child must love the breast
and feeds contentedly
upon the very love
that gave it life, and holds it close
in time, and for eternity.

I love you
as the strings do love the bow
that draws, even from their heart,
sweet tunes that now become
a song of love, with soaring notes,
in time with my heart's melody.

I love you
as the snowdrops love the Spring
and reach with awakening hands
towards fresh days of hope,
and all that's new and possible,
in time to glimpse eternity.

I love you
as the breakers love the shore
and come, drawn by the moon,
now welcomed home again,
to rest awhile and then depart,
in time with rhythmic melody.

I love you
as I loved you from the start,
with all that I can be
and ever will become,
and give my love with all my heart
in time and for eternity.

### Twenty-first Sunday

*Old Testament:* Song of Songs 2:8-13
*Epistle:* James 1:17-27
*Gospel:* Mark 7:1-23

# 54 Off guard

'Mr Campbell. Am I speaking with Mr Campbell?'

'Yes. That's right.'

'Colin Campbell?'

'Yes.'

'Ah, Colin, that's good. How are you today?'

'I'm as well as can be expected, thank you for asking. But who is this?'

'Oh, sorry, Colin. I should have introduced myself. My name's Sonya and I'm calling from *PB Home Improvements*. We're in your area at the moment, Colin, and we wanted to …'

Colin Campbell never waited to find out what Sonya from *PB Home Improvements* actually wanted, or whether he might be in any way interested. He slammed the receiver down in its cradle and cursed yet another interruption from a random telephone sales' company. 'I hate that,' he spat when he rejoined his wife, Mandy, in the kitchen. 'And I hate it all the more when they use my name. When did I give Sonya from *PB Home Improvements* permission to call me Colin? It's as if I was some long-lost friend. And that's the *last* thing I want to be with *PB Home Improvements*, whether it's Sonya or anyone else.'

'Calm down, will you,' his long-suffering wife suggested. 'And anyway, it's a well known sales' technique – use someone's name and it catches them off guard, gets them on your side, makes the sale easier. It's one of the best weapons they have.'

'Off guard, is it? Well I'll damn well be *on* my guard next time. They'll be lucky if they get past Mr Campbell. Or maybe I'll just cut them off at the 'hello'. Getting me on their side? If only. Arrgghh …' And, with that, Colin Campbell was off, muttering under his breath, 'Using someone's name, indeed.'

The incident with Sonya from *PB Home Improvements* became a distant memory as the day wore on. It was all but forgotten when the Campbells spent a pleasurable evening in town. Their monthly visit to the local theatre, followed by a very pleasant meal in their favourite Indian restaurant, left them both in good spirits. It wasn't much short of midnight, as they were returning to their car in the multi-storey car park beside the theatre, when the rumpus started. They could hear it from the far end of the car park – aggressive shouting; loud cursing; the sound of breaking glass.

'Come on, Colin,' Mandy whispered. 'Let's not hang about. Sounds like there's trouble.' But by the time they'd arrived at the ticket-machine and Colin was sorting out cash for the parking fee, the trouble had got a lot nearer. Within seconds, a mob of about a dozen teenagers, brandishing beer cans and wine bottles and high on goodness-knows what else, were approaching. There was no time for Colin and Mandy to retreat to the safety of their car, or hot-foot it up the stairs to the next level. They were caught between the ticket-machine and the staircase, with no escape route in sight. Colin looked around to see if there was anyone else who could help. There was no one to be seen. They were trapped.

'Yo, ho. And what have we here?' one of the yobs shouted. 'A couple of lovers having their end away in the corner, eh lads.'

'Dirty, dirty,' sneered another.

'Hey mate. I think I might like to have your wallet, right?' threatened a third, approaching menacingly.

'An' the handbag from your fancy piece,' mocked the first.

What Colin Campbell *should* have done was to hand over the requested wallet and handbag, hold his hands up as a request for no more trouble, and hope the baying mob would take that as a signal to be on their way. But he didn't. To this day, he doesn't know why.

'Trevor! Trevor Eadie! As I live and breathe … I haven't seen you for ages. How's your sister, Sharon, isn't it? Trevor Eadie. Tommy Eadie's boy.'

'What's he on about, Trev?' spat one of the crowd. 'Let's get the stuff and skedaddle.'

'These your mates, Trevor? How's the apprenticeship coming along? Dad still working on the buses?'

'How d'you know me?' Trevor Eadie asked quizzically, thankfully not moving any closer. The threatening scowl had been replaced by a look of bewilderment.

'Me and your dad used to play in the same darts team, years ago. My sister used to do the odd baby-sit when you were a nipper. Trevor Eadie. Who would have believed it?'

'C'm'on Trev. We're out of here,' someone shouted. And as the crowd obediently started to move away, the clearly dumbstruck Trev went with them.

'Give my best to your folks, Trevor,' Colin shouted after them. The loudness of the teenagers began to rise again, but this time the noise was heading away from a much relieved Colin and Mandy Campbell.

The parking fee duly paid, Colin and Mandy were pleased to get into their car, exit the multi-storey, and head home. Mandy was shaken. Colin wasn't much better. 'I thought we were in deep trouble, Colin,' Mandy confessed when they got home. 'And you, trying to be brave.'

'No, not brave,' Colin smiled. 'Not brave. Just lucky. But anyway, who was it that taught me about a well known sales' technique – use someone's name and it catches them off guard, gets them on your side, makes the thing easier. It's one of the best weapons to have. And it works, don't you think?'

### Naming the demons

Now,
I don't think I'm demon-possessed.
At least, I hope not.
But what I *do* know is that I have demons in my life
that sometimes threaten to take over,
gain control, that kind of thing.
Demons? Yes, I think so.

There's the demon
that never wants me to be late,
and puts pressure on those around me too.
It's hard to control that one.

Then there's the demon
about not wanting to fail,
and working doubly hard
to make sure people still believe in me.
That's a tough one too.

And there's the demon
about always wanting to be right,
and struggling when I'm proved wrong.
Big battles there too.

No,
I'm not demon-possessed.
But I do have my demons to contend with,
and I reckon I always will.

So how do I cope with my demons?
Well, I've done it already, even here.
I single them out.
I give them a name.
I say, 'I know who you are.'
Do they disappear?
No, not altogether.
But it catches them off guard
so they've got less control,
and *much* less chance of taking over completely.

'I know who you are ...
I know where you come from ...
I know what you do ...'
And another demon bites the dust for a while.

### Twenty-second Sunday

*Old Testament:* Proverbs 22:1-2, 8-9, 22-23
*Epistle:* James 2:1-17
*Gospel:* Mark 7:24-37

# 55 Advice

Fraser was a fisherman. He plied his trade along the rocky coast down from his village. Fraser was seventy-two years old and was still at the fishing. Well, if fishing's in your blood, what can you do?

In his heyday – or, more appropriately, when fishing locally was in its heyday – Fraser fished for herring. Along with dozens of other boats from his village, and all the other villages along the coast, Fraser would spend days at sea, first in his uncle's boat and then in his own, far out into the wilds of the North Sea, to harvest the 'silver darlings'. He'd made a good living at the herring, as had many others. But the fishing grounds hadn't been well managed. So the herring fishing had declined and Fraser's trawler had been sold long since. But, if fishing's in your blood ...

So Fraser had turned to fishing for shellfish, then lobsters. Three times a week, Monday, Wednesday and Friday, Fraser would turn the *Mary Anne* out of the harbour and spend five or six hours hauling up his creels, boxing the crabs and precious lobsters, baiting the creels afresh and returning them to the seabed. The crabs were given away when Fraser got back to the harbour to anyone who wanted them. But the lobsters were like gold dust. The prize catch was a one-and-a-half-pounder, just what the fancy hotels and restaurants in town needed to provide an expensive meal for their customers. The daily market paid well for such prize catches.

Fraser seldom fished alone. He wasn't bothered if he had to, but his two daughters had warned him 'within an inch of his life' not to go out alone at his age. So Fraser was usually accompanied by one or other of the nominally retired fishermen who hung around the harbour, payment for a day's work being seldom more than a couple of pints in the *Harbour Bar* and a few 'crabs for the pot'. But when Fraser's grandson was home from college, this was all the crew Fraser ever needed or wanted. Every week Stuart, Fraser's six-foot, strapping, rugby-playing, nineteen-year-old, only grandson would get his cut of the profits – 'Better in the laddie's hands than in the till at the *Harbour Bar*,' Fraser would often say. But the truth of it was that Fraser and Stuart were more than grandfather and grandson, and much more than employer and temporary employee. They'd become best mates, and the bond between them grew stronger with every creel hauled up, emptied and baited.

Fraser loved it when Stuart's youthful strength made light work of hauling in the heavy creels. Stuart loved it when Fraser would tell him tales of the old days, and dubious stories which Stuart had to swear he'd never tell his mother or his gran. Fraser loved it when Stuart confided in him some problem with college and sought his advice. Stuart loved it when Fraser would tell him another story, for he knew that much wise counsel was wrapped up in there somewhere for him to ponder later. Though neither of them would ever admit it to the other, there was a deep love between these two men, a love that transcended generations and culture, knowledge and experience.

One day, after their spell at the creels and the inevitable trip to the market, Stuart persuaded his grandfather to accompany him to the *Harbour Bar* for a pint before teatime. 'Just the one, mind,' Fraser insisted. The two men settled at a table in the corner, and before long the talk turned to Stuart's time at the college. He was struggling, he confided in his grandfather, and was beginning to feel it was all too much. He was contemplating 'dropping out' and coming home – 'Don't dare say a word to mum' – perhaps to spend more time at the fishing. After all, he suggested, it would be easier that way, and safer. There was too much uncertainty about the future. Perhaps it would be better never to have tried, and maybe being back home would be best.

Fraser listened with his usual seriousness, taking an occasional sip of his pint, knowing well enough that his grandson needed to get something off his chest. When Stuart was finished baring his soul, he half turned to his Grandfather and asked, 'I'm sure you've felt like that sometimes, eh? When you'd had a heavy weekend, or the fishing-grounds were empty. I'm sure there were times you wanted to pack it in too, eh?'

Fraser smiled. 'Well, laddie, you may be right enough,' he mused. 'But then, the fishing's in my blood. So there's nothing I can do about that.' He paused, as if the moment required some further weighty comment. The silence lasted for a good while, and Stuart knew not to try to interrupt when his grandfather was thinking. Eventually Fraser reached out for his pint, raised it to his lips, took a fair mouthful, and returned his glass to the table. As he did so, he turned and looked Stuart straight in the eye. 'There was once a man called William Greenough Thayer Shedd. He lived in America in the second half of the 19th century. He was the son of a Reverend, and became a well known Presbyterian theologian.'

Stuart furrowed his brow, wondering momentarily where this was going. He didn't have to wonder for long, as Fraser continued, 'Now, I don't know whether this man was ever a sailor, or had the fishing in his blood. But I've heard tell that he once said this. "A ship is safe in harbour. But that's not what ships are for." So whether it's a great ship, or a little boat like the *Mary Anne*, we could tie her up and keep her safe, or we could take her to sea and have her do her job. William Shedd … "A ship is safe in harbour. But that's not what ships are for." Eh?'

Fraser paused again, but never averted his eyes from his grandson's. The hint of a smile appeared on the old man's face. 'D'you know what I mean, laddie?'

Stuart held the offered gaze, lost his puzzled frown and returned the breaking smile with an expansive smile of his own. 'Yes, Granddad,' he said. 'I know *exactly* what you mean.'

### Wisdom

*(Based on Proverbs 1:20-33)*

Wisdom calls aloud again,
No longer hushed against her will

In busy streets and public squares;
Wisdom's voice is not restrained,
And asks the searching questions still,
When we would pass by unawares.

Wisdom cries once more, out loud,
Demanding our attention now.
Past city gates, down noisy roads,
Wisdom calls us from the crowd,
Rebukes our mockery, and how
We watch as righteousness erodes.

Wisdom pours its generous heart
On those who thirst for knowledge, yet
Would turn from what was once the Way.
Wisdom laughs when Truth departs,
Replaced by trouble, fear and threat;
Calamity and woe, our judgement day.

Wisdom calls us back to Life,
No condemnation hers, but hope;
Redemption's chance is ours to seize!
Wisdom's voice above the strife –
'Here's fullness; look! and endless scope
For healing's touch our souls to ease.'

## Twenty-third Sunday

*Old Testament:* Proverbs 1:20-33
*Epistle:* James 3:1-12
*Gospel:* Mark 8:27-38

# 56 The fairy trail

Tomasz knew his mother cleaned houses. She didn't speak of it much, and, anyway, when Tomasz was in school, he never knew where his mother went or what she did. She was always at home when he got back, and he and his little sister, Franciszka, were always welcomed with a big hug.

Things had been a bit easier since the three of them had come from Poland to their new home. Tomasz had been a bit scared at first. It was all so strange and different, and especially hard when he didn't understand what people were saying. He missed his village back home. Bronowice, just outside Krakow, would always be special to him. But since his dad left... well, things had to change. But his mother had been very reassuring, as she always was. And now he could speak English well and had pals to play football with, he had begun to feel better. Home would always be back in Bronowice, of course, but as a second best this wasn't too bad.

Tomasz knew his mother cleaned houses, but he never thought very much about it until the school holidays came around. His mother hadn't been able to arrange for him and Franciszka to be cared for over a couple of days at the start of the summer break. There were usually summer clubs, and childcare – and, in an emergency, Mrs Henderson from number twenty-two would look after them for an hour or so. But none of that seemed to be possible. So, one morning, Tomasz's mum informed him that he and Franciszka would have to come with her to work. Tomasz wasn't best pleased. He liked the summer clubs and childcare, and even Mrs Henderson was OK. But he didn't say. It wasn't his place. So with his mother and little sister, he travelled in a bus all the way across town until his mother indicated that it was time to get off.

Tomasz was amazed when he looked around after the bus had

pulled away. They were standing in front of big metal gates with carved gold leaves right at the top. On either side there were massive stone pillars, and as far as he could see, to the right and the left, there were high hedges, twice as big as he was. His mother had moved towards the right-hand pillar of the gates and was pressing a button on the side. To Tomasz's surprise, a crackly voice enquired, 'Yes … Who is it?' And to Tomasz's even *greater* surprise, his mother then proceeded to talk to the voice in the wall. 'It is Izolda Markowski … Here to do the cleaning …' There was no reply, but Tomasz was astonished when the big gates slowly began to swing open all by themselves. His mother beckoned them through and the gates slowly swung shut behind them. Tomasz's mother took him and Franciszka by their hands as they made their way along the tree-lined driveway. Soon they'd come upon the biggest house Tomasz had ever seen in his whole life. And there, in the enormous doorway, stood the oldest woman he'd ever seen.

'Ah, good morning, Izolda,' the old woman said. She was dressed from head to toe in black. She had silver hair fastened by clasps at the side – just as Tomasz's grandma back in Bronowice used to have – and she had a spindly pair of glasses perched on the end of her nose.

'Good morning, Mrs McKenzie,' Tomasz's mother responded. 'It is so good you allow me to bring children. I promise they be good.'

'It's a pleasure, my dear,' the old woman responded. 'I haven't had children here for many, many years. Come, now. Inside. You know what you need to do, Izolda. The children will come with me. I have a treat for them.'

'But I do not want fuss. The children will sit, and wait. I do not want bother …' She wasn't allowed to finish.

'It will be no bother, my dear. It will be a pleasure. Come, children. We will go through the house to the garden.'

Tomasz and his sister were taken through what seemed to a little boy to be huge rooms and long corridors. The kitchen was massive, and Tomasz's mother was already at work sweeping and clearing. And then they were in the garden. There were fruit trees along a big wall, laden with what he discovered later were apples, plums and peaches. There were flowers everywhere, huge sunflowers and delicate begonias, tall foxgloves and roses of all colours. And, at the foot of the garden, there was a mass of bushes and shrubs, a great tangle of wild growth, and a little path that disappeared from the edge of the lawn into … well … nowhere, it seemed.

Tomasz was a bit overwhelmed and not a little intrigued. He and his sister had settled down round a little wrought-iron table and were tucking into the orange juice and scones which Mrs McKenzie had provided. And when he had found his tongue at last, he asked his elderly hostess, 'Where does the path at the end of the garden go to, please?

The old lady smiled, put down her glass of juice carefully on the table, and pointed to the foot of the garden. 'That path is the fairy trail,' she announced.

'Fairy trail?' Tomasz asked. 'What is that?'

'The fairy trail has been there since I was a little girl,' Mrs McKenzie replied. 'When I was younger than you and your sister my father called it "the fairy trail", and it's just stuck.'

'But where does it go?' Tomasz enquired.

'It goes anywhere you like,' Mrs McKenzie continued. 'One day it leads to a land of pirates and sailing ships, and another it takes you to a garden centre full of flowers and plants; one day you end up in a festival of music, and another in a land of beautiful stillness; one day you find a beautiful princess in a castle, and another a playroom full of toys. It's a fairy trail, so it can take you anywhere you want.'

That was the only visit Tomasz ever had to Mrs McKenzie's magical house, and the only conversation he ever had with the old woman dressed all in black, with her silver hair fastened by clasps at the side, and with a spindly pair of glasses perched on the end of her nose. He was never invited to explore Mrs McKenzie's fairy trail.

Tomasz now teaches English to Polish immigrants, and works

with organisations for the resettlement of asylum seekers in his neighbourhood. He knows he's found things down his own fairy trail that he never believed were possible, and he hopes he can help other people in a strange, unusual place to find what's at the end of their own fairy trail too.

## Responsible

I take my daughter to the playground in the park.
It's a lovely day,
and she's always so well behaved and responsible.
So, I settle down to read my newspaper,
while she plays happily on her own.

And then, the air is broken by an ear-piercing scream,
and I see the child running towards me,
hysterical,
because she's fallen from the slide
and grazed her knee.

But I'm a responsible adult,
so I know just what to do.
I sit her down on the ground in front of me,
and I say,
'Now, isn't it interesting that your knee should be sore?
You know why?
It's because the nerve-endings at the site of the graze
are sending signals to your brain that something is wrong.
It's all to do with the construction
of the central nervous system ...'

No?
Of course not.
Now, that would be silly.

Instead, as a responsible adult,
knowing what to do,
I tell her that she's now learning
about the meaning of suffering,
and coming to terms with this
could be a crucial moment in her spiritual development.
'You see, philosophers and theologians,
from all religions and cultures,
from the beginning of recorded time,
have wrestled with the meaning of suffering and pain,
and you have to grasp the importance of ...'

No?
Of course not.
Now, that would be *really* silly.

Instead, as a responsible adult,
knowing what to do,
and because it's in the job-description of being a parent,
I scold her because she's interrupted my private time.
'Don't come screaming to me, young lady.
Can't you see I'm busy?
Goodness, do I never get any peace?
Pull yourself together ...'

No?
Of course not.
Now that would be *very* silly *and* insensitive.

So, as a *really* responsible adult
I know what I must do.
I open my arms wide when I see her running to me,
and I lift her up and hold her in her distress.

No explanations, just comfort;
no reasons, just reassurance;
no meaning, just consolation ...
And I hold her in my arms until her tears subside,
and she calms down,
and she feels reassured that the world hasn't come to an end
because she's grazed her knee falling off a slide.
And I dry her eyes and wipe her nose,
and I say 'There, there,' several times.
And when she's ready,
she slips off my knee
and goes back to her swings and her slide,
comforted now ...
and still with the graze on her knee.

I'm responsible,
as a responsible adult should be ...

And I hope that someone will do that for me
when I'm hysterical in the face of my own suffering.

### Twenty-fourth Sunday

*Old Testament:* Proverbs 31:10-31
*Epistle:* James 3:13-48a
*Gospel:* Mark 9:30-37

# 57 Every inch a ruler

Melinda Mary Beatrice Williamson-Smyth was queen bee. Actually, she'd been called worse than that in her day – toffee-nosed, stuck-up, posh totty being among the gentler of labels. But as lady of the manor, she was undoubtedly queen bee, and that was fine by her.

Even 'lady of the manor' was a misnomer, for she was from no landed-gentry stock. She just happened to live in the big house in ten acres of land at the edge of the village; she just happened to be the wife of a self-made millionaire property developer; she just happened to have all the trappings of wealth and success. And that was more than enough to make Melinda Mary Beatrice Williamson-Smyth queen bee.

Her double-barrelled surname was a bit of a con, though Melinda hoped no one knew that. She'd been the 'Williamson' part, daughter of a coal merchant from Leeds. Her husband had been Rob Smith, a bricklayer from Dagenham. Smith to Smyth ... with a Williamson added for good measure ... and a cunningly placed hyphen to make it *really* posh ... It was all she needed. Melinda Mary Beatrice Williamson-Smyth was certainly queen bee.

'Queen bee!' she'd once remarked to her husband. 'Queen bee?' he'd retorted. 'Queen, is it? So, with your height, maybe they'll say "And the queen was twelve inches tall ... she was every inch a ruler!" eh?' And Robert Williamson-Smyth, proud husband of the queen bee, laughed uproariously at his own joke. *'Every inch a ruler,'* Melinda pondered ...

The Williamson-Smyths had a garden party every summer – well, it's what you do when you're queen bee and happen to live in the big house in ten acres of land at the edge of the village. And that's when Melinda first heard about South Matabeleland.

To be honest, she'd never heard of the place before. But when the vicar said that she couldn't stay long because she had to head off to the airport to collect her eldest son, Melinda felt obliged to ask where he'd been. And when the vicar said he'd been working in a project in South Matabeleland, she felt obliged to ask where that was. And when the vicar said it was in Zimbabwe, and that the lad been working in a Christian Aid partnership project there, she felt obliged to ask what it was all about. And when the vicar said that she'd have to rush because she'd be late for the flight, Melinda felt obliged to ask if she had any more information. And when the vicar thrust a dog-eared leaflet into her hand before she headed off, Melinda felt obliged to read it. And when she read it, she felt obliged to ...

**Working in partnership**
*Does your church, school or business*
*want to transform communities in the developing world?*
*Join our Partnership Scheme and you can.*

Our scheme connects you to communities in the developing world and helps you see the real difference your giving and prayers make. We can link you to a Christian Aid project in one of the world's poorest countries, countries like Burkina Faso in West Africa, or Zimbabwe. Interested?

In Zimbabwe, political instability, combined with increasingly erratic rainfall and the impact of HIV, has left many communities across the country facing serious food shortages. This is particularly true in Matabeleland, a dry region stretching across the south and west of the country. Here poor soils, inadequate water supplies and environmental degradation have reduced harvests and increased malnutrition, particularly among children.

However, Christian Aid is now working with local partners ZimPro and Lutheran Development Services and communities in South Matabeleland on a new project to increase the productivity of the soil and introduce new and better crops.

Along with new farming methods, the project is also introducing a greater diversity of crops, livestock – such as chickens and goats – and measures to preserve the soil so that communities have more reliable and varied sources of food.

Support from the European Commission means that for every £1 donated through the Partnership Scheme to this project, the Commission will give an additional £9, therefore multiplying donations by 10!

When Melinda Mary Beatrice Williamson-Smyth announced that she was organising a fundraising event for a Christian Aid project in South Matabeleland, no one was at all surprised. She'd been talking about it for months. No one had heard anything *but* the project ever since the garden party. 'A queen bee with a bee in her bonnet,' her husband had remarked. And the event? A circle of £1 coins on the pavement all the way round the Williamson-Smyths' property … *Every £1 matters. Every inch is progress. Every person is important,*' the posters proclaimed.

Melinda had worked it out …With a £1 coin measuring nearly an inch across, £30,000 and more was needed to complete the circle, and that was an awful lot to be raised. She needn't have been concerned. The people of the village – and for miles around – caught the imagination of the project. It took a while, but, in time, the circle was finished and £32,241 was the result.

Melinda Mary Beatrice Williamson-Smyth had her photograph in the local paper with a ruler in her hand, measuring a line of £1 coins on the pavement outside the gates to her driveway. The headlines praised her for her commitment to the needs of others. What the reports *didn't* say was that Melinda Mary Beatrice Williamson-Smyth had matched the money raised, pound for pound. Well, you don't broadcast that kind of thing, do you? It might make people think you were "every inch a ruler" after all.

### If I ruled the world

If I ruled the world,
there would be no chance whatsoever

of every day being the first day of spring.
Now, come on!
Ruler I might be,
but would I have any control
over the changing of the seasons
or the quality of the weather?
No, I'll leave that to …

But if I ruled the world,
every day would be …
Now, come on!
Ruler I'll never be!
Would I ever have any control
over *anything* that big?
Not the likes of me, I wouldn't think …
No, I'll leave that to …

But if I ruled …
If I *did* rule …
Now, come on!
Maybe, just maybe …
ruler I am already.
I've got responsibility over *some* things,
no matter how limited … No?
Maybe I should just start small
and work outwards from there.

And I can't leave that to anyone else …

### Twenty-fifth Sunday

*Old Testament:* Esther 7:1-10, 9:20-22
*Epistle:* James 5:13-20
*Gospel:* Mark 9:38-50

# 58 The deal

Mario went to Mass every Sunday with Luigi, his grandfather's eldest brother. 'Papa D'Angelo' was very special to Mario. The senior figure in a large, extended Italian immigrant family, he was a constant companion to Mario. Going to Mass was part of that.

Papa D'Angelo was the only one of the family who attended Mass with any kind of regularity. He'd hardly missed a Sunday since he'd settled in the West of Scotland as an immigrant worker after the war. The ice-cream business had gone well, and D'Angelo's Café was soon well established in the town which had become home. And, in recent years, D'Angelo's Pizzas had become as widely known as the famous ice-cream.

The whole family was now involved with the business. Luigi's two brothers – one of them being Mario's grandfather – had come to Scotland too, and the extended D'Angelo family were fully engaged with the ever-expanding ice-cream and pizza trade. It wouldn't be long before Mario got involved. But, till then, he had to be content with spending as much time as possible with his beloved papa.

Nowadays, the old man largely left his business affairs to his sons and nephews and their partners and offspring – including Mario's cousins. So Papa D'Angelo had ample time to spend with Mario, and, of course, to go to Mass.

But there was one problem. When Papa D'Angelo sat down for more than five minutes at a time, he was inclined to fall asleep! Mario was used to that. In fact, he loved to watch his papa when he was asleep and would smile at the old man's grunting, the twitch of his droopy moustache, and the way his glasses would slowly slip down his nose. And it was *very* funny when Papa D'Angelo woke up with a start and tried to pretend he'd never been asleep in the first place –

failing to convince Mario or anyone else!

Now, falling asleep in your armchair by the fire after lunch is one thing. But falling asleep at Mass? Not that Mario minded. He was used to it. And anyway, the spaces in the Mass where Mario and his papa had enough time to sit still for long were very limited. There was always the standing up for the hymns, kneeling for the prayers and moving forward for the Sacrament to curtail periods of possible drowsiness. Even the priest's homily was mercifully short. So if Papa D'Angelo succumbed to sleep for a moment or two, it never bothered Mario ...

It did, however, appear to bother the priest. After all, the priest could clearly see that old Luigi D'Angelo regularly fell asleep during the Mass. And the priest wasn't best pleased!

The first Mario got to know about this was when the priest took him aside after Mass one Sunday for a 'quiet word'. Mario thought he was in trouble and made sure he stayed in full view of his papa who was talking with some of the other men at the church door. But it was soon clear that it wasn't Mario who was in trouble – it was Luigi D'Angelo.

'Do you know your papa falls asleep during Mass?' the priest whispered.

'No,' Mario lied.

'Well, he does,' the priest continued.

'Oh,' responded Mario, not knowing what else to say.

'It's not good enough,' the priest insisted.

'Oh,' repeated Mario.

'... not good enough,' the priest muttered again, and promptly turned and walked away.

Mario wasn't bothered. If his papa fell asleep, what could *he* do about it? *That* question was answered before Mass the following Sunday. When Mario arrived at church with his papa, the priest beckoned him into the corner of the vestibule. 'Listen,' whispered the priest, 'I have an idea.'

'Oh,' replied Mario, in what was rapidly becoming his standard response in any conversation with the priest.

'About Mr D'Angelo falling asleep ... '

'Oh?'

'Yes.'

'Oh.'

'I'll make you an offer you can't refuse.'

'Oh?'

'Yes. So here's the deal ... I'll give you a pound if you keep your papa awake during Mass, OK?'

'Oh.'

'Deal?

'Oh.'

'OK?'

'OK.'

'It's a deal then?'

'OK.'

'OK. Here's your pound. Now, don't let me down.' With that, the priest slipped a pound coin into Mario's hand which the young boy quickly pocketed before Papa D'Angelo came over to take him into Mass. 'What did the priest want?' the old man enquired.

'Nothing much,' Mario lied – again ...

'Didn't *seem* like nothing much,' Luigi continued as the two D'Angelos settled in their places.

'Oh, just some explanation about the Mass,' Mario replied. Whether Luigi D'Angelo was aware of the purpose of Mario's whispered questions during a lapse in the worship, or Mario 'accidentally' dropping his prayer-book on the floor and bumping his papa's legs as he bent down to retrieve it, or Mario surprisingly taking his papa's hand and squeezing it several times ... Mario never knew. But what he *did* know was that the priest winked at Mario and gave him the thumbs up after the Mass, so something had worked ...

The following Sunday the priest slipped Mario a pound when he arrived at the church, and Papa D'Angelo was wide awake during the Mass. The following Sunday, a pound, and Papa D'Angelo was wide awake during the Mass. The following Sunday, a pound, and Papa D'Angelo was wide awake. The following Sunday, a pound, and Papa D'Angelo was wide awake. The following Sunday, a pound, and Papa D'Angelo was *fast asleep* during the Mass again.

The priest wasn't best pleased, and with some vigour called Mario into the corner of the vestibule after Mass to remonstrate with the apparently recalcitrant child. 'Listen,' he began sternly. 'You know it's a sin to cheat?' He never waited for a response. 'Well, you've cheated. We had a deal, didn't we? I give you a pound, and you keep Mr D'Angelo awake. No?'

'I know, Father,' Mario nodded slowly. 'But what could I do? Because on the way to church today Papa promised he'd give me a fiver if I'd let him sleep …'

## And they brought …

And they brought little children,
Some with their brothers and sisters,
And others in their grandfathers' arms,
And a few not really wanting to come,
But having to be there,
Because it had been decided by those who brought them …

And they brought little children,
Some lovely ones, quiet as mice – aahhh …
And others in a very disgruntled state,
Clearly not really wanting to come,
But having to be there,
Though it would have been much more fun to have stayed at home.

And they brought little children,
Some well dressed and smart,
And others ... well ... it was a disgrace,
Though no one had asked them if they'd wanted to come,
But having to be there,
With dirty faces and torn jeans and runny noses ...

And they brought little children,
Some desperate to see the action,
And others hanging back, not so sure,
Because no one had asked them if they wanted to come,
But having to be there,
Though they were not at all sure they understood what was going on.

And they brought little children,
And still they kept bringing them,
And others no one had seen before;
Everyone seemed to be coming,
Having to be there,
Drawn by a magnet of personality and love and welcome.

And they brought little children ...
And what a crowd it was.
But there was no crush or stampede.
Though everyone seemed to be coming,
Having to be there;
Yet every single one of them got undivided attention.

And they brought little children,
And they took them away again, one by one;
While others lingered behind,
Not wanting to leave,
But having to go,
When those who'd brought them had to go home.

And they brought little children …
And some remembered,
While others forgot pretty quickly,
Not choosing to forget,
But having to get on with life,
And figure out what on earth all that had been about.

And they brought their children …
And they heard tell
That the one to whom they had brought them
Had had a great time,
Delighted they had been there,
For he'd held the Kingdom of God in his arms.

### Twenty-sixth Sunday

*Old Testament:* Job 1:1, 2:1-10
*Epistle:* Hebrews 1:1-4, 2:5-12
*Gospel:* Mark 10:2-16

# 59 Presentation

Philip was a PR consultant. He was young and he was arrogant. He was trying to make his mark on the world of public relations. Philip was going to be famous – so Philip said – the best ever, top of his profession, such was his high opinion of himself. He would represent the elite, the celebs, the high-fliers, the people-in-the know. Philip's star was on the rise – so Philip believed.

It was important, Philip considered, to make your mark quickly. *'The world of commerce and business has to be impressed, right away, with the new kid on the block. They have to be well impressed,'* so Philip thought. *'And that starts with the presentation. Presentation is everything. PR men have to get their PR right, don't they?'*

So Philip rented a large office in a prestigious new building in the centre of town. He couldn't really afford it, though who would know it was done on a bank loan? But that was never going to be a problem. After all, *presentation is everything* ... He just had to get started, and the money would *roll* in. *'I just can't lose,'* thought Philip.

He furnished his new office with the most impressive of things – studded leather chairs, gold-framed paintings, and a wonderful antique desk. He filled it with the most up-to-date equipment he could lay his hands on. And his pride and joy was the fanciest of telephones – *'Absolutely, without question, state-of-the-art,'* so Philip considered – which sat on his desk waiting to be connected.

All Philip had to do was wait ... So, on his first day in his sumptuous office, he was delighted – and not at all surprised – when, first thing in the morning, a client was announced, the beginning of what he believed would be a long list of distinguished clients who would come to rely on his *considerable* knowledge, contacts and expertise. Philip rubbed his hands with glee. He almost *drooled* with anticipation.

So, to indicate his busyness and the preciousness of his time – *'You have to get the impression over right away. Presentation is everything,'* Philip said to himself – the aspiring PR star deliberately made the new client wait in the outer office, and left him there for a quarter of an hour. And to create an even bigger impression on the client when he was eventually ushered in, he picked up the receiver of the fancy telephone and pretended to have a conversation. 'But, my dear Rodney, I cannot *possibly* consider taking on your client for *that* kind of derisory fee. I really do think we are both wasting our time. Yes … Yes … Of course … If you absolutely insist that I should take the job … But not for under £20,000. That's the bottom line, for I have many demands on my valuable time … Yes … Please … I'll give you time to the consider the matter … Yes … You can call me back … You have the number … All right then … That's settled. You will be making a wise choice. *Ciao, mio amico.* Goodbye.'

Philip replaced the receiver and noticed, to his considerable pleasure, that the client who stood before him was suitably impressed. Indeed, he appeared to be somewhat taken aback by the PR man's stunning performance, almost overwhelmed, and certainly confused. *'Get the first impressions right. Presentation is everything,'* Philip mused …

So, glowing with pride, the young man looked haughtily at his somewhat incredulous client, 'Well, my man, what can I do for you? You realise I am busy. I have *so* many calls on my time, as you will no doubt have heard. So what can I do for *you* today?

And the man paused for a while, as if not quite knowing where to begin. Then, quietly, nervously, he replied to Philip's question, 'Well, excuse me, sir. But, you see, it's not what you can do for me, it's what I can do for you.'

Philip leapt to his feet, bristling with indignation that such as *this* would feel he had anything to offer the likes of him. *'The audacity of the man,'* Philip fumed.

'And what, my man, what do you consider that *you* can do for *me*?

The man smiled, looked Philip in the eye, and said quietly, 'Oh. I'm sorry to bother you sir. I know you're very busy. But, you see, I'm from BT and I've just come to connect your new telephone.'

## Presentation

It's all in the presentation.
Never mind the substance.
If you make it *look* right,
everything will be fine.

*Whited sepulchres ...*

OK. So presentation matters.
I mean, who's going to see the inside?
When the outside looks so good,
everything's fine, OK?

*Wolves in sheep's clothing ...*

Inside, outside, and all that ...
it's all a bit confusing.
Presentation still matters, though,
To make it all fine, yes?

*You hypocrites ...*

Surely, presentation's everything.
If it looks OK, that's enough,
and no one will bother to ask
whether the inside's as good as the outside.

*Blessed are the pure in heart ...*

## Twenty-seventh Sunday

*Old Testament:* Job 23:1-17
*Epistle:* Hebrews 4:12-16
*Gospel:* Mark 10:17-31

# 60 The best umbrella

Alfie was delighted with his new umbrella. It was just what he'd always wanted – a huge golf umbrella in his family tartan. Not that Alfie was a golfer – 'An annoying way to spoil a brisk walk!' he'd said often enough. But he'd always aspired to have a special golf umbrella. And finding *exactly* what he'd been looking for on a recent trip to St Andrews – the veritable home of golf, he'd been told – the big, tartan golf umbrella was his pride and joy.

The umbrella sat with a couple of old walking sticks below the coat-rack in the hall, just waiting to be used. The weather had been fine since he'd bought it. Not a drop of rain. He'd almost been *willing* the weather to break, even *praying* for the good Lord to offer just a small downpour so he could test out his special umbrella, *and* show it off to an admiring public at the same time.

Praying was a way of life for Alfie. Well, it's kind of expected of a minister, isn't it? Maybe it wasn't *quite* appropriate for Alfie to slip in the odd petition to the Almighty for his own purposes. But, well, if the Lord *could* help, just a little bit, wouldn't that make it OK? A small shower of rain wasn't too much to ask.

Alfie had been struggling that week with his Sunday sermon. It was, by coincidence, on the topic of prayer. But what new insight could he offer? Where was the new angle, the imaginative idea that would be just what his congregation needed? Sermons weren't always a struggle. But this one just didn't seem to be working. He'd been up late on the Saturday night changing a section, adding something new, rewording his conclusion. It was harder than usual, and on Sunday morning he woke with a heavy heart. It was too late to make any more changes. What he had would just have to do. It was far from perfect, but it was all he had.

He was so despondent that he never noticed the rain on the

kitchen window during breakfast. It wasn't till he had opened the front door to go out to the car for the journey to the church that he became aware of the break in the weather. 'It's raining,' he exclaimed. 'IT'S RAINING! AT LAST! My umbrella! Now's the time …' And with that, he spun on his heel, went back into the hall, and retrieved his precious golf umbrella.

'Margaret,' he shouted over his shoulder to his wife. 'Margaret, I'm going to walk to church today. I'll leave you the car, and I'll see you down there later.'

'Walk?' came the incredulous reply from the kitchen. 'Walk? In this weather? You'll get soaked, man!'

'No! There's no danger of that. I've got my new umbrella!' And with that, the bold Alfie ventured into the elements, well protected from the increasing downpour.

He was chuffed to bits. As the rain battered down, he was bone dry, totally protected from the wet. This is what he'd always wanted. Maybe he'd walk to church more often, even in the rain – *especially* in the rain! He was *sure* that passers-by were impressed. He was *convinced* that the people in the bus that drew up at the traffic lights as he crossed the road were transfixed by the sight of man and umbrella coping admirably with that rain! Sermon-struggle despondency had gone! The big, tartan golf umbrella was doing its job!

It was about halfway to the church that Alfie realised his shoes were letting in water. It began with a dampish feeling in his right foot followed quickly by wetness in his left. There was no ignoring it, Alfie was getting wet feet. He paused briefly in a shop doorway to investigate the problem. It didn't take much working out. The hole in the sole of one shoe, and the split in the stitching of the other were the obvious causes of his difficulty. He continued on his walk to the church. He had no choice. By the time he got there his feet were soaking wet.

Wearily climbing the steps of the church – his despondency having now returned in considerably larger measure – he shook the rain from his new umbrella and went in through the front door. He was standing in the doorway shaking the wetness from his feet, when Donald, the church officer, came by. 'Nice day, minister,' he announced. 'New umbrella? Sensible man, right enough. You'll need that above you on a day like this.'

'Aye, Donald, thanks for that. But look at the state of my feet. I'm soaked! Sopping wet! What a state to be in!'

Donald smiled knowingly. He reached over and took Alfie's umbrella. Shaking the last drops of rain from it, he looked admiringly at it as Alfie might have hoped. Then he looked down at Alfie's soaking feet, and smiled again. 'Well, now,' he said, looking Alfie straight in the eye, 'the truth is this, minister. What's the point of having a fancy umbrella when your shoes are letting water in? What's the good of having all that protection "up there"', he announced, pointing skywards, 'when it isn't working "down here"', gesticulating to Alfie's wet shoes. 'Eh? New umbrella and leaking shoes … Not a great combination, eh?'

When it came time for the sermon that morning, Alfie did something he'd never done before. 'The sermon I've prepared for today isn't worth sharing with you,' he confessed. 'Instead, I'm going to tell you a story about a fancy umbrella and leaky shoes. What's the point of having a fancy umbrella when your shoes are letting in water? What's the good of having protection above you when you can't walk in the right way? What's the point of all the prayers in the world, if you've not got things right at ground level?

Someone told him afterwards that it was one of the best sermons he'd ever preached. But Alfie knew it was actually Donald's sermon all the time!

### Work and prayer

'*Laborare est orare*'
Was the truth God did bestow;
'Work is prayer and prayer is work –

For the Bible tells it so …'
This I grasped so long ago.

So I worked and worked some more –
I believed God willed it so.
'Work is prayer, so I can't stop –
Always, always on the go;
'Tis the only prayer I know.'

'Come and rest with me, my child,
Cease your frantic to and fro …'
'Twas the call of God for *me*.
Something else that I should know?
Did I need to have it so?

So, reluctantly, I stopped,
Heard the call – 'Be still and know …
Find the balance, work and prayer …
Look above you – and below …
Look, you need to have it so.'

Work is work and prayer is prayer –
Find the level as you go;
Time to serve and time to rest…
How I wish this *quid pro quo*
Was my lesson long ago!

## Twenty-eighth Sunday

*Old Testament:* Job 38:1–41
*Epistle:* Hebrews 5:1–10
*Gospel:* Mark 10:35–45

# 61 Seeing

Mrs Green just couldn't see it. It was always the same – change, change and more change. If it wasn't enough that she had to put up with the demise of the corner shop and the arrival of the supermarket; the students in her stair in place of nice families and retired couples; the terrible programmes on the television instead of decent stuff; and the Tories who'd lost control of the council in the recent election …

As if that wasn't enough … now the church was changing too. They had a woman minister for one thing; a new hymn book; guitars; and there was talk of chairs replacing the pews. Mrs Green just couldn't see it. Surely the church could stay the same when everything else was changing. Surely … Mrs Green wasn't sure she'd go to church any more. She just couldn't see it.

★ ★ ★

Reuben just couldn't see it. It was always the same – the Palestinians were getting all the positive publicity. People's opinions were beginning to change. His mate had given up his job to go and spend time as a volunteer in an aid programme in the West Bank. He was *full* of the plight of the Palestinian people. All talk …

Reuben had to cope with the distress of his father too. It was what being Jewish was about, at least for his father. Not that Reuben bothered too much about his Jewishness. He never attended the synagogue. He wasn't sure about the God bit at all. But what did still matter were his roots, and his family, and his father's distress. A Palestinian homeland? He just couldn't see it.

★ ★ ★

Constable Jimmy Summers just couldn't see it. It was always the same – all that work put in to giving the local kids a better chance; the programmes and the youth clubs; the educational opportunities and the detached youth workers; the time and energy offered by community police officers like himself. Time and time again, a kid would be on the brink of making something of him- or herself, and then fall by the wayside.

Jimmy Summers was getting round to wondering why he should be bothered. Maybe he should keep to nicking rogues – just like his sergeant always reminded him. Maybe it would be easier just to 'lock 'em up and throw away the key' if the 'softly, softly' approaches weren't working. Why didn't the kids catch on? He just couldn't see it.

★ ★ ★

Colonel Douglas (Rtd, Household Cavalry) got his eyes opened. It was the minister who did it. Or maybe it was the young people from the church youth club who really opened his eyes. It had all happened when he'd been away. He didn't *want* to be away, of course. He was prepared to stick with things for as long as he could. But he was a proud man, and stubborn too. The army had taught him that. So *he* wasn't going to give in and ask for help.

It was the fall that had taken him away from his home. Three months he'd been in hospital, various hospitals indeed; a pin in his hip; rehabilitation; homecare being organised. He never expected his overgrown garden to be transformed while he was away. But it was. He couldn't believe it when he got home. 'The minister' and the 'youth club lot', he'd been told. He wasn't bothered who it was. He just knew he'd got his eyes opened.

★ ★ ★

Joseph Gold got his eyes opened. He knew it would happen at some stage, but he never expected it this way. It was when he had to defend a Muslim on a terrorist charge that his perspective changed. It wasn't mainstream, not a big publicity-generating affair – just a young, naive guy, the son of a local shopkeeper, who'd been associating with a bad crowd. It was the first time he'd really had anything to do with anyone from an Islamic background.

The young man reminded him of his own son, trying to hold himself together in a society full of prejudices – real and perceived; overt and hidden. The charge was dropped, thankfully – and rightly, Joseph reckoned – but not before Joseph had got to know his client a lot better. And he just knew he'd got his eyes opened.

★ ★ ★

Martin Miller got his eyes opened. No matter how hard he tried, he despaired about some of the kids in his care. Well, 'care' was a bit of a misnomer. Being a teacher in the local high school made you a teacher and not a carer, didn't it? But then, Martin Miller *did* care, especially when he saw kids who had little or no chance of breaking out of their social circumstances.

It was reading the Review section from the Sunday paper that gave him hope. 'A new band,' the article said, 'breaking new ground … the freshest on the scene … going to make it … talented singer-songwriter … Andy Welsh … local lad …' That couldn't be the same Andy Welsh who'd been in a Young Offenders' Institution, could it? The Andy Welsh that Martin had worked so hard with, only to be let down so many times? If it was … then Martin Miller just knew he'd got his eyes opened.

### Amazing grace

*Amazing grace, how sweet the sound*
*That saved a wretch like me.*
*I once was lost, but now am found;*
*Was blind, but now I see.*

When I am blinded by things that are different,
save me by a grace that opens my eyes
to truths that are new.

When I am blinded by my own prejudices,
save me by a grace that opens my eyes
to the goodness of others.

When I am blinded by despair and hopelessness,
save me by a grace that opens my eyes
to hope and new possibilities.

When I am blinded by the rightness of my cause,
save me by a grace that opens my eyes
to different points of view.

When I am blinded by my own failures,
save me by a grace that opens my eyes
to forgiveness and beginning again.

When I am blinded by not knowing or believing,
save me by a grace that opens my eyes
to what is beyond my seeing.

### Twenty-ninth Sunday

*Old Testament:* Job 42:1-17
*Epistle:* Hebrews 7:23-28
*Gospel:* Mark 10:46-52

# 62 Something to tell you

When Father Dermot was told that Bridie O'Callaghan was dying, he got round to her home as fast as he could. Bridie had been poorly for some time and her parish priest had been a regular visitor to her bedside. It was no strain for Dermot to spend time with Bridie. For she was one of the holiest, most saintly Christian people Father Dermot had known. A dedicated servant to her church, a regular at Mass, a committed disciple of her Faith, Bridie was all that could ever be expected as a parishioner of St Clement's Parish.

Bridie had been deteriorating for some days now. Surrounded by her devoted family, with her rosary beads constantly in her hands, and with Father Dermot regularly bringing her the Offices of her religion, Bridie was approaching death with all the courage, faith and cheerfulness that could have been expected.

Father Dermot was somewhat breathless when he arrived at the house. He was met on the doorstep by Mary, the eldest of Bridie's four daughters. 'Thanks for coming so quickly, Father,' was Mary's welcome.

'Well, it was my promise,' Dermot replied. 'And is the end close?'

Mary ushered the young priest into the hallway and closed the front door. She gripped Dermot by the sleeve and whispered, 'Well, we thought so.'

'You mean, she's still hanging on?' enquired Dermot.

'Yes. But more than that,' Mary continued. 'She seems to have rallied a bit — and she's asking for you? In fact,' she went on, 'she's said that there's something she wants to tell you — for your ears only — something important — before she goes.' By now Mary was ushering him into Bridie's bedroom. And there was Dermot's favourite parishioner, propped up on pillows, looking desperately frail.

'I'll leave you to it, Father,' said Mary as she closed the bedroom door. Dermot pulled over a chair and was soon sitting by Bridie's bedside holding her hand in his, as he'd done many times before. He'd slipped on his small purple stole before he sat down, and, as Bridie's priest, was ready to be her spiritual companion on her journey to death. But he wasn't ready for what happened next.

'Father,' Bridie whispered faintly but distinctly, 'there's something I have to tell you.'

'Yes, my child, I am ready to hear your confession.' Bridie's old face cracked into a broad smile.

'No, no Father. None of that for now. No, no. It's about my funeral, you see.'

'Funeral?' Dermot responded, genuinely perplexed. 'But you needn't worry about your funeral, Bridie. You're to have a full Funeral Mass. You'll be buried with all the rites of your Church.'

'Father Dermot,' Bridie replied, 'I know that fine. It's not the Mass. It's how I'm to be laid out.'

'Laid out?' the confused young priest enquired. 'Laid out? What do you mean?'

'In my coffin, Father. When I'm laid out in my coffin.'

By now, the St Clement's parish priest was on distinctly foreign territory. So he responded with a heartfelt and genuinely liturgical 'Uh?'

Bridie took this as a sign that her Father Confessor was now on her wavelength. So, taking as deep a breath as she was able, she whispered hoarsely, 'Father, when I'm laid out, you've to put my prayer book and rosary in one hand and a spoon from my kitchen drawer in the other. That's the way I want to go.'

Dermot was clearly unable to hide the confused look that flickered across his face. Bridie grinned. 'You've not heard that before, Father?' she asked. Dermot silently shook his head. 'And you're wondering whether I've gone off my trolley.' Dermot was embarrassed to find himself nodding slightly. Bridie smiled again and squeezed his hand.

'Well, Father,' she began, 'when I was a little girl, I was brought up in a devout but poor household. We were well fed and clothed. But we had no luxuries. Life was simple and plain. We were happy. And when we sat down as a family at our kitchen table, my father would bless the food and give thanks to God. It was always the same. And we ate. And we laughed. And we were thankful.' Her frail grip tightened around Dermot's fingers. He nodded, as an indication for Bridie to continue. And she did.

'But sometimes,' she said, 'just sometimes when I sat down at the kitchen table with the others, as well as the knife and fork at my place there would be a spoon. A spoon! And a spoon could only mean one possible thing. A spoon meant ... that there would be afters.'

Bridie turned her head on the pillow and looked straight at her priest. And with a voice firmer than Dermot had heard from her for some time, she affirmed, 'So when I'm laid out, put a spoon in my hand – because I'm going to be excited that there will be afters.'

When Bridie died, she was indeed laid out with her prayer book and rosary in one hand and a dessert spoon from her kitchen drawer in the other. Only a few people knew why. And the congregation at the funeral were puzzled at first when the priest began his tribute to Bridie by saying that she had taught him that a meal wasn't really complete unless there was a dessert ... until, that is, they heard the story about the spoon and the afters ...

### Heaven

'Wot's heaven like?' Nathan asked.
He was always asking about stuff,
and sometimes he didn't wait for an answer.
But this time, he wasn't running away.
'Wot's heaven like?' Nathan repeated,

just in case his question
hadn't actually been heard the first time.
'Why are you asking that?' came the reply,
because grown-ups are clever, you see,
and it's always a good technique
to answer a question with another question
because it gives you time to think,
and respond properly to Mr Questioning.
'Well, you said my nana had gone to heaven.
So, wot's heaven like, if Nana's there?'
I suppose I could have answered his question
with another question of my own.
But I couldn't think of one.
And anyway, it didn't sound much like he was in the mood
to be fobbed off.
'I suppose it's kind of nice,' was all I could say.
Kind of feeble, really, I reckoned.
But I hoped it might help.
'Nicer than here?' Nathan went on.
'I suppose,' I replied – sounding really feeble now.
'Nicer than our house?' he continued.
'I expect so,' the increasingly feeble grown-up response.
'So, where is it then?' Nathan asked.
Feeble responses appeared to be no deterrent
to Mr Questioning's current line of enquiry.
So I reverted to type – again –
reduced to answering a question with another question
trying desperately to negotiate time to think.
'What do you reckon?' I asked.
'Dunno,' Nathan shot back.
Why did it not sound feeble when *he* was honest?
'Dunno …' he repeated.

Clearly, he wasn't finished with his answer.
'See, I was thinking about my nana, right?
And it's just that … I don't want her to be in heaven,
'cause that must be far away,
and if *you* don't know where it is
and *I* can't find it anywhere,
even though I've looked and looked and looked,
I don't want my nana to be
in a place I can't find,
like far away, see?
And if I knew where heaven was
I could pop over and see how she was getting on,
just like we did before she went away.
But I can't, 'cause I can't find heaven
and you don't know either, eh?
So I just think about my nana,
and there she is, OK?'
He paused …
The current line of enquiry appeared
to be temporarily suspended.
'OK … I suppose …' I replied, feebly,
not supposing anything was OK at all.
'So you can find your nana when you think about her …'
I continued, feebly,
reduced now to repeating what I'd just been told,
because there wasn't a question to use
to respond to a question, any more …
but I still needed time to think.
'Yeah. When I think about my nana,
she just feels close, eh?'
I was going to reply
but I really had nothing to say.

Neither had Nathan, really,
apart from a final contribution to our
heaven-centred discussion.
'I suppose, if my nana and me are together
when I think about my nana,
then I'm in heaven with her, eh?
So heaven is ... when Nana is with me ...'
*'Wot's heaven like?'*
I was still stuck with his original question.
He was always asking about stuff,
and sometimes he'd work out his own answer,
that usually turned out to be helpful to me too –
like this time ...
And now he was running away.

## All Saints

*Old Testament:* Daniel 7:1, 9-10, 13-14
*Epistle:* Revelation 7:9-17
*Gospel:* Matthew 5:1-12

# 63 The Kid

The Kid always seemed to be watching. He stood at the gate ... and, well ... just watched. Paul had not long moved into the cottage in the village. It had been a surprise when he'd learned that he'd been left the little hideaway in his aunt's will. But then, Paul and his Aunt Matilda had always been close and ... she'd always understood. It was years now since she'd first suggested that Paul take his partner to 'my little retreat house' for the weekend. It had been the best gift she could have given him, for that weekend had been the first of many weekends and holiday breaks for Paul and Tim in Aunt Matilda's cottage.

She was the only one who knew about Tim – *really* knew, that is. Paul never understood how she'd figured it out. To his mother, Aunt Matilda's elder sister, Tim was just a good friend whom Paul had met in the army and kept up with back in civvy street. Well, having a mate was good for Paul after his marriage had fallen apart. Not that his mother had ever *liked* his wife. And, for that matter, not that Paul had ever really liked his wife much either. He'd kind of fallen into marriage, and no one was that surprised that it hadn't lasted long.

So time with Tim was deemed to be good for Paul. No one ever questioned the relationship – at least, not that Paul ever heard. And, until the day she died, Paul's mother never asked any questions, and Paul never felt he could come out to her in the way he wanted.

But with Aunt Matilda it was different. Not that she ever questioned it either. But Paul just knew she'd figured it out, and that made him feel good. 'Why not bring that nice young man round for tea,' was how it had begun. Then it was the offer of the cottage ...

Maybe giving Paul the cottage in her will was Aunt Matilda's way of saying she'd always understood. But, whatever her reasons, it gave Paul and Tim a chance to settle down to a new life together. Both of them had been planning early retirement when the cottage came their way. The timing was just right. So, two months ago, the cottage had become Paul and Tim's permanent and loving home.

Then Paul began to notice … the Kid. He'd first come to his attention when Paul and Tim were moving in. As books and kitchen utensils, lampshades and fireside rugs, pictures and suitcases were being unloaded from the car after the removal men had left, the Kid had been standing by the gate. He was about eight years old, and wore knee-length black shorts, scruffy trainers, a Denis-the-Menace jumper and a far-from-new baseball cap at a jaunty angle. He never said anything and never got in the way. He stood at the gate … and … well … just watched. Paul had tried to engage him in conversation. 'Want to help?' he'd enquired. The Kid never replied. 'What's your name, then?' The Kid never responded. 'You live round here?' The Kid stayed dumb.

And, as the weeks had passed, every time Paul went down the path and out the gate, the Kid was there again. When he was planting his bedding plants in preparation for summer flowering, the Kid was back. When Paul and Tim were sitting together on the garden bench with their newspapers and having their Sunday morning coffee, the Kid was in his usual place. The Kid always seemed to be watching. He stood at the gate … and … well … just watched. Paul didn't really mind, but it was beginning to get to Tim. 'Disconcerting,' he'd confessed one day.

Paul decided enough was enough. So the next Sunday morning, when he had come out with his Sunday papers and his coffee and the Kid was back by the gate, he decided to have a quiet word. 'Look here,' he began, gently, so as not to create a scene, 'why are you always here? Haven't you got better things to do? Come on, speak up, eh, what're you here for, eh? Cat got your tongue?' The Kid never moved. His expression never changed. He just … well … carried on watching. Paul could feel his hackles rise. 'Disconcerting …' was the least of it! And he was just about to raise his enquiries – and his voice – a notch or two when the Kid spoke for the very first time.

'I knew Tillie,' he said. 'She was my friend. She came here lots, ever since I was little. She'd talk to me and tell me stuff, funny stuff and sad stuff, stories, and that. We'd have juice and biscuits together.' The Kid stopped, as if struggling to figure out what to say next. Paul said nothing, allowing the silence to encourage the Kid to carry on now he'd started. And he did.

'Tillie stopped coming. My mum said she was dead. I cried and cried. And when I stopped crying I came back here. I wanted Tillie to come back again. I didn't want what my mum told me to be true. But when you came, and moved in, that was that. It wasn't Tillie's house any more. She was never, ever going to come back …'

The Kid started to cry, and Paul did too. A nameless kid knew his Aunt Matilda as he did, as an accepting, welcoming, loving human being. And the Kid was missing her as well.

So Paul told the Kid about Aunt Matilda, and the cottage, and what kind of person she'd been to himself and Tim. And the Kid dried his eyes, and Paul did too. After a time he said, 'What's your name?' 'Alexander,' came the reply, 'but Tillie always called me Alexander the Great. What's your name?' 'Benjamin, and my Aunt Matilda always called me Paul.'

'I should go now,' Alexander said. 'Thanks Tillie – sorry, Paul …' He smiled. 'I like you,' he whispered. 'I like talking about Tillie. It's like she's still here, like she hasn't gone for good …' and, turning on his heel, the Kid skipped off down the path and Paul went back to Tim and their coffee and Sunday papers, and said a silent 'thank you' to his Aunt Matilda for her special gift.

## Love's treasure store

No words can say what's right when sorrow's hand still clings;
No truth can offer light when pain new darkness brings,
Unless love's healing touch is known.
No walls can be torn down when we remain apart,
No stumbling blocks o'ercome when heart speaks not to heart,
Unless love's fond embrace is shown.

No hope can be renewed when deep despair brings grief;
No faith can be reviewed when doubts destroy belief,
Unless love gives its treasure store.
No gulf can be traversed when discord is our creed,
No hostile views reversed when conflicts still succeed,
Unless love risks itself once more.

No fury can be quelled when fear still holds its sway,
No loneliness dispelled when terror has its way,
Unless love's triumph is sustained.
Unless love's gift is given, no life will know it's blessed;
Unless we reach for heaven, no hell can be suppressed;
Unless Love lives, we live in vain.

### Thirtieth Sunday

*Old Testament:* Ruth 1:1-18
*Epistle:* Hebrews 9:11-14
*Gospel:* Mark 12:28-34

# 64 Recuerdo; Recordamos

Chavez had fought in the Spanish Civil War. It wasn't the first thing Elizabeth learned about Chavez Alvarado. Indeed, the first thing she learned was that Chavez did not wish to have anything to do with her at all.

Such was the way of things in the hospice. Sometimes the chaplain would be invited to see someone, and sometimes there would be a request from a patient or a family for some of the chaplain's time. But there were times, too, when Elizabeth was discouraged from spending time with someone. That was OK. She had enough on her plate in a busy hospice without imposing herself on people who'd made up their mind about her anyway. Chavez Alvarado was one of those. Indeed, he made his views clear the first time he and Elizabeth met.

Chavez had been admitted to the hospice on a Monday. Given the availability of beds, he had to share a three-bedded room. With the third bed still unoccupied, there was only one other patient in the room when Chavez arrived – an old, frail man by the name of Willie Anderson. So, while the nurses settled their new patient and helped him feel at home, appropriate care and attention continued to be given to the other man in the room. Willie's wife was with him most of the time. While the old man was peaceful, his wife was anxious and distressed. That's why Elizabeth was involved, and throughout the Monday she was in and out of the room, offering comfort and support to a grieving wife. And, of course, she couldn't pass the bed of a new patient without saying 'hello', now could she?

Elizabeth said 'hello' several times as she passed by, aware that there was a lot of necessary activity around Chavez as nurses, doctors and others went about their appropriate regimes. Eventually, towards the end of the day, she stopped to introduce herself properly. 'Hello,' she said cheerily, extending her hand in greeting, 'I'm Elizabeth. Are you settling in OK?'

Chavez Alvarado never lifted his hands from his lap to return her greeting. Instead, he looked up and said, 'And who may you be?'

'I'm Elizabeth ... the chaplain ... part of the team here ... and I was just passing by and realised we hadn't met.'

'And I am Chavez Alvarado. My friends call me Chavez. But you and the others may call me Dr Alvarado. And if you were just passing by, I would wish you to *keep* passing by, for I want nothing to do with the likes of you.'

Elizabeth wasn't unused to this as an initial response to her welcome. So, with a smile, she responded, 'Non problemo, señor. I'm around if you need me.'

Chavez offered the hint of a smile. 'You speak Spanish?'

'No, not really. I can do *hola* and *gracias* and *Real Madrid,* and that's about it, I'm afraid,' Elizabeth offered apologetically.

'Clearly, you are no linguist. For if you had said *No un problema, señor,* then you would have been correct.' Again, the flicker of a smile.

'Oh! Your Spanish is obviously better than mine,' Elizabeth responded, clearly realising that she wasn't now being dismissed as promptly as a moment or two before.

'With a name like Chavez Alvarado, might it not be?' was the reply. 'I was professor of Spanish at the University, until I retired ten years ago.'

By now, Elizabeth had slipped into the chair at the side of Dr Alvarado's bed. He didn't seem to have noticed. 'You say you are the chaplain?' the patient asked.

'Yes, I am,' Elizabeth responded.

'A priest? A woman? How can this be?'

'No, not a priest ... well, a kind of priest ... but here for everyone, of all religions and none.'

'I do not wish for a priest,' the man said firmly.

It was Elizabeth's time to smile. 'I'm with you, Dr Alvarado. I would reckon to do without some of the priests and ministers I know too.' It was a bold – and risky – thing to say to someone she'd just met. But it was worth the risk, for her new acquaintance was softening gently. There was a long silence. And then the story came ...

'I do not wish for a priest. I do not wish for a priest at any time, from any church. I am an atheist, and I do not wish for a god-pedlar.' He paused again. Elizabeth chose to sit in silence. It was the right thing to do. 'I do not wish to have anything to do with the church of Franco's Spain.' Elizabeth could see deepening furrows appear on her informant's brow. Still, she chose silence as the appropriate response. Still she was right.

'When I was twenty, I fought in my country's civil war. I fought on the Republican side, for freedom from fascism, with the Popular Front and the International Brigades. For three years I fought Franco's forces. And the church stood with them. And they defended the church. And I saw my brother killed and my friends die. And the church sided with the powers that caused those deaths. *Recuerdo*. I remember ... I remember ...'

'*Recuerdo*,' Elizabeth spontaneously repeated, instantly liking the sound of the word. '*Recuerdo ... Recuerdo ...*' Then it was her time to pause. Looking her patient in the eye, she said, 'I remember too, Dr Alvarado. I remember those who died in all wars, some of whom were my own family and from families I have worked with. I remember times when I too have been angry with the church. I remember, all too vividly, when I have wanted nothing to do with God.' She waited a moment before she went on. 'But I remember other things too. I remember good people I've met. I remember good people like you who've stood up for what they believed in. And I remember people who've worked for peace and justice and reconciliation.' She stopped suddenly. 'I'm sorry. I didn't mean to offer a sermon.'

'But you are a priest. It is what you do.'

Both chaplain and patient smiled, and silence embraced their fledgling togetherness. Elizabeth reckoned enough had been said. She rose to her feet and held out her hand once again. 'It's been good to meet you, Dr Alvarado.'

A once-reluctant patient took Elizabeth's hand and said, '*Gracias.*'

Elizabeth smiled. 'Tell me, Dr Alvarado. If *recuerdo* is 'I remember', what would 'we remember' be?'

Still holding Elizabeth's hand, Chavez responded, '*Recordamos, we remember.*'

'So,' Elizabeth replied, 'perhaps it might be *recordamos* when we share more time together, no?'

Dr Chavez Alvarado squeezed Elizabeth's hand. 'I think I'd like that. *Recordamos. Recordamos.* We will remember – together.'

### We will remember

*They shall grow not old as we that are left grow old.*
*Age shall not weary them nor the years condemn.*
*At the going down of the sun and in the morning,*
*We will remember them.*

We stand, in respectful silence
at our cenotaphs and war memorials,
on a Remembrance Sunday
or an Armistice Day,
and we remember.

We remember as we should,
and, as hymns are sung and bugles sound,
as flags are lowered and tears are shed,
we remember,
respectfully,
deeply,

sadly,
painfully.

We will remember them –
in the horrors of Ypres
and on the beaches of Normandy;
in the hills of the Falklands
and the sands of Afghanistan;
from our own shores
and from foreign lands …
We will remember them,
for that is our promise.

But when respectful silences
are over for another year;
when bugles no longer sound
and poppy wreaths are faded by the rain;
when medals are unpinned
and flags are stowed away,
will we still take time to remember?

Will we read the names on our war memorials
on other days of the year?
Will we weep for the fallen
who did not die in battle?
Will we carry in our daily deliberations
the saints and sinners of all our generations past?
Will we be silent
when no two minutes are called for,
and bow our heads
when no 'Last Post' rings out?
Will we commit ourselves to cherish
the legacy of goodness and truth,

of justice and peace
offered as a gift
by those who have gone before?
Will we?
Will we remember like that?

They shall grow not old as we that are left grow old.
Age shall not weary them nor the years condemn.
At the going down of the sun and in the morning ...
and in all the times in between,
we will remember them,
because they matter so much.

## Remembrance Sunday

*Appropriate readings might be chosen from*

*Old Testament*
2 Samuel 23:13-17, Isaiah 2:1-5, 25:1-9, 26:1-4, Micah 4:1-5
*Epistle*
Romans 8:31-39, Ephesians 4:25-5:2, 6:10-18, Revelation 21:1-7
*Gospel*
Matthew 5:1-12, John 15:9-17

# 65 Taking the biscuit

All Tiffany's mother had to spare in the kitchen cupboard for the school harvest festival was a packet of chocolate-coated digestive biscuits. She *could* have told Tiffany that she'd forgotten to buy something special. She *could* have said that she'd meant to prepare a colourful fruit basket as she'd done in previous years, but the shop had run out of fruit. She *could* have said something convincing that wouldn't disappoint an enquiring child. She *could* have lied. The simple truth was that she couldn't afford anything special. The household budget didn't run to any extras – not this week – and not for several weeks recently. Not since Jim had lost his job.

Actually, Jim hadn't really 'lost' his job. He'd left of his own accord. The accusations of the foreman that he wasn't fast enough on the production line were the last straw. The constant nagging had got to him. He could have punched the abusive so-and-so. But he chose the easier option – he just downed tools and walked off the job.

Easier option? Maybe not. For now Jim had to wait the requisite twenty-six weeks before he could receive his Jobseekers' Allowance because he had deliberately left his work 'without good reason' – even though Jim believed having a sod for a foreman was good reason enough. And, try as he did, Jim couldn't find work anywhere. The little savings the family had were rapidly dwindling. And while Tiffany's mum's job as a part-time cleaner in the Community Centre helped a bit, limited hours and the minimum wage didn't bring much into the household budget.

Tiffany knew little of this, of course, other than knowing that her dad was at home now – and the fact that her mum couldn't provide a colourful basket of fruit for the school harvest festival like she'd done last year. So a packet of digestive biscuits would just have to do, her mum had said. '*A packet of biscuits?*' Tiffany thought. '*What good is that among all the lovely things that will be on the tables in the school hall?*'

So it was with a heavy heart that Tiffany set off on her walk to school. She had plenty of time. She knew the way well. She always met with her friends at the corner of the park for the last part of the journey. But this time she held back. If she was going to be embarrassed by the meagreness of her offering for the harvest festival, she was going to be embarrassed alone.

That's when she saw Johnny Anderson fall off his bike. Johnny was a boy in the class below Tiffany, and he was always scooting about on his bike. Tiffany saw the little dog before Johnny did. But by the time Johnny had seen the mad pooch, it was too late to take evading action. So, at the last minute, Johnny had to swerve suddenly … And, as the yelping dog went one way back to its master at the edge of the park, Johnny went the other, and he and the bike fell in a heap at the edge of the path. He'd grazed his knee. He'd banged his arm. He'd severely hurt his pride.

By the time Tiffany arrived, he was sitting on the path clutching his elbow and crying profusely. Tiffany didn't know what to do. So she sat down on the path and cried as well. Johnny didn't seem to have broken anything. But he couldn't stop sobbing … So when Tiffany had done with her crying, she reached into her school bag and unearthed … a packet of chocolate-coated digestive biscuits. As carefully as possible, she stripped back the packaging at one end, took out two biscuits, offered one to Johnny and kept the other herself. And she and Johnny sat in silence on the path beside a fallen bike, and found comfort in digestive biscuits and quiet companionship. Johnny stopped crying, and after a time he smiled weakly, picked up his fallen steed and rode off, leaving Tiffany to fold down the packaging of her biscuits as best as she could, and return the packet to her bag.

Why she shared a biscuit with old Mrs McAlister who always sat on the bench under the big oak tree she couldn't tell you … But she

liked Mrs McAlister and, well, the packet of biscuits was open already
… and, well, Mrs McAlister looked lonely … and, well, sharing biscuits was easier than finding something to say.

Karen Palmer's wee one got two biscuits to break into pieces and
throw for the ducks … Well, she was screaming, wasn't she, because
her big brother had taken the whole eight slices of bread and thrown
them into the pond in one lump … just because he could … creating
a frenzy of activity in the pond as the ducks fought over their feast,
with a distressed sister in a pushchair at the edge who had nothing to
give the ducks …

There had never been a journey to school like it. Tiffany had long
since stopped trying to pretend the packet of biscuits could be
resealed so that no one would know there were any biscuits missing.
By the time she got to school, there were only two chocolate-coated
digestive biscuits left. So she ate them – well, what else was she to do?

It was Tiffany's teacher who found out about the biscuits. When
the class was assembling at the classroom door ready to go to the
school hall for the harvest festival, with all the children clutching
their fruit baskets and shopping bags with typical pride and excitement, Tiffany's teacher saw the usually enthusiastic youngster lin-
gering at the back of the line looking very sheepish and carrying
nothing. 'You OK, Tiffany?' was all she asked, but it was enough to
reduce Tiffany to tears. And in a quiet corner at the back of the classroom, and through wracking sobs, out came the whole story of the
journey to school that morning – the biscuits that had comforted
Johnny Anderson; and the biscuits that had calmed Karen Palmer's
little girl; and the biscuits that had brought a smile to Mrs McAlister's
face. 'Where's the evidence?' the teacher asked. And Tiffany
unearthed from her school bag the torn, sorry remains of the biscuit
packaging, and handed it over.

The harvest festival went off without any fuss. The class teacher
made sure Tiffany wasn't embarrassed in front of the others because

she had nothing to bring, having handed over her own basket of fruit so that Tiffany had something to place on the table at the front. But, at the close of the service, Tiffany was surprised to see her teacher go to the front of the hall and lay a crumpled and torn biscuit wrapper on the table. And, turning to the children, she announced, 'Boys and girls. Thank you for all you've brought today. You've been very kind and generous. But let me tell you a story of someone who had very little to bring ... but made that the most generous gift of all ...' And Tiffany was delighted to hear a story of an old woman in a church who'd done the same with her two coins as she'd done with her packet of biscuits ...

## Giving

I walked through a station
with a friend the other day.
There was a homeless man
sitting at the entrance,
a mangy dog beside him
and a paper cup in his hand.
I went to walk by –
I'd already doled out
my charitable giving for the week.
And, anyway,
we were in a hurry.
But my friend stopped,
and opened his wallet
and stuffed a £20 note
into the battered cup.
The guy was speechless –
even more than I was –
and looked up and mouthed

a silent 'thank you'.
When I got my voice back
I complained to my friend.
'Why did you do that?
He'll only spend it on drink,'
I said, sternly.
And my friend just smiled.
'So, today, for once,
he'll have a choice, then,'
my friend said.
'We make choices all the time.
But he can't, can he?
I can spend twenty quid
without thinking.
Today, £20 is his whole world.'
So I looked across at my friend
and tried to give him a silent 'thank you'.
But I didn't have it in me to give –
not yet.

### Thirty-first Sunday

*Old Testament:* Ruth 3:1-5, 4:13-17
*Epistle:* Hebrews 9:24-28
*Gospel:* Mark 12:38-44

# 66 Eccentric, or what?

Eric's mother's clock was as eccentric as Eric's mother. The old thing sat on the mantelpiece in the dining room – the clock, that is, not Eric's mother – and had been there for as long as Eric could remember. He was told in later years that it was an Art Deco kind of thing. But as far as Eric was concerned it was a brown, wooden clock with a faded face and with the most eccentric chime of any clock in the history of chiming timepieces.

It didn't chime thirteen on 'a bright cold day in April' as in Orwell's *1984*. But on every other day, and in every kind of weather you'd care to mention, it did its eccentric best to be equally strange. For a start, it never chimed on the hour. Sometimes it chimed at two minutes after the hour and sometimes at ten minutes before ... But never, *ever* exactly on the hour. For another thing, it wasn't always guaranteed to offer the right number of chimes to correspond to the actual hour. At twelve it would chime four, at four it would chime two, and at two it might decide not to chime at all. Never thirteen, mind, but anything else was possible. But the most eccentric behaviour of all was the chiming on the half hour and the quarter. No unpredictability here, however. The clock *always* chimed with the same eccentric combination at the quarter past, half past and quarter to ... It was accurate, to the minute. Bang on fifteen, thirty and forty-five, it was always the same.

Click ... Pause ... *Bong, Bong, Bong, Bong* ... Click ... *Bong, Bong, Bong, Bong* ... Click ... *Bong, Bong, Bong, Bong* ... Click ... *Bong, Bong, Bong, Bong* ... Click ... Pause ... Click ... Pause ... *Bong* ... Click ... Pause ... Click ... *Bong, Bong, Bong, Bong* ... Click ... And the whole damned thing would go through its terrible, eccentric cycle one more time!

There *was* a switch inside the casing that allowed the chiming mechanism to be switched off. But Eric didn't discover that till he was forty-three. There was a hammer in his father's toolbox, though.

Eric discovered that when he was eight. Eric's father discovered Eric just in time before the hammer was used to silence the clock's chimes for ever, and Eric was warned *never* to touch the hammer again, and never, *ever* to touch the clock on the mantelpiece in the dining room.

So Eric lived with an eccentric clock that was the treasured possession of his eccentric mother. His mother had her ways, her strange ways, which is what made Eric's mother Eric's mother, and why he loved her so much. Eric was fourteen when he discovered that not everyone's mother mixed orange juice with cola to create the foulest brown drink you could care to imagine – to offer to her unsuspecting children. Who else could be found sitting in the lotus position in the middle of the rose garden in the belief that the creation of a peaceful aura would do the roses a world of good? And did Eric not discover that, inspired by Salvador Dali, his mother wore her shoes a size too small so that she could 'keep herself alert'? Eric's mother was as eccentric as Eric's mother's clock, perhaps even more so.

In later years, eccentricity and dementia got all mixed up together. At the start, bizarre behaviour was deemed to be just that – bizarre ... But when putting your purse in the oven gravitated to throwing a full tin of beans on the fire in an attempt to burn your rubbish, and the can exploding all over the living room ... and when stripping off in the kitchen and putting everything you're wearing into the washing machine deteriorated into thinking the bundle of ironing on the settee was your GP and introducing him as such to everyone, including Eric, when they came to visit ... well ... bizarre just didn't explain it all.

The effects of the dementia were as rapid as they were deep. The time came when Eric's mother didn't know him when he came to visit her in the care facility that had become her home. She was seven years like that. Eric reckoned she'd died seven years before her body gave up its slender grip on life. Eric was glad when it was all over. But he missed his mother more than he ever believed he would.

If the seven years had been a limbo time for Eric's mother, it was a limbo time for Eric too. How could he grieve for the loss of his eccentric mother, how could he tell the world this wonderfully strange, amazing, unique, larger-than-life bundle of madness was dead when the bizarre creature she'd become was still there? So when Eric's mother died, Eric's seven-year wait to grieve was over, and he could feel the loss of the mother he loved.

Not surprisingly, the eccentric clock helped him with that. Now it sits on the big dresser in the upstairs hall in his house in town. He knows where the switch is, of course, and he keeps the chiming silent most of the time. But sometimes he switches it on, and when it chimes eleven when it's two o'clock, he smiles and remembers his mother. And when it goes through its eccentric ritual of bongs and clicks and pauses at the quarter and half-hours, he cries and misses his mother and wishes she was still her living, eccentric self.

Eric's mother's clock is still as eccentric as Eric's mother. But then, it reminds him of his mother, and every valued second of her eccentric life.

### The priest

*A reflection on Hebrews 10:11*

Day after day he stands,
Up by the high altar of his rightful place,
Performing his duties,
Again and again with the same words,
The same eccentric ideas,
Offering the security of familiarity.

Day after day he stands,
Up by the high altar of his calling,
Performing his rites,
Again and again the same movements and gestures,
The same staged presentation,
Offering the sacrifice of his bounden duty.

Day after day he stands,
Up by the high altar of his responsibilities,
Performing his offices,
Again and again with the same conclusion,
The same dénouement to the plot,
Offering a culmination to the presented drama.

Day after day he stands,
Up by the high altar of his connections,
Performing as the *pontifex,*
Again and again the same entrancing skill,
The same beauty and form,
Offering a bridge-building to the sacramental.

Day after day he stands,
Up by the high altar of his giving,
Performing his priestly role,
Again and again with the same commitment,
The same absolute belief,
Offering his all for the love of it all.

Day after day he is entranced,
Up by the high altar of his faith,
Performing not for his own glory,
Again and again the same looking beyond,
The same pointing upwards,
Offering, for a moment, a glimpse of the divine.

### Thirty-second Sunday

*Old Testament:* 1 Samuel 1:4–20
*Epistle:* Hebrews 10:11–25
*Gospel:* Mark 13:1–8

# 67 Nostalgia

'But nostalgia's not a thing of the past.' It was Jim's wife's final desperate contribution to a minor tiff over the breakfast table.

'Oh yes it is,' Jim retorted. 'Or at least it is with me. I can't be bothered with all of that. And I'm *not* going. And that's it … final! I'm definitely not going, OK?'

It had begun earlier that morning when Jim had received a letter from his old school. And 'old' was a pretty apt description, Jim reckoned. After all, it had been over fifty years since the school had benefited from Jim's presence. The high school had been pretty decrepit even then. And, despite repairs and extensions, refurbishment and new equipment over the years, the school had clearly been well past its sell-by date for some time. That's why, according to the letter now lying on the kitchen table, the Education Authority had decided that the school was due for demolition. A brand new, state-of-the-art secondary school, a mile away towards the edge of the town, was close to completion. At the end of the summer holidays it would be ready for occupation. A new term would see eight hundred pupils move to their new school. The 'old' high school would be no more, and demolition would commence as soon as the final pupils had departed.

So, the letter continued, as a farewell celebration, the final week of the summer term was to contain all kinds of events to mark an ending and a new beginning. There was to be a 'staff-versus-former-pupils' sports' tournament. The students were to offer a 'musical extravaganza', showing off their skills through performances by the school choir, the wind ensemble, the jazz orchestra and the rock band. A 'singalong *Pirates of Penzance*' was designed to draw in all those who over the years had sung in school productions of Gilbert & Sullivan operas, with senior pupils taking the lead parts. The school was to host a week-long art exhibition, with present and past artists showing off their wares. And, of course, there was to be a display of photographs, to chart the school's history from then until now.

'You should go back and see the old place,' Jim's wife had suggested. But Jim had made up his mind. 'I'm not going, and that's it,' had closed the fledgling debate.

Jim's wife was surprised, therefore, when the household debating society reconvened over the lunch table, to find that Jim had unearthed a copy of an ancient school photograph. It was, Jim explained, the only memento he had kept from his school days. '*Choir at school concert. May 1961. James Wood third from the left, back row*' was written in pencil on the back. And Jim was studying the photograph intently when his wife came into the kitchen.

'I thought you weren't interested in nostalgia,' she offered as an opening gambit.

'I'm not,' Jim retorted. 'It's looking at this lot that makes me even more convinced that I shouldn't go back. It would be a major dose of "Where-are-they-now?" discussions. And anyway, I haven't kept up with any of them. Half of them could be dead for all I know. Whatever happened to Ginger Tomkins, I wonder? Destined for great things, we always reckoned. And there's "Slim Jim" Simmers, grinning away as usual. I'll bet that's because he'd had a big win at the poker-school he always organised during the lunch break. And, blow me, there's Tubby and Posh Grenville … Inseparable, they were. "The Likely Lads" we called them.' So it continued … and Jim's wife was quietly amused that a man who'd left school fifty-odd years before was pretty animated *and* pretty knowledgeable about members of a school choir from 1961. 'And there's old "Joe Loss", grinning like a Cheshire cat!' Jim blurted.

'Oh, come on,' his wife intervened, 'who's "Joe Loss"? Another of your erstwhile school chums?'

'No, don't be daft,' Jim responded. 'That's the school music teacher. We called him "Joe Loss", after the band-leader, right? I don't think I could even remember his real name. He was always "Joe Loss" to us, right enough …' A thoughtful silence ensued. 'I wonder where they all are now. I wonder … I wonder where they are …'

Jim Wood's wife was not at all surprised when her husband announced a week later that he'd changed his mind. 'I think I'll pop along on one of the open days, just for old time's sake, to say goodbye to the old place, kind of thing.' And that's why Jim and Elsie Wood were walking round the old school two days before its demolition. Much of the building Jim didn't recognise at all. Rooms had been changed. What had been the Art Department, was now French. Where the library had been was now offices. And there were bits that had been built long after an eighteen-year-old Jim Wood had walked through the school gates for the last time. But Jim was pleased to discover that the 'lower corridor' was still much as it had been. Part of the original building, the lower corridor had been the centre of Jim's world for six years. With Geography at one end, History in the middle rooms, and English in rooms six and seven; with the senior boys' cloakroom and the prefects' study across the corridor; with the boys' loos through the middle swing-doors, where many a clandestine cigarette had been shared at break-time … it was all still there.

Jim was not prepared for the effect stepping back in time would have on him. When he took his first tentative steps into the lower corridor, his heart skipped a beat. There it was, the old place, not much different from what he remembered. But it was empty now, and about to be gone for good. Jim Wood just stood, and looked. He took it all in, absorbing the atmosphere one last time. And as he did, the strangest of things happened … Absorbed as he was in recalling 'the old days', he was sure he could see Ginger Tomkins, steeped in a book as usual, in the corner of the cloakroom. Jim blinked hard, but, right enough, there was Ginger, as large as life. And as Jim stared, he realised that on a bench at the other side sat none other than … Slim Jim Simmers, dealing another poker hand to two unsuspecting pupils. And there,

further along, were the Likely Lads, Tubby and Posh, in animated conversation about who-knows-what. And there was Andy Miller, crib-
bing homework from Brainy, and some money changing hands to
boot. And Trev, and Willie, and Mel, and Jinky, and Lofty, and … Down
the corridor, whistling an air from *The Pirates of Penzance* came … no,
it couldn't be … but, yes, it was … the one and only … Joe Loss …

Jim's wife wasn't at all surprised when Jim announced at teatime
that he was going to frame the old school photo and put it on display.
And when a photograph of a *'Choir at school concert. May 1961. James
Wood third from the left, back row'* was placed on the Wood-household
mantelpiece, she suggested, 'It's a shame you don't know where any of
them are now.' But Elsie Wood was somewhat taken aback when her
husband announced, '*Au contraire, Madame, au contraire.* I know *exactly*
where they all are, every single one.'

**Where are they now?**

The people I've met with; the folk that I've fought;
The ones that I've cared for; and those that I've not;
The people who matter; the ones I'd disown;
Pray tell me – but where have they gone?

    They come along with you in memory's store,
    They're part of your life since they've come through your door;
    Their influence stays with you, never to go;
    They'll always be with you, you know.

What, even the bad ones I'm happy to shun;
And those that I've damaged, who hate what I've done?
I want them to leave me, to let me alone;
Please tell me that they have all gone.

I'm sorry to tell you, but that's not the case;
The worst of encounters has not gone to waste.
You're moulded and shaped by experience; so
They'll always come with you, you know.

The people I've failed with; the folk who've done wrong;
The ones who've rejected me, laughed at my song?
You tell me they matter, whatever their tone?
You mean that they'll never be gone?

It's not just your saints who will shape you and mould
Your character, purpose and future; so hold
To the truth of the matter, and watch how you go –
You are what they've made you, you know.

## Final Sunday of the year

*Old Testament:* 2 Samuel 23:1-7
*Epistle:* Revelation 1:4b-8
*Gospel:* John 18:33-37

**A Blessing to Follow**

*Contemporary parables for living*

A companion volume to *With An Open Eye*, with stories relating to lectionary cycle C.

**Welcoming Each Wonder**

*More contemporary stories for reflection*

Another companion volume to *With An Open Eye*, with stories relating to lectionary cycle A.

**A Need for Living**

*Signposts on the journey of life and beyond*

Everyone has a need for meaning in life. For most of us, it is only when we are facing a life crisis, or the loss of a loved one, or the reality of our own death that the search for meaning becomes real. How then do we express what really matters?

Facing this in his work as a hospice chaplain, Tom Gordon has created a book for people facing a life crisis and for those who care for the dying. Ultimately it is for everyone, especially those for whom traditional words and symbols have failed, and who need new images to help them live again.

**New Journeys Now Begin**

*Learning on the path of grief and loss*

Bereavement is a journey to be travelled, not an illness to be treated or a problem to be solved. Tom Gordon writes with sensitivity and clarity about real people as they begin to understand their journeys of bereavement, helping us understand the unplanned and often frightening twists and turns grief forces the bereaved to face.

# The Iona Community is:

- An ecumenical movement of men and women from different walks of life and different traditions in the Christian church
- Committed to the gospel of Jesus Christ, and to following where that leads, even into the unknown
- Engaged together, and with people of goodwill across the world, in acting, reflecting and praying for justice, peace and the integrity of creation
- Convinced that the inclusive community we seek must be embodied in the community we practise

Together with our staff, we are responsible for:

- Our islands residential centres of Iona Abbey, the MacLeod Centre on Iona, and Camas Adventure Centre on the Ross of Mull

and in Glasgow:

- The administration of the Community
- Our work with young people
- Our publishing house, Wild Goose Publications
- Our association in the revitalising of worship with the Wild Goose Resource Group

The Iona Community was founded in Glasgow in 1938 by George MacLeod, minister, visionary and prophetic witness for peace, in the context of the poverty and despair of the Depression. Its original task of rebuilding the monastic ruins of Iona Abbey became a sign of hopeful rebuilding of community in Scotland and beyond. Today, we are about 250 Members, mostly in Britain, and 1500 Associate Members, with 1400 Friends worldwide. Together and apart, 'we follow the light we have, and pray for more light'.

*For information on the Iona Community contact:*
*The Iona Community, Fourth Floor, Savoy House, 140 Sauchiehall Street, Glasgow G2 3DH, UK. Phone: 0141 332 6343*
*e-mail: admin@iona.org.uk; web: www.iona.org.uk*

*For enquiries about visiting Iona, please contact:*
*Iona Abbey, Isle of Iona, Argyll PA76 6SN, UK. Phone: 01681 700404*
*e-mail: ionacomm@iona.org.uk*